D0430543

Hey, Whipple,
Squeeze This

pg. 98
272-portfolio

Adweek Books address the challenges and opportunities of the marketing and advertising industries, written by leaders in the business. We hope readers will find these books as helpful and inspiring as *Adweek*, *Brandweek*, and *Mediaweek* magazines.

Great Books from the Adweek Series Include:

Disruption: Overturning Conventions and Shaking Up the Marketplace, by Jean-Marie Dru

Truth, Lies and Advertising: The Art of Account Planning, by Jon Steel

Perfect Pitch: The Art of Selling Ideas and Winning New Business, by Jon Steel

Eating the Big Fish: How Challenger Brands Can Compete Against Brand Leaders, 2nd Edition, by Adam Morgan

Life after the 30-Second Spot: Energize Your Brand With a Bold Mix of Alternatives to Traditional Advertising, by Joseph Jaffe

Pick Me!: Breaking Into Advertising, and Staying There, by Janet Kestin and Nancy Vonk

Hey, Whipple, Squeeze This: A Guide to Creating Great Advertising, 3rd Edition, by Luke Sullivan

Hey, Whipple, Squeeze This

Squeeze This

A Guide to Creating Great Ads

Third Edition

LUKE SULLIVAN

AdweekMedia

WILEY

John Wiley & Sons, Inc.

Copyright © 2008 by Luke Sullivan All rights reserved.

Published by John Wiley & Sons, Inc., Hoboken, New Jersey.
Published simultaneously in Canada.

No part of this publication may be reproduced, stored in a retrieval system, or transmitted in any form or by any means, electronic, mechanical, photocopying, recording, scanning, or otherwise, except as permitted under Section 107 or 108 of the 1976 United States Copyright Act, without either the prior written permission of the Publisher, or authorization through payment of the appropriate per-copy fee to the Copyright Clearance Center, Inc., 222 Rosewood Drive, Danvers, MA 01923, (978) 750-8400, fax (978) 750-4470, or on the web at www.copyright.com. Requests to the Publisher for permission should be addressed to the Permissions Department, John Wiley & Sons, Inc., 111 River Street, Hoboken, NJ 07030, (201) 748-6011, fax (201) 748-6008, e-mail: permcoordinator@wiley.com.

Limit of Liability/Disclaimer of Warranty: While the publisher and author have used their best efforts in preparing this book, they make no representations or warranties with respect to the accuracy or completeness of the contents of this book and specifically disclaim any implied warranties of merchantability or fitness for a particular purpose. No warranty may be created or extended by sales representatives or written sales materials. The advice and strategies contained herein may not be suitable for your situation. The publisher is not engaged in rendering professional services, and you should consult a professional where appropriate. Neither the publisher nor author shall be liable for any loss of profit or any other commercial damages, including but not limited to special, incidental, consequential, or other damages.

For general information on our other products and services please contact our Customer Care Department within the U.S. at (800) 762-2974, outside the United States at (317) 572-3993 or fax (317) 572-4002.

Wiley also publishes its books in a variety of electronic formats. Some content that appears in print may not be available in electronic books. For more information about Wiley products, visit our web site at www.wiley.com.

ISBN 9780470190739

Printed in the United States of America

10 9 8 7 6 5

TO MY DEAR WIFE,
CURLIN,
AND OUR GROWING BOYS,
REED AND PRESTON

CONTENTS

FOREWORD BY ALEX BOGUSKY
xi

PREFACE
xiii

CHAPTER 1
Salesmen Don't Have to Wear Plaid
Selling without selling out
1

CHAPTER 2
A Sharp Pencil Works Best
Some thoughts on getting started
16

CHAPTER 3
A Clean Sheet of Paper
Making an ad—the broad strokes
36

CHAPTER 4
Write When You Get Work
Making an ad—some finer touches
80

CHAPTER 5
In the Future, Everyone Will Be Famous for 30 Seconds
Some advice on making television commercials
116

CHAPTER 6

But Wait, There's More!

Does direct-response TV have to suck?

130

CHAPTER 7

Radio Is Hell. But It's a Dry Heat.

Some advice on working in a tough medium

148

CHAPTER 8

Big Honkin' Ideas

Hitting on every cylinder

174

CHAPTER 9

"Toto, I Have a Feeling
We're Not in McCann-Erickson Anymore."

Working out past the edge

198

CHAPTER 10

Only the Good Die Young

The enemies of advertising

206

CHAPTER 11

Pecked to Death by Ducks

Presenting and protecting your work

236

CHAPTER 12

A Good Book or a Crowbar

Some thoughts on getting into the business

270

CHAPTER 13

Making Shoes versus Making Shoe Commercials

Is this a great business or what?

296

SUGGESTED READING

307

BIBLIOGRAPHY
311

ONLINE RESOURCES
315

NOTES
317

ACKNOWLEDGMENTS
323

INDEX
325

FOREWORD BY ALEX BOGUSKY

I'm late. Way late.

I just got another e-mail from Luke Sullivan asking when this foreword to *Hey, Whipple, Squeeze This* would be done. I was also late reading his earlier e-mail about being late because there were about 200 other e-mails in front of that one, most of them about something I owed somebody and they were asking why it was late.

The thing is, I'm not one of those "late people." Really. I love work and I hate being late and I pretty much never miss a deadline. I think being late is poor form, so I'm feeling a little like a dolt right now.

It's just that I've been so damn busy. So busy I wasn't even able to fit a martini into my lunch break. Damn. Actually, I haven't had a martini lunch in my entire career. I eat lunch at my desk. Those three-martini lunches are long gone, and they've been replaced with a business that's more competitive and fast-paced than even the movie industry.

These days, there's simply a lot more to do. The single television spot or print ad has been replaced by the integrated campaign—a single big idea that works across every media. An idea that can draw the consumer out and compel him or her to spend some time with the brand, and maybe even some money. It's a lot of work and it ain't for the faint of heart. But as my Dad used to say, "It's better than diggin' ditches."

In the end, it's rarely the deadlines or the amount of work that keep us from getting the job done. Hell, it's never even the lack of a big idea. You see, *new media, untraditional media, integration,*—they may be the buzzwords we read every day in the hype that surrounds our business. But so far as I know, they've yet to come up with a powerful form of communication that does not at least begin life as *words*.

Failure in advertising most often comes from the lack of this basic skill in finding the right words. The ability to find the words to write down an idea or to present an idea in the most compelling way possible. That's the wisdom that's in this book—in words. It's why everybody here at Crispin Porter + Bogusky has read it at least once. And it's why some of the really brilliant and successful people I've met in this business have read it two, even three times.

Which reminds me, I'm going to read it again. When I get the time.

PREFACE

THIS IS MY FANTASY.

———

We open on a tidy suburban kitchen. Actually, it's a room off the side, one with a washer and dryer. On the floor is a basket full of laundry. The camera closes in.

Out of the laundry pops the cutest little stuffed bear you've ever seen. He's pink and fluffy, has a happy little face, and there's one sock stuck adorably to his left ear.

"Hi, I'm Snuggles, the fabric-softening bear. And I . . ."

The first bullet rips into Snuggles's stomach, blows out of his back in a blizzard of cotton entrails, and punches a fist-sized hole in the dryer behind. Snuggles grabs the side of the Rubbermaid laundry basket and sinks down, his plastic eyes rolling as he looks for the source of the gunfire.

Taking cover behind $^1/_{16}$th-inch of flexible acrylic rubber, Snuggles looks out of the basket's plastic mesh and into the living room. He sees nothing. The dining room. Nothing.

Snuggles is easing over the backside of the basket when the second shot takes his head off at the neck. His body lands on top of the laundry, which is remarkably soft and fluffy. Fade to black.

———

We open on a woman in a bathroom, clad in apron and wielding brush, poised to clean her toilet bowl. She opens the lid.

But wait. What's this? It's a little man in a boat, floating above the sparkling waters of Lake Porcelain. Everything looks clean already!

With a tip of his teeny hat, he introduces himself. "I'm the Ty-D-Bowl Man, and I . . ."

Both hat and hand disappear in a red mist as the first bullet screams through and blows a hole in curved toilet wall behind the Ty-D-Bowl Man. Water begins to pour out on the floor as the woman screams and dives for cover in the tub.

Ty-D-Bowl Man scrambles out of the bowl, but when he climbs onto the big silver lever, it gives way, dropping him back into the swirling waters of the flushing toilet. We get two more glimpses of his face as he orbits around, once, twice, and then down to his final reward.

———

We open on a grocery store, where we see the owner scolding a group of ladies for squeezing some toilet paper. The first shot is high and wide, shattering a jar of mayonnaise.

Hey, Whipple,
Squeeze This

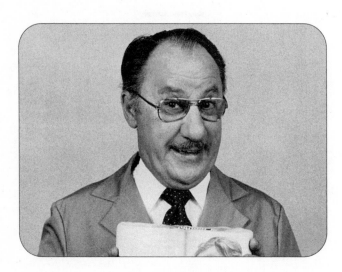

Fig. 1.1   Whipple

1

Salesmen Don't Have to Wear Plaid

Selling without selling out

I GREW UP POINTING A FINGER GUN at Mr. Whipple. He kept interrupting my favorite shows. The morning lineup was my favorite, with its back-to-back *Dick Van Dyke* and *Andy Griffith* shows. But Whipple kept butting in on Rob and Laura Petrie.

He'd appear uninvited on my TV, looking over the top of his glasses and pursing his lips at the ladies in his grocery store. Two middle-aged women, presumably with high school or college degrees, would be standing in the aisle squeezing rolls of toilet paper. Whipple would wag his finger and scold, "Please don't squeeze the Charmin." After the ladies scurried away, he'd give the rolls a few furtive squeezes himself.

I used to shoot him the second he appeared, but later discovered greater satisfaction in waiting till the 27th second, when he was squeezing the Charmin. *Bang!* and he was gone.

Now, years later, I am armed like millions of other Americans with a remote control. I still go looking for Whipple, and if I see him, I'm takin' him out.

To be fair, Procter & Gamble's Charmin commercials weren't the worst thing that ever aired on television. They had a concept, though contrived, and a brand image, though irritating—irritating even to a ninth grader.

If it were just me who didn't like Whipple's commercials, well, I might write it off. But the more I read about the campaign, the more consensus I discovered. In Martin Mayer's book *Whatever Happened to Madison Avenue?*, I found this:

> [Charmin's Whipple was] one of the most disliked . . . television commercials of the 1970s. [E]verybody thought "Please don't squeeze the Charmin" was stupid and it ranked last in believability in all the commercials studied for a period of years . . .[1]

In a book called *How to Advertise*, I found:

> When asked which campaigns they most disliked, consumers convicted Mr. Whipple. . . . Charmin may have not been popular advertising, but it was number one in sales.[2]

And there is the crux of the problem. The mystery. How did Whipple's commercials sell so much toilet paper?

These shrill little interruptions that irritated nearly everyone, that were used as fodder for Johnny Carson on late-night TV, sold toilet paper by the ton. How? Even if you figure that part out, the question then becomes, why? Why would you irritate your buying public with a twittering, pursed-lipped grocer when cold, hard research told you everybody hated him? I don't get it.

Apparently, even the agency that created him didn't get it. John Lyons, author of *Guts: Advertising from the Inside Out*, worked at Charmin's agency when they were trying to figure out what to do with Whipple.

> I was assigned to assassinate Mr. Whipple. Some of New York's best hit teams before me had tried and failed. "Killing Whipple" was an ongoing mission at Benton & Bowles. The agency that created him was determined to kill him. But the question was how to knock off a man with 15 lives, one for every year that the . . . campaign had been running at the time.[3]

No idea he came up with ever replaced Whipple, Lyons noted.

Next up to assassinate Whipple, a young writer: Atlanta's Joey Reiman. In a phone conversation, Reiman told me he tried to sell P&G a concept called "Squeeze-Enders"—an Alcoholics Anonymous kind of group where troubled souls struggled to end their visits to Mr. Whipple's grocery store, and so perhaps end the Whipple dynasty. No sale. Procter & Gamble wasn't about to let go of a winner. Whipple remained for years as one of advertising's most bulletproof personalities.

As well he should have. He was selling literally billions of rolls of toilet paper. *Billions.* In 1975, a survey listed Whipple's as the second-most-recognized face in America, right behind that of Richard Nixon. When Benton & Bowles's creative director, Al Hampel, took Whipple (actor Dick Wilson) to dinner one night in New York City, he said "it was as if Robert Redford walked into the place. Even the waiters asked for autographs."

So on one hand, you had research telling you customers hated these repetitive, schmaltzy, cornball commercials. And on the other, you had Whipple signing autographs at the Four Seasons.

It was as if the whole scenario had come out of the 1940s. In Frederick Wakeman's 1946 novel, *The Hucksters,* this was how advertising worked. In the middle of a meeting, the client spat on the conference room table and said: "You have just seen me do a disgusting thing. Ugly word, spit. But you'll always remember what I just did."[4]

The account executive in the novel took the lesson, later musing: "It was working like magic. The more you irritated them with repetitious commercials, the more soap they bought."[5]

With 504 different Charmin toilet tissue commercials airing from 1964 through 1990, Procter & Gamble certainly "irritated them with repetitive commercials." And it indeed "worked like magic." P&G knew what they were doing.

Yet I lie awake some nights staring at the ceiling, troubled by Whipple. What vexes me so about this old grocer? This is the question that led me to write this book.

What troubles me about Whipple is that he isn't *good.* As an idea, Whipple isn't good.

He may have been an effective salesman. (Billions of rolls.) He may have been a strong brand image. (He knocked Scott tissues out of the number one spot.) But it all comes down to this: If I had created Mr. Whipple, I don't think I could tell my son with a straight face what I did at the office. "Well, son, you see, Whipple tells the lady shoppers not to squeeze the Charmin, but then, then he squeezes it *himself.* . . . Hey, wait, come back!"

As an idea, Whipple isn't good.

To those who defend the campaign based on sales, I ask, would you also spit on the table to get my attention? It would work, but would you? An eloquent gentleman named Norman Berry, once a British creative director at Ogilvy & Mather, put it this way:

> I'm appalled by those who [judge] advertising exclusively on the basis of sales. That isn't enough. Of course, advertising must sell. By any definition it is lousy advertising if it doesn't. But if sales are achieved with work which is in bad taste or is intellectual garbage, it shouldn't be applauded no matter how much it sells. Offensive, dull, abrasive, stupid advertising is bad for the entire industry and bad for business as a whole. It is why the public perception of advertising is going down in this country.[6]

Berry may well have been thinking of Mr. Whipple when he made that comment in the early 1980s. With every year that's passed since, newer and more virulent strains of vapidity have been created: I'm Digger the Dermatophyte Nail Fungus—Ring Around the Collar—Snuggles, the fabric softening bear—Dude, you're getting a Dell!—He loves my mind *and* he drinks Johnny Walker Red—Don't hate me because I'm beautiful—I'm not a doctor, but I play one on TV—Head on! Apply directly to forehead!—I've fallen and I can't get up!

Writer Fran Lebowitz may well have been watching TV when she observed: "No matter how cynical I get, it's impossible to keep up."

Certainly, the viewing public is cynical about our business, due almost entirely to this parade of idiots we've sent into their living rooms. Every year, as long as I've been in advertising, Gallup publishes their poll of most- and least-trusted professions. And every year, advertising practitioners trade last or second-to-last place with used car salesmen and members of Congress.

It reminds me of a paragraph I plucked from our office bulletin board, one of those e-mailed curiosities that makes its way around corporate America:

> Dear Ann: I have a problem. I have two brothers. One brother is in advertising. The other was put to death in the electric chair for first-degree murder. My mother died from insanity when I was three. My two sisters are prostitutes and my father sells crack to handicapped elementary school students. Recently, I met a girl who was just released from a reformatory where she served time for killing her puppy with a ball-peen hammer, and I want to marry her. My problem

is, should I tell her about my brother who is in advertising? Signed, Anonymous

THE 1950S: WHEN EVEN X-ACTO BLADES WERE DULL.

My problem with Whipple (effective sales, grating execution) isn't a new one. Years ago, it occurred to a gentleman named William Bernbach that a commercial needn't sacrifice wit, grace, or intelligence in order to increase sales. And when he set out to prove it, something wonderful happened.

But we'll get to Mr. Bernbach in a minute. Before he showed up, a lot had already happened.

In the 1950s, the national audience was in the palm of the ad industry's hand. Anything that advertising said, people heard. TV was brand new, "clutter" didn't exist, and pretty much anything that showed up in the strange, foggy little window was kinda cool.

In *Which Ad Pulled Best?*, Ted Bell wrote: "There was a time in the not too distant past when the whole country sat down and watched *The Ed Sullivan Show* all the way through. To sell something, you could go on *The Ed Sullivan Show* and count on everybody seeing your message."[7]

World War II was over, people had money, and America's manufacturers had retooled to market the luxuries of life in Levittown. But as the economy boomed, so too did the country's business landscape. Soon there were more than one big brand of aspirin, more than two soft drinks, more than three brands of cars to choose from. And advertising agencies had more work to do than just get film in the can and cab it over to Rockefeller Center before Milton Berle went on live.

They had to convince the audience their product was the best in its category. And modern advertising as we know it was born.

On its heels came the concept of the *unique selling proposition*, a term coined by writer Rosser Reeves in the 1950s, and one that still has some merit. It was a simple, if ham-handed, notion. "Buy this product and you will get this specific benefit." The benefit had to be one that the competition either could not or did not offer, hence the *unique*.

This notion was perhaps best exemplified by Reeves's aspirin commercials, in which a headful of pounding hammers was relieved "fast, fast, fast" only by Anacin. Reeves also let us know that because of the unique candy coating, M&M's were the candy that "melts in your mouth, not in your hand."

Had the TV and business landscape remained the same, perhaps simply delineating the differences between one brand and another would suffice today.

But then came The Clutter. A brand explosion that lined the nation's grocery shelves with tens of thousands of logos and packed every episode of *Bonanza* wall-to-wall with commercials for me-too products.

Then, in response to The Clutter, came The Wall. The Wall was the perceptual filter that consumers put up to protect themselves from this tsunami of product information. Many products were at parity. Try as agencies might to find some unique angle, in the end, most soap was soap, most beer was beer.

Enter the Creative Revolution. And a guy named Bill Bernbach, who said: "It's not just what you say that stirs people. It's the way you say it."

"WHAT?! WE DON'T *HAVE* TO SUCK?!"

Bernbach founded his New York agency, Doyle Dane Bernbach, on the then radical notion that customers aren't nitwits who need to be fooled or lectured or hammered into listening to a client's sales message. This is Bill Bernbach:

> The truth isn't the truth until people believe you, and they can't believe you if they don't know what you're saying, and they can't know what you're saying if they don't listen to you, and they won't listen to you if you're not interesting, and you won't be interesting unless you say things imaginatively, originally, freshly.[8]

This was the classic Bernbach paradigm.

From all the advertising texts, articles, speeches, and awards annuals I've read over my years in advertising, everything that's any good about this business seems to trace its heritage back to this man, William Bernbach. And when his agency landed a couple of highly visible national accounts like Volkswagen and Alka-Seltzer, he brought advertising into a new era.

Smart agencies and clients everywhere saw for themselves that advertising didn't have to embarrass itself in order to make a cash register ring. The national TV audience was eating it up. Viewers couldn't wait for the next airing of VW's "Funeral" or Alka-Seltzer's

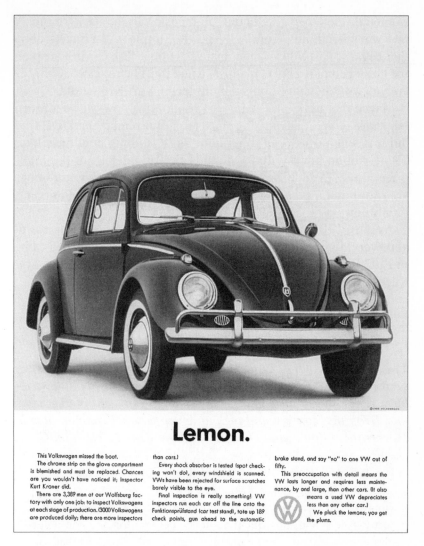

Lemon.

This Volkswagen missed the boat.

The chrome strip on the glove compartment is blemished and must be replaced. Chances are you wouldn't have noticed it; Inspector Kurt Kroner did.

There are 3,389 men at our Wolfsburg factory with only one job: to inspect Volkswagens at each stage of production. (3000 Volkswagens are produced daily; there are more inspectors than cars.)

Every shock absorber is tested (spot checking won't do), every windshield is scanned. VWs have been rejected for surface scratches barely visible to the eye.

Final inspection is really something! VW inspectors run each car off the line onto the Funktionsprüfstand (car test stand), tote up 189 check points, gun ahead to the automatic brake stand, and say "no" to one VW out of fifty.

This preoccupation with detail means the VW lasts longer and requires less maintenance, by and large, than other cars. (It also means a used VW depreciates less than any other car.)

We pluck the lemons; you get the plums.

Figure 1.2   In the beginning, there was the word. And it was "Lemon."

"Spicy meatball." The first shots of the Creative Revolution of the 1960s had been fired.*

How marvelous to have actually been there when DDB art director Helmut Krone laid out one of the very first Volkswagen ads (Figure 1.2). A black-and-white picture of that simple car, no

---

*You can study these two seminal commercials and many other great ads from this era in Larry Dubrow's fine book on the Creative Revolution, *When Advertising Tried Harder*, New York, Friendly Press, 1984.

women draped over the fender, no mansion in the background. A one-word headline: "Lemon." And the simple, self-effacing copy that began: "This Volkswagen missed the boat. The chrome strip on the glove compartment is blemished and must be replaced. Chances are you wouldn't have noticed it; Inspector Kurt Kroner did."

Maybe this ad doesn't seem earth-shattering now; we've all seen our share of great advertising since then. But remember, DDB first did this when other car companies were running headlines like: "Blue ribbon beauty that's stealing the thunder from the high-priced cars!" And "Chevrolet's 3 new engines put new fun under your foot and a great big grin on your face!" Volkswagen's was a totally new voice.

As the 1960s progressed, the revolution seemed to be successful and everything was just hunky-stinkin'-dory for a while. Then came the 1970s. The tightening economy had middle managers everywhere scared. And the party ended as quickly as it had begun.

———

THE EMPIRE STRIKES BACK.

The new gods wore suits and came bearing calculators. They seemed to say, *"Enough of this Kreativity Krap-ola, my little scribblers. We're here to meet the client's numbers. Put 'new' in that headline. Drop that concept and pick up an adjective: Crunch-a-licious, Flavor-iffic, I don't care. The client's coming up the elevator. Chop, chop."*

In *Corporate Report*, columnist William Souder wrote:

> Creative departments were reined in. New ads were pre-tested in focus groups, and subsequent audience-penetration and consumer-awareness quotients were numbingly monitored. It seemed that with enough repetition, even the most strident ad campaigns could bore through to the public consciousness. Advertising turned shrill. People hated Mr. Whipple, but bought Charmin anyway. It was Wisk for Ring-Around-the-Collar and Sanka for your jangled nerves.[9]

And so after a decade full of brilliant, successful examples like Volkswagen, Avis, Polaroid, and Chivas Regal, the pendulum swung back to the dictums of research. The industry returned to the blaring jingles and crass gimmickry of decades previous. The wolf was at the door again. Wearing a suit. It was as if all the agencies were run by purse-lipped nuns from some Catholic school. But instead of whacking students with rulers, these Madison Avenue schoolmarms whacked creatives with rolled-up research reports like "Burke scores," "Starch readership numbers," and a whole bunch of other useless left-brain crap.

Creativity was gleefully declared dead, at least by the big fat agencies that had never been able to come up with an original thought in the first place. And in came the next new thing—positioning.

"Advertising is entering an era where strategy is king," wrote the originators of the term *positioning*, Al Ries and Jack Trout. "Just as the me-too products killed the product era, the me-too companies killed the image advertising era."[10]

Part of the positioning paradigm was the notion that the consumer's head has a finite amount of space to categorize products. There's room for maybe three. If your product isn't in one of those slots, you must de-position a competitor in order for a different product to take its place. The Seven-Up Company's classic campaign from the 1960s remains a good example. Instead of positioning it as a clear soft drink with a lemon-lime flavor, 7UP took on the big three brown colas by positioning itself as "The Uncola."

Ted Morgan explained positioning this way: "Essentially, it's like finding a seat on a crowded bus. You look at the market place. You see what vacancy there is. You build your campaign to position your product in that vacancy. If you do it right, the straphangers won't be able to grab your seat."[11] As you might agree, Ries and Trout's concept of positioning is valid and useful.

Not surprisingly, advertisers fairly tipped over the positioning bandwagon climbing on. But a funny thing happened.

As skillfully as Madison Avenue's big agencies applied its principles, positioning by itself didn't magically move products, at least not as consistently as advertisers had hoped. Someone could have a marvelous idea for positioning a product, but if the commercials sucked, sales records were rarely broken.

Good advertising, it has been said, builds sales. But great advertising builds factories. And in this writer's opinion, the "great" that was missing from the positioning paradigm was the original alchemy brewed by Bernbach.

"You can say the right thing about a product and nobody will listen," said Bernbach (long before the advent of positioning). "But you've got to say it in such a way that people will feel it in their gut. Because if they don't feel it, nothing will happen." He went on to say, "The more intellectual you grow, the more you lose the great intuitive skills that really touch and move people."[12] Such was the state of the business when I joined its ranks in 1979. The battle between these opposing forces of hot creativity and cold research rages to this hour.

It makes for an interesting day at the office.

As John Ward of England's B&B Dorland noted, "Advertising is a craft executed by people who aspire to be artists, but is assessed by those who aspire to be scientists. I cannot imagine any human relationship more perfectly designed to produce total mayhem."[13]

WELCOME TO ADVERTISING. GRAB AN ADJECTIVE.

When I was in seventh grade, I noticed something about the ads for cereal on TV. (Remember, this was before the FTC forced manufacturers to call these sugary puffs of crunchy air "part of a complete breakfast.") I noticed the cereals were looking more and more like candy. There were flocks of leprechauns or birds or bees flying around the bowl, dusting sparkles of sugar over the cereal or ladling on gooey rivers of chocolate-flavored coating. The food value of the product kept getting less important until it was finally stuffed into the trunk of the car and sugar moved into the driver's seat. It was all about sugar.

One morning in study hall, I drew this little progression (Figure 1.3), calling it "History of a Cereal Box."

I was interested in the advertising I saw on TV but never thought I'd take it up as a career. I liked to draw, to make comic books, and to doodle with words and pictures. But when I was a poor college student, all I was sure of was that I wanted to be rich. I went into the premed program. The first grade on my college transcript, for chemistry, was a big, fat, radioactive "F." I reconsidered.

I majored in psychology. But after college I couldn't find any businesses on Lake Street in Minneapolis that were hiring skinny chain-smokers who could explain the relative virtues of scheduled versus random reinforcement in behaviorist theory. I joined a construction crew.

When the opportunity to be an editor/typesetter/ad salesperson for a small neighborhood newspaper came along, I took it, at a salary of $80 every two weeks. (Thinking back, I believe I deserved $85.) But the opportunity to sit at a desk and use words to make a living was enough. Of all my duties, I found that selling ads and drawing them up were the most interesting.

For the next year and a half, I hovered around the edges of the

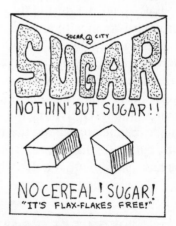

Figure 1.3   Too much hype doesn't persuade anybody, even seventh graders. When I was 12, I was appalled by all the cereal commercials featuring "sugar sparkles" and drew this progression of cereal box designs.

advertising industry. I did paste-up for another small newsweekly and then put in a long and dreary stint as a typesetter in the ad department of a large department store. It was there, during a break from setting type about "thick and thirsty cotton bath towels: $9.99," that I first came upon a book featuring the winners of a local advertising awards show.

I was bowled over by the work I saw there—mostly campaigns from Tom McElligott and Ron Anderson from Bozell & Jacobs's Minneapolis office. Their ads didn't say "thick and thirsty cotton bath towels: $9.99." They were funny or they were serious—startling sometimes—but they were always intelligent.

Reading one of their ads felt like I'd just met a very likable person at a bus stop. *He's smart, he's funny, he doesn't talk about himself. Turns out he's a salesman. And he's selling? . . . Well, wouldn't you know it, I've been thinking about buying one of those. Maybe I'll give you a call. Bye.* Walking away you think, *nice enough fella. And the way he said things: so funny.*

Through a contact, I managed to get a foot in the door at Bozell. What finally got me hired wasn't my awful little portfolio. What did it was an interview with McElligott—a sweaty little interrogation I attended wearing my shiny, wide 1978 tie and where I said "I see" about a hundred times. Tom later told me it was my enthusiasm that convinced him to take a chance on me. That and my promise to put in 60-hour weeks writing the brochures and other scraps that fell off his plate.

Tom hired me as a copywriter in January of 1979. He didn't have much work for me during that first month, so he parked me in a conference room with a three-foot stack of books full of the best advertising in the world: the One Show and *Communication Arts* awards annuals. He told me to read them. "Read them all."

He called them "the graduate school of advertising." I think he was right, and I say the same thing to students trying to get into the business today. Get yourself a three-foot stack of your own and read, learn, memorize. Yes, this is a business where we try to break rules, but as T.S. Eliot said, "It's not wise to violate the rules until you know how to observe them."

PORTRAIT OF THE ARTIST AS A YOUNG HACK.

As hard as I studied those awards annuals, most of the work I did that first year wasn't very good. In fact, it stunk. If the truth be

known, those early ads of mine were so bad I have to reach for my
volume of Edgar Allan Poe to describe them with any accuracy:
"...a nearly liquid mass of loathsome, detestable putridity."

But don't take my word for it. Here's my very first ad. Just look at
Figure 1.4 (for as long as you're able): a dull little ad that doesn't so

INVESTORS. THIS SHOULD ATTRACT YOUR INTEREST.

We'll admit, up till now, Savings & Loans have
been able to offer you that one-quarter percent more interest.
But now, because the Federal Reserve Bank has amended
its law, that's all changed.

Now we can offer you the *same* interest rate as any
Savings & Loan when the Federal rate is 9% or more on a
26-week certificate.

And with a minimum deposit of $10,000, you have a
risk-free way of capitalizing on the highest interest
rate allowed by law: 9.437%.* No other bank, no other
Savings & Loan can offer you a higher rate.

Ask about it. It's our
Investor Certificate.

*Interest rate week of April 2.
†Federal regulations prohibit the
compounding of interest during the
term of non-negotiable deposits
of $10,000 or more.
‡†Substantial penalty for early withdrawal.

We'll take the time to know you

First Savings Bank of Mankato

Member F.D.I.C.
© 1979   Bank System, Inc.

Figure 1.4   My first ad. (I know . . . I know.)

much revolve around an overused play on the word *interest*, as it limps.

Rumor has it they're still using my first ad at poison control centers to induce vomiting. *("Come on now, Jimmy. We know you ate your sister's antidepressant pills and that's why you have to look at this bank ad.")*

The point is, if you're like me, you might have a slow beginning. Even my friend Bob Barrie's first ad was terrible. Bob is arguably one of the best art directors in the history of advertising. But his first ad? The boring, flat-footed little headline read: "Win A Boat." We used to give Bob all kinds of grief about that. It became his hallway nickname: "Hey, Win-A-Boat, we're goin' to lunch. You comin'?"

There will come a time when you'll just start to get it. When you'll no longer waste time traipsing down dead ends or rattling the knobs of doors best left locked. You'll just start to get it. And suddenly, the ads coming out of your office will bear the mark of somebody who knows what the hell he's doing.

Along the way, though, it helps to study how more experienced people have tackled the same problems you'll soon face. On the subject of mentors, Helmut Krone said:

> I asked one of our young writers recently, which was more important: Doing your own thing or making the ad as good as it can be? The answer was "Doing my own thing." I disagree violently with that. I'd like to pose a new idea for our age: "Until you've got a better answer, you copy." I copied [famous Doyle Dane art director] Bob Gage for five years.[14]

The question is, who are you going to copy while you learn the craft? Whipple? For all the wincing his commercials caused, they worked. A lot of people at Procter & Gamble sent kids through college on Whipple's nickel. And these people can prove it; they have *charts* and everything.

Bill Bernbach, quoted here, wasn't big on charts.

> However much we would like advertising to be a science—because life would be simpler that way—the fact is that it is not. It is a subtle, ever-changing art, defying formularization, flowering on freshness and withering on imitation; what was effective one day, for that very reason, will not be effective the next, because it has lost the maximum impact of originality.[15]

There is a fork in the road here. Mr. Bernbach's path is the one I invite you to come down. It leads to the same place—enduring brands and market leadership—but gets there without costing anybody their dignity. You won't have to apologize to the neighbors for creating that irritating interruption of their sitcom last night. You won't have to explain anything. In fact, all most people will want to know is: "That was so cool. How'd you come up with it?"

This other road has its own rules, if we can call them that. Rules that were first articulated years ago by Mr. Bernbach and his team of pioneers like Bob Levenson, John Noble, Phyllis Robinson, Julian Koenig, and Helmut Krone.

Some may say my allegiance to the famous DDB School will date everything I have to say in this book. Perhaps. Yet a quick glance through their classic Volkswagen ads from the 1960s convinces me that the soul of a great advertisement hasn't changed in these years.* Those ads are still great. Intelligent. Clean. Witty. Beautiful. And human.

So with a tip of my hat to those pioneers of brilliant advertising, I offer the ideas in this book. They are the opinions of one writer, the gathered wisdom of smart people I met along the way during a career of writing, selling, and producing ideas for a wide variety of clients. God knows, they aren't rules. As copywriter Ed McCabe once said, "I have no use for rules. They only rule out the brilliant exception."

---

*Perhaps the best collection of VW advertisements is a small book edited by the famous copywriter David Abbott: *Remember Those Great Volkswagen Ads?* Holland, European Illustration, 1982.

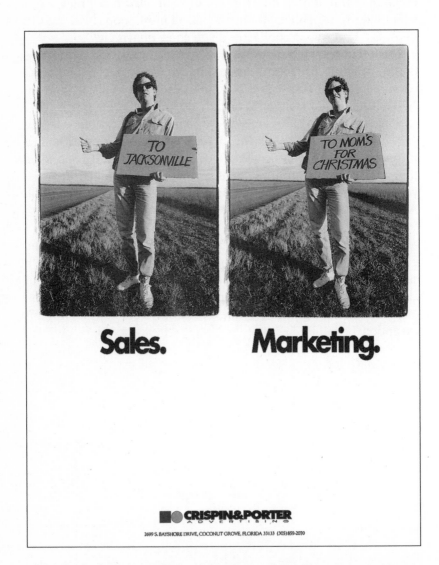

*Figure 2.1   This early ad for my friend Alex Bogusky's agency in Miami
makes a good point. A smart strategy can take the same
message and make it work better.*

2

A Sharp Pencil
Works Best

Some thoughts on getting started

IS THIS A GREAT JOB OR WHAT?

As an employee in an agency creative department, you will spend most of your time with your feet up on a desk working on an ad. Across the desk, also with his feet up, will be your partner-in my case, an art director. And he will want to talk about movies.

In fact, if the truth be known, you will spend a large part of your career with your feet up talking about movies.

The ad is due in two days. The media space has been bought and paid for. The pressure's building. And your muse is sleeping off a drunk behind a dumpster or twitching in a ditch somewhere. Your pen lies useless. So you talk movies.

That's when the traffic person comes by. Traffic people stay on top of a job as it moves through the agency. Which means they also stay on top of *you*. They'll come by to remind you of the horrid things that happen to snail-assed creative people who don't come through with the goods on time.

So you try to get your pen moving. And you begin to work. And working, in this business, means staring at your partner's shoes.

That's what I've been doing from nine to five for over 20 years. Staring at the bottom of the disgusting tennis shoes on the feet of my partner, parked on the desk across from my disgusting tennis shoes. This is the sum and substance of life at an agency.

In movies, they almost never capture this simple, dull, workaday reality of life as a creative person. Don't get me wrong, it's not an easy job. In fact, some days it's almost painful coming up with good ideas. As author Red Smith said, "There's nothing to writing. All you do is sit down at a typewriter and open a vein."[1] But the way movies show it, creative people solve complicated marketing problems between wisecracks and office affairs.

Hollywood's agencies are always kooky sorts of places where odd things are nailed to or stuck on the walls, where weirdly dressed creative people lurch through the hallways metabolizing last night's chemicals, and the occasional goat wanders through in the background.

But that isn't what agencies are like. At least not the four or five agencies where I've worked. Again, don't get me wrong. An ad agency is not a bank. It's not an insurance company. There is a certain amount of joie de vivre in an agency's atmosphere.

Which isn't surprising. Here you have a tight-knit group of young people, many of them making significant salaries just for sitting around with their feet up, solving marketing problems. And talking about movies.

It's a great job because you'll never get bored. One week you'll be knee-deep in the complexities of the financial business, selling market-indexed annuities. The next, you're touring a dog food factory asking about the difference between a "kibble" and a "bit." You'll learn about the business *of* business by studying the operations of hundreds of different kinds of enterprises.

The movies and television also portray advertising as a schlocky business—a parasitic lamprey that dangles from the belly of the business beast. A sort of side business that doesn't really manufacture anything in its own right, where it's all flash over substance, and where silver-tongued salespeople pitch snake oil to a bovine public, sandblast their wallets, and make the 5:20 for Long Island.

Ten minutes of work at a real agency should be enough to convince even the most cynical that an agency's involvement in a client's business is anything but superficial. Every cubicle on every floor at an agency is occupied by someone intensely involved in improving the client's day-to-day business, in shepherding its assets more wisely, sharpening its business focus, widening its market, even improving the product.

Ten minutes of work at a real agency should be enough to convince a cynic that you can't sell a product to someone who has no need for it. That you can't sell a product to someone who can't afford it. And that advertising can't save a bad product.

In ten minutes the cynic will also see there's no back room where snickering airbrush artists paint images of breasts into ice cubes, no slush fund to buy hookers for the clients' conventions, and no big table in the conference room where employees have sex during the office Christmas party. (Um, scratch that last one.)

Advertising isn't just some mutant offspring of capitalism. It's one of the main gears in the machinery of a huge economy, responsible in great part for one of the highest standards of living the world has ever seen. That Diet Coke you had an hour before you bought this book? It's just one of about 30,000 success stories of marketer and agency working together to bring a product—and with it, jobs and industry—to life.

Diet Coke didn't just happen. Coca-Cola didn't simply roll it out and hope that people would buy it. Done poorly, they could have cannibalized their flagship brand, Coke. Done poorly, it could have been just another one of the well-intentioned product start-ups that fail in six months. It took a lot of work by both Coca-Cola and its agency, SSCB, to decipher market conditions, position the product, name it, package it, and pull off the whole billion-dollar introduction.

Advertising, like it or not, is a key ingredient in a competitive economy and has created a stable place for itself in America's business landscape. Advertising is now a mature industry. And for most companies, a business necessity.

Why most of it stinks remains a mystery.

Carl Ally, founder of one of the great agencies of the 1970s, had a theory: "There's a tiny percentage of all the work that's great and a tiny percentage that's lousy. But most of the work—well, it's just there. That's no knock on advertising. How many great restaurants are there? Most aren't good or bad, they're just adequate. The fact is, excellence is tough to achieve in any field."[2]

WHY NOBODY EVER CHOOSES BRAND X.

There comes a point when you can't talk about movies anymore and you actually have to get some work done.

You are faced with a blank sheet of paper, and you must, in a fixed amount of time, fill it with something interesting enough to be remembered by a customer who in the course of a day will see, somewhere, thousands of other ad messages.

You are not writing a novel somebody pays money for. You are not writing a sitcom somebody enjoys watching. You are writing something most people try to avoid. This is the sad, indisputable truth at the bottom of our business. Nobody wants to see what you are about to put down on paper. People not only dislike advertising, they're becoming immune to most of it—like insects building up resistance to DDT.

The way Eric Silver put it was this: "Advertising is what happens on TV when people go to the bathroom."

When people aren't indifferent to advertising, they're angry at it. If you don't believe me, go to the opening night of a big Hollywood movie. When the third commercial comes up on the screen and it's not the movie, those moans you hear won't be audience ecstasy. People don't want to see your stinkin' ad. Your ad is the comedian who comes on stage before a Rolling Stones concert. The audience is drunk and they're angry and they came to see the Stones. And now a comedian has the microphone? You had better be great.

So you try to come up with some advertising concepts that can defeat these barriers of indifference and anger. The ideas you try to conjure, however, aren't done in a vacuum. You're working off a strategy—a sentence or two describing the key competitive message your ad must communicate.

In addition to a strategy, you are working with a brand. Unless it's a new one, that brand brings with it all kinds of baggage, some good and some bad. Ad people call it a brand's *equity*.

A brand isn't just the name on the box. It isn't the thing in the box, either. A brand is the sum total of all the emotions, thoughts, images, history, possibilities, and gossip that exist in the marketplace about a certain company.

What's remarkable about brands is that in categories where products are essentially all alike, the best-known and most well-liked brand has the winning card. In *The Want Makers*, Mike Destiny, former group director for England's Allied Breweries, was quoted: "The many competitive brands [of beer] are virtually identical in terms of taste, color and alcohol delivery, and after two or three pints even an expert couldn't tell them apart. So the consumer is literally drinking the advertising, and the advertising is the brand."[3]

A brand isn't just a semantic construct, either. The relationship between the brand and its customers has monetary value; it can amount to literally billions of dollars. Brands are assets, and companies rightfully include them on their financial balance sheets. When you're writing for a brand, you're working with a fragile, extraordinarily valuable thing. Not a lightweight job. Its implications are marvelous.

The ad you're about to do may not make the next million for the brand's marketer nor bring them to Chapter 11. Maybe it's just a half-page ad that runs one time. Yet it's an opportunity to sharpen that brand's image, even if just a little bit. It's a little like being handed the Olympic torch. You won't bear this important symbol all the way from Athens. Your job is just to move it a few miles down the road. Without dropping it in the dirt along the way.

STARING AT YOUR PARTNER'S SHOES.

For me, writing an ad is unnerving.

You sit down with your partner and put your feet up. You read the account executive's strategy, draw a square on a pad of paper, and you both stare at the damned thing. You stare at each other's shoes. You look at the square. You give up and go to lunch.

You come back. The empty square is still there.

So you both go through the product brochures and information folders the account team left in your office. Hmmm. You point out to your partner that this bourbon you're working on is manufactured in a little town with a funny name.

Your partner looks out the window, stares at some speck in the distance, and says, "Oh."

Down the hallway, a phone rings.

Reading from the client's web site, your partner points out that the distillers rotate the aging barrels a quarter turn to the left every few months. You go, "Hmmm." You read that moss on trees happens to grow faster on the sides that face a distillery's aging house. That's interesting.

You feel the glimmer of an idea move through you. You poise your pencil over the page. And it all comes out in a flash of creativity. *(Whoa. Someone call 9-1-1. Report a fire on my drawing pad 'cause I am SMOKIN' hot.)* You put your pencil down, smile, and read what you've written. It's complete rubbish. You call it a day and slink out to see a movie.

This process continues for several days, even weeks, and then one day without warning, an idea just shows up at your door, all nattied up like a Jehovah's Witness. You don't know where it comes from. It just shows up.

That's how you come up with ideas. Sorry, there's no big secret. That's basically the drill.

A guy named James Webb Young, a copywriter from the 1940s, laid out a five-step process of idea generation that holds water today.

1. You gather as much information on the problem as you can. You read, you underline stuff, you ask questions, you visit the factory.
2. You sit down and actively attack the problem.
3. You drop the whole thing and go do something else while your subconscious mind works on the problem.
4. "Eureka!"
5. You figure out how to implement your idea.[4]

Step two is what this book is about: attacking the problem.

This process of creativity isn't just an aimless sort of blue-skying—a mental version of bad modern dance. Rather, it's what author Joseph Heller (a former copywriter) called "a controlled daydream, a directed reverie." It's imagination disciplined by a single-minded business purpose.

So you start to write. Or doodle. (It doesn't matter which. Good copywriters can think visually; good art directors can write.) You just pick up a pencil and begin. All beginnings are humble, but after several days you begin to translate that flat-footed strategy into something interesting.

The final idea may be a visual. It may be a headline. It may be both. It may arrive whole, like Athena arising out of Zeus's head. Or in pieces—a scribble made by the art director last Friday fits beautifully with a headline the writer comes up with over the weekend. Eventually you get to an idea that dramatizes the benefit of your client's product or service. *Dramatizes* is the key word. You must dramatize it in a unique, provocative, compelling, and memorable way.

And at the center of this thing you come up with must be a promise. The reader must get something out of the deal. Steve Hayden, most famous for penning Apple Computer's "1984" commercial, said, "If you want to be a well-paid copywriter, please your client. If you want to be an award-winning copywriter, please your-self. If you want to be a great copywriter, please your reader."[5]

Here's the hard part. You have to please your reader and you have to do it in a few seconds.

Paul Keye, a well-known West Coast creative, had a good way of putting this: "How to write an interesting ad? Try this: 'Hello. I want to tell you something important or interesting or useful or funny. It's about you. I won't take very long and there's a prize if you stay till the very end.'"[6]

The way I picture it is this: It's as if you're riding down an elevator with your customer. You're going down only 15 floors. So you have only a few seconds to tell him one thing about your product. One thing. And you have to tell it to him in such an interesting way that he thinks about the promise you've made as he leaves the building, waits for the light, and crosses the street. You have to come up with some little *thing* that sticks in the customer's mind.

By "thing," I don't mean gimmick. Anybody can come up with an unrelated gimmick. Used car dealers are the national experts with their contrived sales events—"The boss went on vacation and our accountant went crazy!"—You might capture somebody's attention for a few seconds with a gimmick. But once the ruse is over and the salesman comes out of the closet in his plaid coat, the customer will only resent you.

Bill Bernbach: "I've got a great gimmick. Let's tell the truth."

The best answers always arise out of the problem itself. Out of the product. Out of the realities of the buying situation. Those are the only paints you have to make your picture, but they are all you need. Any shtick you drag into the situation that is not organically part of the product or customer reality will ring false.

You have more than enough to work with, even in the simplest advertising problem. You have your client's product with its brand equities and its benefits. You have the competition's product and its weaknesses. You have the price-quality-value math of the two prod-ucts. And then you have what the customer brings to the situation—pride, greed, vanity, envy, insecurity, and a hundred other human emotions, wants, and needs, one of which your product satisfies.

———

THE SUDDEN CESSATION OF STUPIDITY.

"You've got to play this game with fear and arrogance."

That's one of Kevin Costner's better lines from the baseball movie *Bull Durham*. I've always thought it had an analog in the advertising business.

There has never been a time in my career I have faced the empty page and not been scared. I was scared as a junior-coassistant-copy-cub-intern. And I'm scared today. Who am I to think I can write something that will interest 10 million people?

Then, a day after winning a medal in the One Show (just about the toughest national advertising awards show there is), I feel bulletproof. For one measly afternoon, I am an Ad God. The next day I'm back with my feet up on the table, sweating bullets again.

Somewhere between these two places, however, is where you want to be—a balance between a healthy skepticism of your reason for living and a solar confidence in your ability to come up with a fantastic idea every time you sit down to work. Living at either end of the spectrum will debilitate you. In fact, it's probably best to err on the side of fear.

A small, steady pilot light of fear burning in your stomach is part and parcel of the creative process. If you're doing something that's truly new, you're in an area where there are no signposts yet—no up and down, no good or bad. It seems to me, then, that fear is the constant traveling companion of an advertising person who fancies himself on the cutting edge.

You have to believe that you'll finally get a great idea. You will.

And there is nothing quite like the feeling of cracking a difficult advertising problem. What seemed impossible when you sat down to face the empty white square now seems so obvious. It is this very obviousness of a great idea that prompted Polaroid camera inventor, E.H. Land, to define creativity as "the sudden cessation of stupidity." You look at the idea you've just come up with, slap your forehead, and go, "Of course, it *has* to be this."

———

"YOU LIKE ME. YOU REALLY LIKE ME."

Solving a difficult advertising problem is a great feeling. Even better is the day, weeks or months later, when an account executive pops his head in your door and says sales are up. It never ceases to amaze me when that happens. Not that I doubt the power of advertising, but sometimes it's just hard to follow the thread from the scratchings on my pad all the way to a ringing cash register in, say, Akron, Ohio. Yet it works.

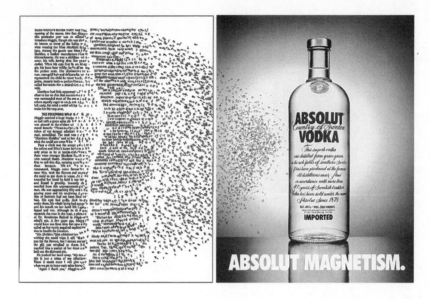

Figure 2.2   A campaign with more legs than the Rockettes.

People generally deny advertising has any effect on them. They'll insist they're immune to it. And perhaps, taken on a person-by-person basis, the effect of your ad is indeed modest. But over time, the results are undeniable. It's like wind on desert sands. The changes occurring at any given hour on any particular dune are small. A grain here, a handful there. But over time, the whole landscape changes.

Try this on: 1980—Absolut Vodka is a little nothing brand. Selling 12,000 cases a year. That's nothing. (I'm sure 6,000 of that was *me*.) Ten years and one campaign later, this colorless, nearly tasteless, and odorless product is the preferred brand, selling nearly 3 million cases a year. All because of the advertising (Figure 2.2).

More anecdotal, but equally impressive, were the results of the trade campaign created to attract advertisers to the pages of *Rolling Stone* magazine. After Fallon McElligott's famous "Perception/ Reality" campaign was up and running (Figure 2.3), publisher Jann Wenner was reported as saying, "It was like someone came in with a wheelbarrow of money and dumped it on the floor."

It's a great business, make no mistake. I see what copywriter Tom Monahan meant when he said, "Advertising is the rock 'n' roll of the business world."

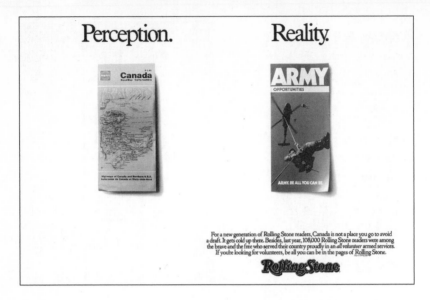

*Figure 2.3   First scribbled on a napkin in a New York City diner by
writer Bill Miller, this campaign went on to be named one of the
10 best campaigns of the 1980s.*

BRAND = ADJECTIVE.

Each brand has its own core value. Dan Wieden says it another way:
Brands are verbs. "Nike exhorts, IBM solves, and Sony dreams."
Even Mr. Whipple, as bad as he was, helped Charmin equal soft.

This is an important point, and before we talk about strategy, it
bears some discussion.

People don't have time to figure out what your brand stands for.
It is up to you to make your brand stand for something. The way to
do it is to make your brand stand for *one* thing. Brand = adjective.
Everything you do with regard to advertising and design—whether
it's creating the product or designing the web site—adheres to
absolutely draconian standards of simplicity.

Recently, I was on the phone with a client who works for a
nationwide chain of grocery stores. This director of marketing mentioned in passing that the number of brands on the shelves in his
stores had just passed 50,000.

That's 50,000 brands competing for a customer's attention.

50,000.

This number alone should take the spring from the step of any advertising person whose job it is to make the silhouette of a brand show up on a customer's radar. Until recently, it's been reasonable to assume that the way to make customers remember a brand is to differentiate it from its competitors: "The model of car we're selling has incredible styling and the other guy's brand doesn't."

But your competition isn't just the other guy's car.

When you sit down to do an ad, you are competing with *every* brand out there. You're competing with the 50,000 packaged-good brands on the shelves at the grocery store, as well as every other product and service and logo in the country. You're competing for attention with every TV commercial that has ever aired, with each billboard on every mile of highway, with the entire bandwidth across the radio, and every one of the 100 trillion pixels on the Web. All those other advertisers want a piece of your customer, and they're going to get it at your client's expense. Looked at from this perspective, through the teeming forest of brands vying for customers' attention, cutting through the clutter may require more than giving a sharp knife-edge to your brand. It calls for a big, noisy, smoking chain saw.

But a kick-ass Super Bowl commercial isn't what I mean by a chain saw.

The chain saw you need is simplicity.

SIMPLE = GOOD.

When you think about it, what other antidote to clutter can there possibly *be* except simplicity?

Perhaps we should try cutting through the clutter with clutter that's extremely entertaining? Should we air clutter that tests well? Or clutter that wins awards or clutter with a big 800 number?

I propose that the only possible antidote to clutter is draconian simplicity.

Draconian simplicity involves stripping your brand's value proposition down to the bone and then again to the marrow, carving away until you get down to brand = adjective. Make your brand stand for one thing. Pair it with one adjective.

But which adjective?

If you ask consumers in focus groups to talk about buying a car, with sufficient amounts of Dr Pepper and M&M's, they will amaze you with their complex analysis of the auto-buying process. I'm not kidding. These groups go on for hours, days. But if you ask a guy in a bar, "Hey, talk to me about cars," he'll break it down to a word—usually an adjective.

"Yeah, gonna get me a Jeep. They're tough."

Porsches, they're fast. BMWs perform. And Volvos, they're . . . what?

If you said "safe," you've given the same answer I get from literally every person I've ever asked. Ever.

In every speech I've ever given, anywhere around the world, when I ask audiences, "What does Volvo stand for?" I hear the same answer every time: "*Safety*." Audiences in Berlin, Los Angeles, Helsinki, Copenhagen, New York City all give the same answer. The money Volvo has spent on branding has paid off handsomely. Volvo has successfully spot welded that one adjective to their marque. And here's the interesting bit: In the past couple of years, Volvo hasn't even made it onto the top 10 list of safest cars on the market. So here's a brand that, having successfully paired its logo to one adjective, rides the benefit of this simple position in customers' minds long after its products no longer even *merit* the distinction. Such is the power of simplicity.

The adjective you choose is key. Once it's married to a brand, divorce can be ugly. On the good side, once it's paired with the brand, that one square foot of category space is taken. If all the good adjectives are taken, don't settle for the second best. (*"'Refreshing' is taken? Oh well . . . gimme 'Quenching.'"*) Second best won't be different enough. Try a polar opposite. Or consider a flanking move. In ketchup, the adjective everyone fought over for a long time was to be the "tomato-iest." Then one day Heinz came along claiming it was the "slowest," and sales went up—and stayed up. You can also try creating a whole new adjective that alters the playing field in your favor. (Axe cologne's "Bom Chicka Wah Wah" comes to mind.) The right adjective, the answer, will come out of the product. Or from your customers. Ask them. They know the answer.

Find an adjective and stick to it. But it's the sticking to it that so many brands seem to have trouble with. The problem may be that, from a client's perspective, there are many things to admire about the product.

"How can we narrow down our brand's value proposition to a word? Our product lasts longer, it's less expensive, it works better. *All* that stuff's important." Yes, those secondary benefits are important, and, yes, they have a place: in the brochures, on the packaging, or two clicks into the web site. All those other benefits will serve to shore up the aggregate value proposition of a brand, once customers try it. But what they're going to remember a brand for, the way they're going to file it on their desktops, is with a *word*.

Find that word.

You may argue that I have oversimplified here. And I have; I'll accept the criticism. Because I'm arguing for purism in an area where it's often impossible to think that way. Many brands simply do not lend themselves to such clean theoretical distinctions. But at least try; try to find that one word.

You're going to thank me when it comes time to sit down and think up an ad.

———

BEFORE YOU PUT PEN TO PAPER.

Before you do any new thinking, there's some background work to do. You won't be doing it alone, though. You'll have help from the people in account service.

The account folks are the people in charge of an account at an agency. They analyze the market, study the competition, and arrange for and interpret the research. They formulate strategy, set budgets, and do a whole bunch of other stuff, some of it boring. They also help you present work to the client. Overall, they're the liaison between client and agency, explaining one to the other.

Some account people are great, some so-so, and some bad. It will pay to hitch up with the smart ones as soon as you can. The good ones have the soul of a creative person and will share your excitement over a great ad. They're articulate, honest, and inspiring, and they have a better batting average at selling your work.

Here are some things I've learned from the great account people I've worked with.

Start by examining the current positioning of your product.

There's a book called *Positioning: The Battle for Your Mind*, one I recommend with many caveats. (Though the strategic thinking of the authors is sound, I have many differences with them on the subject of creativity, which they declare irrelevant.)

The authors, Ries and Trout, maintain that the customer's head has a finite amount of space in which to remember products. In each category, there's room for perhaps three brand names. If your product isn't in one of those slots, you must "de-position" a competitor to take its place.

Before you start, look at the current positioning of your product. What positions do the competitors occupy? What niches are undefended? Should you concentrate on defining your client's position, or do some de-positioning of the competition? Do they have an adjective? What's your adjective?

Get to know your client's business as well as you can.

Bill Bernbach said, "The magic is in the product. . . . You've got to live with your product. You've got to get steeped in it. You've got to get saturated with it."

The moral for writers and art directors is: Do the factory tour. I'm serious. Go if you get the chance. Ask a million questions. How is the product made? What ingredients does it have? What are their quality control criteria? Read every brochure. Read every memo you can get your hands on. You may find ideas waiting in the middle of a spec sheet ready to be transplanted kit-and-caboodle into an ad. Learn their business.

Your clients are going to trust you more if you can talk to them about their industry in *their* terms. They'll quickly find you boring or irrelevant if all you can speak about with authority is Century Italic. Your grasp of the client's marketing situation has to be as well versed as any account executive's. There are no shortcuts. Know the client. Know their product. Know their market. It will pay off.

Louis Pasteur said, "Chance favors the prepared mind."

On the other hand, there's value in staying stupid.

This dissenting opinion was brought to my attention by a great copywriter, Mark Fenske. Mark says, "Don't give into the temptation to take the factory tour. Resist. It makes you think like the client. You'll start to come up with the same answers the client does."

Mark thinks, as many do, that keeping your "tabula" extremely "rasa" makes your thinking fresher. He may be right. There's also this to consider: When you're on the factory floor watching the caps get put on the bottles, you are a long way from the customer's reality. All the customer cares about is "What's in it for me?"

Get to know the client's customers as well as you can.

Once you get into the agency business, you'll meet another member on the team, a person called a *planner*.

It's the job of planners to learn as much as they can about the client's customers and feed it back to both client and agency. Read everything your planners give you before putting pen to paper. Remember, most of the ads you do will be targeted to people outside your small social circle, people with whom you have no more in common than U.S. citizenship.

Take farming. I've written TV commercials selling herbicides to soybean farmers, but what do I know about farming? As a kid, I couldn't even keep an *ant* farm alive a week after it arrived in the mail. Getting into the mind-set of a soybean farmer took plenty of work—lots of videotaped interviews and plenty of reading. Your account planners can give you piles of material to study.

But don't just read it. Feel it. Take a deep breath and sink slowly into the world of the person you're writing to. Maybe you're selling a retirement community. You're talking to an older person. Someone living on a fixed income. Maybe they're worried about becoming dependent on their kids. It hurts when they get out of a chair. The idea of shoveling snow has dark-red cardiac overtones. How does it *feel* to be them?

Ask to see the entire file of the client's previous advertising.

The client or the account executives will have it somewhere. Study it. Maybe they tried something that was pretty cool, but they didn't do it right. How could you do it better? It will get your wheels turning. It'll also keep you from presenting ideas the client has already tried.

Insist on a tight strategy.

Creative director Norman Berry wrote: "English strategies are very tight, very precise. Satisfy the strategy and the idea cannot be faulted even though it may appear outrageous. Many . . . strategies are often too vague, too open to interpretation. "The strategy for this product is taste,' they'll say. But that is not a strategy. Vague strategies inhibit. Precise strategies liberate."[7]

Poet T.S. Eliot never worked at an ad agency, but his advice about strategy is right on the money: "When forced to work within a strict framework, the imagination is taxed to its utmost and will produce its richest ideas. Given total freedom, the work is likely to sprawl."

Dude nailed it. You need a tight strategy.

On the other hand, a strategy can become too tight. When there's no play in the wheel, an overly specific strategy demands a very narrow range of executions and becomes by proxy an execution itself. Good account people and planners can fine-tune a strategy by moving it up and down a continuum that ranges between broad, meaningless statements and little purse-lipped creative dictums masquerading as strategies.

When you have it just right, the strategy should be evident in the campaign but the campaign should not be evident in the strategy. Jean-Marie Dru put it elegantly in his book *Disruption*:

> There are two questions that need to be asked. The first is: Could the campaign I'm watching have been created without the brief? If the answer is yes, the odds are that the campaign is lacking in content. You have to be able to see the brief in the campaign. The second question is a mirror image of the first. . . . Is the campaign merely a transcription of the brief? If the answer is yes, then there has been no creative leap, and the campaign lacks executional force.[7]

Ultimately, a good strategy is inspiring. You can pull a hundred rabbits out of the same hat, creating wildly different executions all on strategy. Goodby, Silverstein & Partners' magnificent "milk deprivation" strategy called forth a long string of wonderful "Got milk?" executions.*

Insist on a tight strategy. Will you always get one? No. In fact, in this business, they sometimes seem to be the exception, not the rule. But you must push for one as hard as you can.

The final strategy should be simple.

Advertising, as my friend Mark says, isn't "rocket surgery."

People live and think in broad strokes. Like we said earlier, ask some guy in a mall about cars. He'll tell you Volvos are safe, Porsches are fast, and Jeeps are rugged. Boom. Where's the genius here? There isn't.

---

*Go online to one of the ad archive sites and study the campaign. Or see *Communication Arts*, December 1995, for examples.

You want people who feel X about your product to feel Y. That's about it. We're talking one adjective here. Most of the time, we're talking about going into a customer's brain and spot welding one adjective onto a client's brand. That's all. DeWalt tools are tough. Coke is refreshing.

I'm reminded of how Steven Spielberg said he preferred movie ideas that could be summed up in a sentence. "Lost alien befriends lonely boy to get home."

The moral is: Keep it simple. Don't let the account executives or the client make you overthink it. Try not to slice too thin. Think in bright colors.

Make sure what you have to say matters.

It must be relevant. It must matter to somebody, somewhere. It has to offer something customers want or solve a problem they have, whether it's a car that won't start or a drip that won't stop.

If you don't have something relevant to say, tell your clients to put their wallets away. Because no matter how well you execute it, an unimportant message has no receiver. The tree falls in the forest.

Testing strategy is better than testing executions.

This is the best of all possible worlds, and the day hell freezes over, all clients will be testing this way. A few do this now. Here's how it works.

You sit down with the client, the planners, and the account team. You explore all the possible strategies available to your brand. You settle on 5 or 6—10, if you want.

Then you make what are called "benefit boards." Simple, flat-footed layout things that look and feel like ads but aren't. Usually a picture with a headline that spells out with little fanfare exactly the strategy you'd like to test.

For example, say the client manufactures aspirin. The pictures could be anything really—a shot of a person nursing a headache or a close-up of two aspirins on a tabletop. Next to the picture on each board is a headline pitching a different angle on the product: "Faster-acting Throbinex." "Throbinex is easy on the stomach." "Smaller, easier-to-swallow pills." Just crank them out. These aren't ads. They're benefits.

Show 10 different boards like these to a focus group and you'll come away with a good idea of which messages resonate with customers. It's a great place to start. In fact, it's the only place to start.

Go to the focus groups.

Every chance you get to hear what customers are saying, take it. If there's a web site or chat room about a product or brand, go there. Eavesdropping is the best way to learn what customers think.

Less useful (and usually more infuriating) is to hear what customers are saying about your work—in focus groups. I used to hate doing this; I still do. There are *few* things I hate more than listening to focus group people complain about my ideas.* I think pretesting concepts by showing rough layouts and storyboards to people off the street is a bane to the industry. (But more on that later, in Chapter 11.)

For now, I say go to the groups, if only for the reason that it helps you sell work to the client. Because once you've put in the hours at the groups, you can say, "Yes, I sat there and stared through the glass at those people. I think I have a very good idea of what strategies work, what they like, and what they don't, and in my opinion this campaign will work."

Read the publications your ads will be in.

Check out the articles. See what your target customer is reading. Case the joint. Get a feel for the place your ad will be appearing.

Read the awards books.

Take a little inspiration from the excellence you see there. Then get ready to do something just as great. The best awards books are from the One Show and *Communication Arts*, as well as the British D&AD annuals. There are also the ad sites online. (I list several of the better ad sites in the back of this book, but keep in mind that they come and go.)

---

*The Three Things I Hate More Than Going to Focus Groups: (1) sawing off my feet and walking into town on the stumps, (2) sticking an Alka-Seltzer tablet under my eyelid, and (3) kissing the side of a moving train that's made out of sandpaper and then bobbing for razor-blade-filled apples in a tub of boiling alcohol.

Look at the competitors' advertising.

Each category quickly manages to establish its own brand of bor-ing. Learn the visual clichés. Visit their web sites. Watch their com-mercials. Creep through the woods, part the branches, and study the ground your competitors occupy. What is their strategy? What is their look? Those schmucks. They don't know what's coming.

Now comes the fun part. Sharpening your pencil and sitting down to come up with a cool idea.

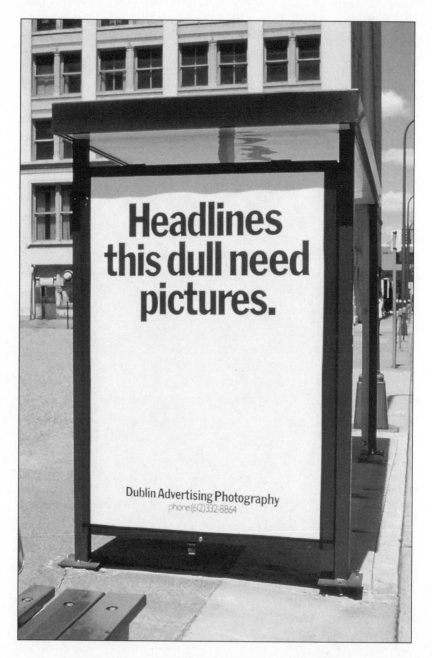

Figure 3.1   A short, five-word course in advertising.

3

A Clean Sheet of Paper

Making an ad—the broad strokes

LET'S BEGIN THIS PART OF OUR DISCUSSION with a quotation from Helmut Krone, the man who did what I think is the industry's first good ad: "I start with a blank piece of paper and try to fill it with something interesting." So if I'm working on a print ad, that's what I do. I get a clean sheet of paper and draw a small rectangle. I figure if an idea doesn't work in a small space, it's not going to work.

And then I start.

SAYING THE RIGHT THING THE RIGHT WAY.

Remember, you have two problems to solve: the client's and yours.

Imagine this circle (Figure 3.2) is the target's bull's-eye of what the brand stands for. Any ad you do that lands inside this area is perfect. The client will love it. If it's outside the circle, they won't. Nor should they.

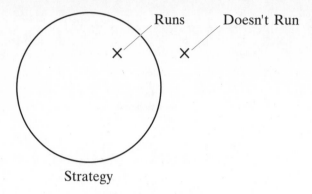

Figure 3.2   *If your idea lands inside the client's*
brand space, they'll love it. If not, buh-bye.

Okay, now imagine you have two circles, overlapping (Figure 3.3).

The one on the left is the client's bull's-eye and on the right is the bull's-eye for what *you* think is a great ad.

The trick is to hit that sweet spot where the two circles overlap.

You solve the account team's and the client's problem by saying exactly the right thing. That's relatively easy; it's the strategy. But you aren't finished until both problems are solved. By nailing the sweet spot.

Bernbach once said, "Dullness won't sell your product, but neither will irrelevant brilliance." Here, dullness is represented on the far left side of the left circle, and irrelevant brilliance on the far right side of the right.

The moral? Do both perfectly. Hit the overlap.

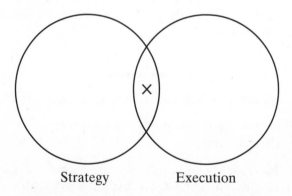

Figure 3.3   *If your idea is only in the left circle, it*
might be boring. Only on the right, it might be
stupid. Hit the sweet spot to win cash and prizes.

Pose the problem as a question.

Creativity in advertising is problem solving. When you state the problem as a bald question, sometimes the answers suggest themselves. Take care not to simply restate the problem in the terms in which it was brought to you; you're not likely to discover any new angles. Pose the question again and again, from entirely different perspectives.

In his book *The Do-It-Yourself Lobotomy,* Tom Monahan puts it this way: "Ask a better question." By that he means a question to which you don't know the answer. He likens it to "placing the solution just out of your reach," and in answering it, you stretch yourself.[1]

As philosopher John Dewey put it: "A problem well-stated is a problem half-solved." It can work. Eric Clark reminds us just how it works in his book *The Want Makers.*

> In the 1960s, a team wrestled for weeks for an idea to illustrate the reliability of the Volkswagen in winter. Eventually they agreed that a snowplow driver would make an excellent spokesman. The break-through came a week later when one of the team wondered aloud, "How does the snowplow driver get to his snowplow?"[2]

If you've never seen it, the VW "snowplow" commercial is vintage Doyle Dane. A man gets in his Volkswagen and drives off through deep snow into a blizzard. At the end, we see where he's driving: the garage where the county snowplows are parked. The voice-over then asks, "Have you ever wondered how the man who drives a snowplow . . . drives to the snowplow? This one drives a Volkswagen. So you can stop wondering."

Don't be afraid to ask dumb questions.

That blank slate we sometimes bring to a problem-solving session can work in our favor. We ask the obvious questions that people too close to the problem often forget. In the question's very naïveté, we sometimes find simple answers that have been overlooked.

Ask yourself what would make you want to buy the product.

A simple enough piece of advice and one I often forget about while I'm busy trying to write an ad. Sit across from yourself at your desk.

Quiet your mind. And ask, "What would make me want to buy this product?"

Then try the flip side: What would you do if you were the one bankrolling the campaign?

There was a writer at my agency who was also an investor in a new product—some kind of running gear. He was both the writer and the client. When he sat down to do ads for a company whose failure would cost him a significant amount of money, he saw how some of the things he hated hearing from clients had merit.

Copywriter John Matthews wrote, "You learn a lot more about poker when you play for money and not for chips."

Find the central truth about your product.

Find the central truth about your whole product category. The central *human* truth. Hair coloring isn't about looking younger. It's about self-esteem. Cameras aren't about pictures. They're about stopping time and holding life as the sands run out.

There are ads to be written all around the edges of any product. But get to the ones written right from the essence of the thing. In *Hoopla*, Alex Bogusky is talking about this essence when he says, "We try to find that long-neglected truth in a product and give it a hug."[3] Notice he says they "find" this truth, not invent it. Roy Spence of GSD&M hits on the same point when he says, "Visionary ideas are discovered, not created." They're discovered. The best

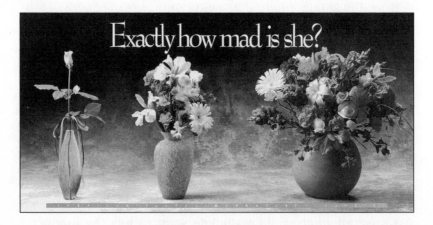

Figure 3.4   The headline could have been something boring like:
"We're proud of our wide variety of beautiful flower arrangements.
One's just right for your budget."

ideas are old truths brought to light in fresh, new ways. As an example, check out this ad by my friend Dean Buckhorn for the American Floral Marketing Council (Figure 3.4). He could have done something about how "purdy" flowers are. He didn't, and instead focused on one of the central human truths about this category—the use of flowers as a ticket out of the Casa di Canine.

Try the competitor's product.

What's wrong with it? More important, what do you like about it? What's good about their advertising?

Then try this trick. In *Marketing Warfare*, Ries and Trout suggested, "Find a weakness in the leader's strength and attack at that point."[4]

A good example comes to mind, again from the pens of Bernbach's crew. Avis Rent A Car was only number two. So Avis suggested you come to them instead of Hertz because "The line at our counter is shorter."

Dramatize the benefit.

Not the features of the product, but the benefit those features provide the user, or what some call "the benefit of the benefit." There is an old advertising maxim that expresses this wisdom in a way that's hard to improve: "People don't buy quarter-inch drill bits. They buy quarter-inch holes."

Avoid style; focus on substance.

Remember, styles change; typefaces and design and art direction, they all change. Fads come and go. But people are always people.

They want to look better, to make more money; they want to feel better, to be healthy. They want security, attention, and achievement. These things about people aren't likely to change. So focus your efforts on speaking to these basic needs, rather than tinkering with the current visual affectations. Focus first on the substance of what you want to say. Then worry about how.

Make the claim in your ad something that is incontestable.

Make it something that can't be argued about. Facts can't be refuted. There are some products to which this advice won't apply.

Products that are all image. Or products with no real difference worth hanging your hat on, like, I don't know, paper clips.

But when you have a fact at your command, use it. When you can say, "This product lasts 20 years," what's to argue with? State fact, not manufactured nonsense about, oh, say, how "We Put the 'Qua' in Quality."

GET SOMETHING, ANYTHING, ON PAPER.

The artist Nathan Oliveira wrote, "All art is a series of recoveries from the first line. The hardest thing to do is put down the first line. But you must."

Here are some ideas to help you get started.

First, say it straight. Then say it great.

To get the words flowing, sometimes it helps to simply write out what you want to say. Make it memorable, different, or new later. First, just say it.

Try this. Begin your headline with: "This is an ad about . . ." And then keep writing. Who knows? You might find, by the time you get to the end of a sentence, you have something just by snipping off the "This is an ad about" part. Even if you don't, you've focused. A good first step.

Whatever you do, just start writing. Don't let the empty page (what Hemingway called "the white bull") intimidate you. Go for art later. Start with clarity.

Restate the strategy and put some spin on it.

Think of the strategy statement as a lump of clay. You've got to sculpt it into something interesting to look at. So begin by taking the strategy and saying it some other way, any way. Say it faster. Say it in English. Then in slang. Shorten it. Punch it up. Try anything that will change the strategy statement from something you'd overhear in an elevator at a sales convention to a message you'd see spray painted on an alley wall.

Club Med's tagline could have been "A Great Way to Get Away." It could have been "More Than Just a Beach." Fortunately, Ammirati & Puris had the account, and it became: "Club Med. The Antidote for Civilization."

Be careful, too, not to let your strategy show. Many ads suffer from this transparence, and it happens when you fail to put enough creative spin on the strategy. Your ad remains flat and obvious, there's no magic to it, and reading it is a bit of a letdown. It's like Dorothy discovering that the Wizard of Oz is just some knucklehead behind a curtain.

In his book *Disruption,* Jean-Marie Dru described this kind of ad:

> You can tell when ads are trying too hard. Their intentions are too obvious. They impose themselves without speaking to you. By contrast, there are some that grab your attention with their executional brio, but their lack of relevance is such that after you've seen them they leave you kind of empty. Great advertising combines density of content with the elegance of form.[5]

Density of content and elegance of form. Great advice.

What's the mood you want your reader or viewer to feel?

This is a decision you can sometimes make early on in the process. It's likely based on the kind of product you are working with. If you're working on a web site for a hospital, well, pie-in-the-face humor probably shouldn't be on the list of likely solutions. Pick a mood. A feeling. You can change your mind later, but sometimes it helps give you focus when you decide, "Okay, this campaign is gonna be . . . thoughtful." Or angry, or stark, or . . . well, you decide. What's right for your client? What's right for the customer?

Allow yourself to come up with terrible ideas.

In *Bird by Bird,* her book on the art of writing fiction, Anne Lamott says:

> The only way I can get anything written at all is to write really, really crappy first drafts. That first draft is the child's draft, where you let it pour out and then let it romp all over the place, knowing that no one is going to see it and that you can shape it later. You just let this childlike part of you channel whatever voices and visions come through and onto the page. If one of the characters wants to say, "Well, so what, Mr. Poopy Pants?," you let her.[6]

Same thing in advertising. Start with "Free to qualified customers" and go from there.

Remember, notebook paper is not made only for recording gems of transcendent perfection. A sheet of paper costs about one-squillionth of a cent. It isn't a museum frame. It's a workbench. Write. Keep writing. Don't stop.

Allow your partner to come up with terrible ideas.

The quickest way to shut down your partner's contribution to the creative process is to roll your eyes at a bad idea. Don't. Even if the idea truly and most sincerely blows, just say, "That's interesting," scribble it down, and move on. Remember, this is not a race. (Well, if it is, it's one of those nerdy three-legged races at the company picnic where you and your partner win or lose together.) You are not in competition with your partner. You are competing with your client's rival brands.

No matter what your partner says, see if you can take it and shape it and mold it. Then throw it back to him or her with your idea tacked on. In a wonderful book called *Creative Advertising,* author Mario Pricken likens this conceptual back-and-forth to a game: " . . . a kind of ping-pong ensues, in which you catapult each other into an emotional state resembling a creative trance."[7]

Feed a baby idea lots of milk and burp it regularly.

Nurture a newly hatched idea. Until it grows up, you don't know what it's going to be. So don't look for what's wrong with a new idea, look for what's right. And no playing the devil's advocate just yet. Instead, do what writer Sydney Shore suggests: Play the "angel's advocate." Coax the thing along.

Share your ideas with your partner, even the kinda dumb half-formed ones.

Just because an idea doesn't work yet, it might work eventually. I sometimes find I get something that looks like it might go somewhere, but I can't do anything with it. It just sits there. Some wall inside prevents me from taking it to the next level. That's when my partner scoops up my miserable little half-idea and runs with it over the goal line.

Remember, the point of teamwork isn't to impress your partner by sliding a fully finished idea across the conference room table. It's about how $1 + 1 = 3$.

That said, I feel the need to remind you not to say aloud *every* stinking thing that comes into your head. It's counterproductive. I worked with someone like this once, and I ended up with a bad case of "idea-rrhea" that lasted the whole weekend.

Spend some time away from your partner, thinking on your own.

I know many teams who actually prefer to start that way. It gives you both a chance to look at the problem from your own perspective before you bring your ideas to the table.

Let your subconscious mind do it.

Where do ideas come from? I have no earthly idea. Around 1900, a writer named Charles Haanel said true creativity comes from "a benevolent stranger, working on our behalf." Novelist Isaac Singer said, "There are powers who take care of you, who send you patience and stories." And film director Joe Pytka said, "Good ideas come from God." I think they're probably all correct. It's not so much our coming up with great ideas as it is creating a canvas where a painting can appear.

So do what Marshall Cook suggests in his book *Freeing Your Creativity*: "Creativity means getting out of the way. . . . If you can quiet the yammering of the conscious, controlling ego, you can begin to hear your deeper, truer voice in your writing. . . . [not the] noisy little you that sits out front at the receptionist's desk and tries to take credit for everything that happens in the building."[8]

Stop the chatter in your head. Go into Heller's "controlled daydream." Breathe from your stomach. If you're lucky, sometimes the ideas just begin to appear.

What does the ad want to say? Not you, the ad.

Shut up. Listen.

In *The Creative Companion*, David Fowler says, "Maybe if you walked around the block you could hear it more clearly. Maybe if you went and fed the pigeons they'd whisper it to you. Maybe if you stopped telling it what it needed to be, it would tell you what it wanted to be. Maybe you should come in early, when it's quiet."[9]

Try writing down words from the product's category.

Most of the creative people I know have their own special system for scribbling down ideas. Figure out what works for you. For me—let's say we're selling outboard engines—I start a list on the side of the page: Fish. Water. Pelicans. Flotsam. Jetsam. Atlantic. Titanic. Ishmael.

What do these words make you think of? Pick up two of them and put them together like Tinkertoys. You have to start somewhere. Sure, it sounds stupid. The whole creative *process* is stupid.

It's like washing a pig. I'm serious. It's exactly like washing a pig. It's messy; it has no rules, no clear beginning, middle, or end; it's kind of a pain in the ass, and when you're done, you're not sure if the pig is clean or even why you were washing a pig in the first place. Welcome to the creative department.

Stare at a picture that has the emotion of the ad you want to do.

Have you ever tried to write an angry letter when you weren't angry? Oh, you manage to get a few cusswords on paper, but there's no fire to it. The same can be said for writing a good ad. You need to be in the mood.

I once had to do some ads for a new magazine called *Family Life*. The editors said this wasn't going to be just another "baby magazine," which are very much like diapers—soft, fluffy, and full of . . . My point is, they wanted ads that captured the righteous emotion of the editorial. Raising a child is the most moving, most important thing you'll ever do.

To get in the mood, I did two things. I reread a wonderful book by Anna Quindlen on the joys and insanities of parenting called *Living Out Loud*. I'd soak up a couple of pages before I sat down to write. When I was ready to put pen to paper, I propped up a number of different stock photos of children, including a picture of a child in a raincoat, sitting in a puddle (Figure 3.5).

As you can see in the ad reprinted here, the idea didn't come directly out of the photo, but in a way it did. It's worked for me. You might want to try it.

Explore Jim Aitchison's format: "Do I want to write a letter or send a postcard?"

In his book *Cutting Edge Advertising*,[10] Aitichison offers up this early fork in the road. Do you want to write a letter or just drop a postcard?

Fig 3.5   The headline was inspired by the photograph.
The copy reads: "The years from age 3 to 12 go by so fast.
Only one magazine makes the most of them."

A postcard, says Aitchison, is an ad that's visually led. A single visual and a small bit of copy are all that are needed to make the point. For example, to get across the spirit and drive of the new Beetle, Arnold Communications did this simple postcard (Figure 3.6): "0–60? Yes."

On the other hand, a letter is an ad that's predominantly copy-driven. It's probably better for ads that have to deliver a more complex message. Just the sheer weight of the body copy adds a sense of gravitas to the product regardless of whether the consumer reads a word of the copy. Check out the beautiful ad for Land Rover done by my friends at GSD&M (Figure 3.7).

There are both letter ads and postcard ads throughout this book. Take a look at how each visual or verbal format serves the different messages the brands are trying to convey.

Find a villain.

Find a bad guy you can beat up in the stairwell. Every client has an enemy, particularly in mature categories, where growth has to come out of somebody else's hide.

Your enemy can be the other guy's scummy, overpriced product.

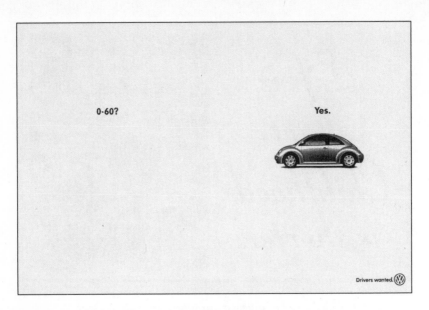

Figure 3.6   An example of a postcard ad. Write a postcard, says Aitchison,
when you have "just a little something" you want the customer to hear.
(Photographer: Bill Cash)

It can also be some pain or inconvenience the client's product spares you. If the product's a toothpaste, the villain can be tooth decay, the dentist, the drill, or that little pointy thing Laurence Olivier used on Dustin Hoffman in *Marathon Man*. ("Is it safe?") A villain can come from another product category altogether, in the form of what's called an *indirect competitor*. Parker Pens, for example, could be said to have an indirect competitor in word processors.

A gracefully raised knee to a villain's groin isn't just fun, it's profitable. Because competitive positioning is implicit in every villain paradigm.

It's also an easy and fun place from which to write. Mom was always telling us about "constructive criticism." Yeah, well highly underrated and much more fun is the concept of "destructive criticism."

"Tell the truth and run."

This old Yugoslavian proverb is a reminder of the power of truth. Even if you have an unpleasant truth, say it.

"We're Avis. We're only number two. So we try harder." Totally

Figure 3.7 "If we've learned one thing in 20 years of building Range Rovers, it is this. An ostrich egg will feed eight men." Followed by 630 words of Gold One Show body copy.

believable. More important, I like a company that would say this about themselves. America loves an underdog.

Perhaps the biggest underdog of all time was Volkswagen. VW was the king of self-deprecation. The honest voice Doyle Dane Bernbach created for this odd-looking little car turned its weaknesses into strengths. This ad is a perfect example (Figure 3.8).

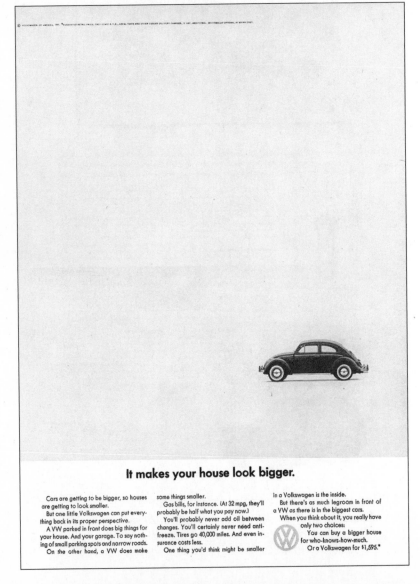

It makes your house look bigger.

Cars are getting to be bigger, so houses are getting to look smaller.

But one little Volkswagen can put everything back in its proper perspective.

A VW parked in front does big things for your house. And your garage. To say nothing of small parking spots and narrow roads.

On the other hand, a VW does make some things smaller.

Gas bills, for instance. (At 32 mpg, they'll probably be half what you pay now.)

You'll probably never add oil between changes. You'll certainly never need anti-freeze. Tires go 40,000 miles. And even insurance costs less.

One thing you'd think might be smaller in a Volkswagen is the inside.

But there's as much legroom in front of a VW as there is in the biggest cars.

When you think about it, you really have only two choices:

You can buy a bigger house for who-knows-how-much.

Or a Volkswagen for $1,595.*

Figure 3.8   Many other clients would've urged the agency to avoid, hide, or deny the small size of their car. Not VW.

Does the medium lend itself to your message?

Some great ads have been done playing off of the very place they appear. This is well-tilled ground, so take care that your idea hasn't been done a hundred times before. But when it works, it works.

The ad from Australia's Taronga Zoo is a great example and is reprinted at actual size (Figure 3.9).

Be provocative.

Sometimes the best way to bring the message home is to gallop into town and splash mud all over decent citizens.

Provocative is good. It gets your client talked about. Go over the line once in a while, when it seems right. Just a couple of steps. Going way over the line may backfire on you. And please, don't take this as permission to do a "pee-pee" joke. If I see even one more ad with a sly nudge-nudge-wink-wink reference to penises, I think I shall retire to my chambers, close the door, and gently weep until dusk.

Remember, being provocative just because you *can* isn't the point. Like Bernbach said, "Be sure your provocativeness stems

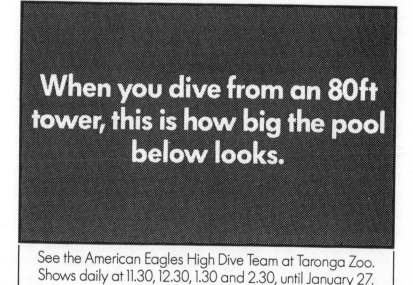

Figure 3.9   *Spinning your concept off the shape or placement of the ad is fun. This is well-tilled ground, so do your homework to make sure your idea hasn't been done a hundred times already.*

*Figure 3.10   Being provocative is good. Particularly when you
need to make people mad about something.*

from your product." This ad for the truth® youth-smoking prevention campaign qualifies (Figure 3.10). Here's a client that wants to
use the natural rebellious tendencies of teenagers and turn them on
the lies of tobacco companies. It's exactly the right time to pull out
all the stops.

"DO I HAVE TO DRAW YOU A PICTURE?"

Be visual and go short on the copy.

The screen saver on the computers at London's Bartle Bogle
Hegarty reads, "Words are a barrier to communication." Creative
director (CD) John Hegarty says, "I just don't think people read
ads."

I don't think most people read ads, either—at least not the body
copy. There's a reason they say a picture is worth a thousand words.
When you first picked up this book, what did you look at? I'm bet-
ting it was the pictures.

Granted, if you interest readers with a good visual or headline,
yes, they may go on to read your copy. But the point is, visuals
work fast. As the larger brands become globally marketed, visual

solutions will become even more important. They translate, not surprisingly, better than words.

Visual solutions are so universal, they work even after years in a deep freeze. Look at the 1879 ad for the Diebold Safe & Lock Company of Cleveland, Ohio (Figure 3.11). Putting aside the issue of whether this is a good ad or not, I'll bet it's a lot better than any verbal equivalent from other safe manufacturers of the times. (*"Doers of Evil and Kriminal Minds agree, Monies safekept in an Acme Vault are ne'er Pilfered For Gambling & Likker."*)

The ad for Mitsubishi's Space Wagon (Figure 3.12) from Singapore's Ball Partnership is one of my all-time favorites. The message is delivered entirely with one picture and a thimbleful of words. What could you possibly add to or take away from this concept?

Relying on one simple visual means it assumes added responsibilities and a bigger job description. You can't bury your main selling idea down in the copy. If readers don't get what you're trying to say from the visual, they won't get it. The page is turned.

Don't take my word for it. Watch someone in the airport read a magazine. They whip through, usually backward, at about two sec-

Figure 3.11   A visual ad from the 1800s.

Figure 3.12   Long-copy ads can be great. This is not one of them.

onds per page. They glance at the clock on the wall. They turn a page. They think about the desperate, pimpled loneliness of their high school years. They look at a page. They see your ad.

If you can get them to take in your visual (or read your headline), your ad is a resounding success. Break out the Champale. Call your parents. You are a genius.

Coax an interesting visual out of your product.

One day when he was a little boy, my son Reed and I went through this mental exercise using his toy car. I held the car in its traditional four-wheels-to-the-ground position and asked him, "What's this?" "A car," he said. I tipped it on its side. Two wheels on the ground made the image "a motorcycle." I tipped the car on its curved top. He saw a hull and said, "Boat." When I set it tailpipe to ground, pointing straight up, he saw propulsion headed moonward and told me, "It's a rocket!"

Look at your product and do the same thing. Visualize it on its side. Upside down. Make its image rubber. Stretch your product visually six ways to Sunday, marrying it with other visuals, other icons, and see what you get—always keeping in mind you're trying to coax out of the product a dramatic image with a selling benefit.

What if it were bigger? Smaller? On fire? What if you gave it legs? Or a brain? What if you put a door in it? What is the wrong way to use it? How else could you use it? What other thing does it look like? What could you substitute for it? Take your product, change it visually, and by doing so, dramatize a customer benefit.

Get the visual clichés out of your system right away.

Certain visuals are just old. Somewhere out there is a Home for Tired Old Visuals. Sitting there in rocking chairs on the porch are visuals like Uncle Sam, a devil with a pitchfork, and a proud lion, just rocking back and forth waiting for someone to use them in an ad once again. And grousing, "When we were young, we were in all kinds of ads. People used to *love* us."

Remember: Every category has its own version of Tired Old Visuals. In insurance, it's grandfathers flying kites with grandchildren. In the tech industries, it's earnest people looking at computer screens. And in beer, it's boobs. Learn what iconography is overused in your category, and avoid it.

Check out the ad for Polaris watercraft in Figure 3.13. It's just a wild guess, but I'm thinkin' this is probably the first use of a hippo in the Jet Ski category.

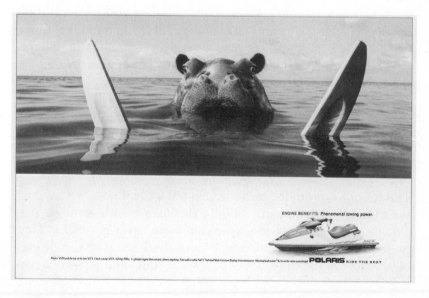

Figure 3.13   In the watercraft category, a Tired Old Visual might be a happy, wet family having a grand time waterskiing. That is why this marvelous ad stands out.

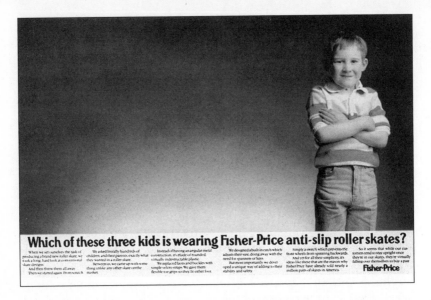

Which of these three kids is wearing Fisher-Price anti-slip roller skates?

Figure 3.14   The mental image this ad paints of two kids landing on their duffs is more powerful than actually showing them that way.

Show, don't tell.

Telling readers why your product has merit is never as powerful as showing them. I could take all day explaining how well a certain brand of vacuum cleaner works, but you'll sit up and take notice when I plug it in and show how it empties a sandbox in under a minute. Showing the benefit of your product also allows readers to reach their own conclusions. It's more involving.

This great ad by BMP in London for Fisher-Price's antislip roller skates (Figure 3.14) is a good example of the benefits of showing your story, not telling it. It's one of my all-time favorites.

Saying isn't the same as being.

This is a corollary to the previous point. If a client says, "I want people to think our company is cool," the answer isn't an ad saying, "We're cool." The answer is to be cool. Nike never once said, "Hey, we're cool." They just *were* cool. C'mon, think about it. The Beatles didn't meet in the third-floor conference room and go over a presentation about how they were going to become known as cool. They just *were* cool.

The folks at Crispin Porter + Bogusky think the same way, focusing often on what they call "proof points." As an example, for their auto client MINI Cooper they could have run a TV commercial that said, "Hey America, this is one unconventional car that puts the fun back in driving!" Instead, they mounted a MINI on *top* of an SUV (typically the space you strap down the fun stuff like bikes and surf-boards) and drove the hulking gas-guzzler around town with a message that said, "What are you doing this weekend?" The damn car *fit* up there. And when you saw this thing drive by you on the street, it was more than just a claim of unconventionality and fun. It was proof.

As Miss Manners politely points out, "It is far more impressive when others discover your good qualities without your help."

"THE REVERSE SIDE ALSO HAS A REVERSE SIDE."

When everybody else is zigging, you should zag.

There was this really dumb supervillain in the old Superman comics, Bizzaro-Man. He did everything . . . opposite. It was really stupid (and cool). Try being Bizzaro-Man.

If your product is white sheets, write the headlines in mud. If your product is beautiful, show something ugly. If your product is an insurance ad, design it like a poster for a rock concert. Try writing your copy backward. Encircle the logo for your bank client with hot dogs. I'm not saying all this Bizzaro crap makes your idea great. But you should at least search as far outside the boundaries of convention as you can. It's likely you'll end up pulling back a bit, but you won't know what's out there until you go.

Steve Dunn, a fabulous art director from London, put it this way: "One thing I recommend is at some point you should turn everything on its head. Logos usually go lower right, so put them top left. Product shots are usually small, make them big. Instead of headlines being more prominent than the body copy, do the opposite. It's perverse, but I'm constantly surprised how many times it works."[11]

Don't be different just to be different.

You must have a reason to "zag," one beyond just the desire to be different. Bill Bernbach said it best:

> Be provocative. But be sure your provocativeness stems from your product. You are not right if in your ad you stand a man on his head just to get attention. You are right if [it's done to] show how your

product keeps things from falling out of his pockets. Merely to let your imagination run riot, to dream unrelated dreams, to indulge in graphic acrobatics is not being creative. The creative person has harnessed his imagination. He has disciplined it so that every thought, every idea, every word he puts down, every line he draws . . . makes more vivid, more believable, more persuasive the . . . product advantage.[12]

Consider the opposite of your product.

What doesn't the product do? Who doesn't need the product? When is the product a waste of money? Study the inverse problem and see where negative thinking leads.

I saw a great opposite idea in a student book. It was a small poster for a paint manufacturer that painters could put up after their job was finished. Above the company's logo, this warning: "Dry Paint." Recently, I saw another good one in the *New York Times Magazine*. It's called *reverse graffiti*. If you wipe or sand the grime off the wall of derelict property, words and images can be formed by the cleaned area. The kid described in the article was accused by the local city council of breaking the law. "For what?" he asked. "Cleaning without a permit?"[13]

Avoid the formula of saying one thing and showing another.

"Your kids deserve a licking this summer" . . . and then you have a picture of some kids with lollipops. Get it?

Again, this isn't a rule. But if you use this sort of setup, make sure the difference between word and picture is breathtaking. The polarity between the two should fairly crackle. This ad from Leagas-Delaney in London is a good example (Figure 3.15).

Move back and forth between wide-open, blue-sky thinking and critical analysis.

It's like this: Up there in my brain, there's this poet guy. Smokes a lot. Wears black. He's so creative. And "chicks dig 'im." He's got a million ideas. But 999,000 of them suck. He knows this because there's also a certified public accountant up there who tells him so.

"That won't work. You *suck*."

The CPA is a no-nonsense guy who clips coupons and knows how to fix the car when the poet runs it into the ditch on his way to

Figure 3.15   A very good example of picture playing off word, done by two very naughty British boys.

Beret World. Between the two of them, though, I manage to come up with a few ideas that actually work.

The trick is to give each one his say. Let the poet go first. Be loose. Be wild. Then let the CPA come in, take measurements, and see what actually works. I sense that I'm about to run this metaphor into the ground, so I'll just bow out here by saying, go back and forth between wild dorm-room creativity and critical dad's-basement analysis, always keeping your strategy statement in mind.

See if you can avoid doing the old "exaggeration" thing.

Sometimes I think there's this tired old computer program inside every copywriter's and art director's head. I call this programming circuitry the *Exaggeration chip.*

Say you're doing an ad for, oh, a water heater. The Exaggeration chip's first 100 ideas will be knee-jerk scenarios about how cold the water will be if you don't buy this water heater: *"Water heater? Easy. What you do is, like, you have* ice *cubes comin' out of the water faucet. See? 'Cause it's so cold the water faucet will have like* ice *cubes, see? Ice cubes . . . 'cause they're cold."*

Now, granted, there are plenty of great commercials out there that use exaggeration to great effect. I'll just warn you that the E-chip is typically the first mental program many creatives will apply to a problem.

Buy a lottery ticket and you'll be so rich that _____.
  (Fill in with I'm-really-rich joke here.)

Buy this car and you'll go so fast that _____.
  (Insert acceleration/cop-giving-ticket joke.)

It's just a little too easy. But here's the other thing. The E-chip will rarely lead you to a totally unexpected solution. You will end up somewhere in the same neighborhood as you started, maybe a little further out to the edge, but still nearby. A place you will likely share with everybody else who's working on the problem with an E-chip. In which case, it'll simply come down to who has the wackiest exaggeration.

Interpret the problem using different mental processes.

See what happens. From a book called *Conceptual Blockbusting*, by James Adams, I excerpt this list:[14]

build up	dissect	transpose
eliminate	symbolize	unify
work forward	simulate	distort
work backward	manipulate	rotate
associate	transform	flatten
generalize	adapt	squeeze
compare	substitute	stretch
focus	combine	abstract
purge	separate	translate
verbalize	vary	expand
visualize	repeat	reduce
hypothesize	multiply	understate
define	invert	exaggerate

Put on different thinking caps.

How would the folks at today's top agencies solve your problem? Chiat/Day, for instance. How would they solve it at Crispin? At

Goodby? How would they approach your problem at Disney? At Apple? At Amblin?

Shake the Etch A Sketch in your head, start over constantly, and come at the problem from wildly different angles. Don't keep sniffing all four sides of the same fire hydrant. Run through the entire neighborhood.

Metaphors must've been invented for advertising.

They aren't always right for the job, but when they are, they can be a quick and powerful way to communicate. Shakespeare did it: "Shall I compare thee to a summer's day?"

In my opinion (and the neo-Freudian Carl Jung's), the mind works and moves through and thinks in and dreams in symbols. Red means ANGER. A dog means LOYAL. A hand coming out of water means HELP. Ad people might say that each of these images has "equity," something they mean by dint of the associations people have ascribed to them over the years. You may be able to use this equity to your client's advantage, particularly when their product or service is intangible like, say, insurance. A metaphor can help make it real.

What makes metaphors particularly useful to your craft is they're a sort of conceptual shorthand and say with one image what you might otherwise need 20 words to say. They get a lot of work done quickly and simply.

The trick is doing it well. Just picking up an image/symbol and plopping it down next to your client's logo won't work. But when you can take an established image, put some spin on it, and use it in some new and unexpected way that relates to your product advantage, things can get pretty cool.

As soon as I put those words on paper, I remembered the marvelous British campaign for the *Economist*. In the one reprinted here (Figure 3.16), an unadorned keyhole is simply plopped down next to the logo. One stroke is all it takes to give the impression that this business magazine has inside information on corporations. So much for rules.

Still, I stand by the advice. Symbols lifted right off the rack usually won't fit your communication needs and typically need some spin put on them.

Example: By overlaying the image of stairs descending into the ocean, the creative team is able to paint a very quick picture of what awaits you at the Sydney Aquarium (Figure 3.17).

Verbal metaphors can work equally well, too. I remember a great ad from Nike touting their athletic wear for baseball. Below the

The Economist

Figure 3.16   Metaphor as ad. Keyhole = competitive business information.

picture of a man at bat, the headline read, "Proper attire for a curveball's funeral." In Figure 3.18, another verbal metaphor is put to good use to describe the feeling of flooring it in a Porsche.

"Wit invites participation."

Part of what makes metaphors in ads so effective is that they involve the reader. They use images already in the reader's mind, twist them to the message's purpose, and ask the reader to close the loop for us. There are other ways you can leave some of the work to the reader, and when you do it correctly, you usually have a better ad.

Here's an example. Nikon cameras ran an ad with the headline: "If you can picture it in your head, it was probably taken with a Nikon." Above this headline were four solid black squares, and inside each square was a small headline in white type describing a famous photograph.

"A three-year-old boy saluting at his father's funeral."

"A lone student standing in front of four tanks."

"An American President lifting his pet beagle up by the ears."

"A woman crying over the body of a student shot by the National Guard."

Instead of showing these famous photos, the negatives are developed in the reader's head. The reader sees JFK Jr. He sees Tiananmen Square. He sees LBJ and Kent State. "Hey, I know all

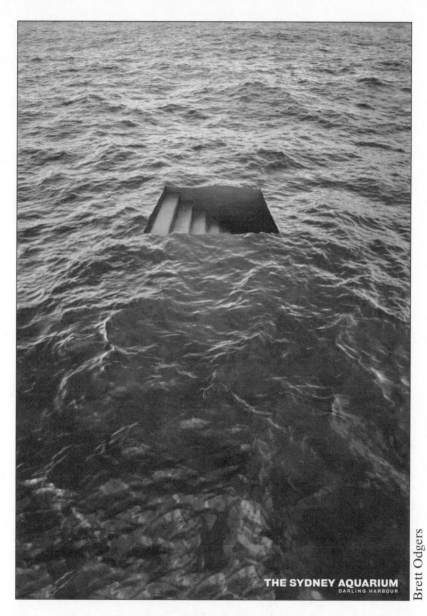

THE SYDNEY AQUARIUM
DARLING HARBOUR

Brett Odgers

Figure 3.17   Metaphors use concepts you already understand
to help you see new ones.

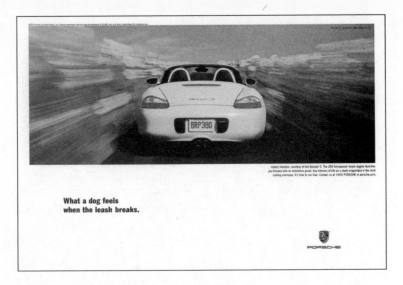

Figure 3.18   Verbal metaphors work just as well as visual ones.*

these photos." The reader connects the dots and in doing so is rewarded for applying his intelligence, rewarded for staying with the ad. The client is rewarded, too, with a reader actively closing the loop between the famous photos and the cameras that took them.

In a great book called *A Smile in the Mind: Witty Thinking in Graphic Design*, authors McAlhone and Stuart say that "wit invites participation."

> When wit is involved, the designer never travels 100% of the way [towards the audience.] . . . The audience may need to travel only 5% or as much as 40% towards the designer in order to unlock the puzzle and get the idea . . . it asks the reader to take part in the communication of the idea. It is as if the designer throws a ball which then has to be caught. So the recipient is alert, with an active mind and a brain in gear.[15]

Their point about traveling "only 5% or as much as 40%" is an important one. If you leave too much out, you'll mystify your audience. If you put too much in, you'll bore them.

---

*The PORSCHE CREST, PORSCHE and BOXSTER are registered trademarks and the distinctive shapes of PORSCHE automobiles are trade dress of Dr. Ing. h.c.F. Porsche AG. Used with permission of Porsche Cars North America, Inc. Copyrighted by Porsche Cars North America, Inc. Photographer: Georg Fischer.

Testing the borders of this sublime area will be where you spend much of your time when you're coming up with ads. Somewhere between showing a picture of a flaming zebra on a unicycle and an ad that reads "Sale ends Saturday" is where you want to be.

The wisdom of knock-knock jokes.

Consider these one-liners from stand-up comedian Steven Wright: "If a cow laughed, would milk come out her nose? . . . When you open a new bag of cotton balls, are you supposed to throw the top one away? . . . When your pet bird sees you reading the newspaper, does he wonder why you're just sitting there staring at carpeting?"

Well, I think it's funny. In the last bit, for instance, the word *newspaper* begins as reading material and ends as cage-bottom covering. A shift has happened and everything is slightly off. I don't know why these shifts and the sudden introduction of incongruous data make our computers spasm; they just do.

You may find that jumping from one point of view to another to introduce a sudden new interpretation is an effective way to add tension and release to the architecture of an ad. That very tension involves the viewer more than a simple expository statement of the same facts.

Creative theorist Arthur Koestler noted that a person, on hearing a joke, is "compelled to repeat to some extent the process of inventing the joke, to recreate it in his imagination." Authors McAlhone and Stuart add, "An idea that happens in the mind, stays in the mind . . . it leaves a stronger trace. People can remember that flash moment, the click, and recreate the pleasure just by thinking about it."

A good example is this famous poster for VW from the United Kingdom (Figure 3.19). As a viewer, you don't need it spelled out; in your head you quickly put together what happened, backward.

"And that, dear students," said the professor of Humor 101, "is why the chicken crossed the road." Suddenly, that's how this section on humor feels to me. Pedantic. So I'll just close by saying that jokes make us laugh by introducing the unexpected. An ad can work the same way.

Don't set out to be funny. Set out to be interesting.

Funny is a subset of interesting. Funny isn't a language. Funny is an accent. And funny may not even be the right accent.

I find it interesting that the Clios, a highly overrated awards show

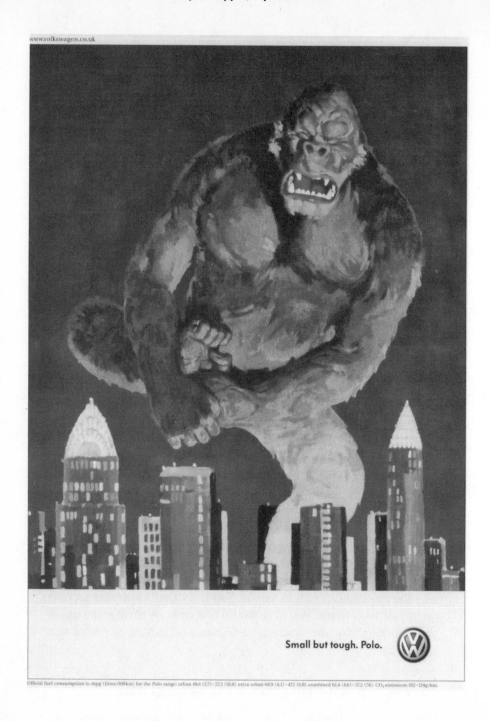

Figure 3.19   Does this ad rock, or what?

with far too many categories, had a category called "Best Use of Humor." And, curiously, no "Best Use of Seriousness." Funny, serious, heartfelt—none of it matters if you aren't interesting first. Howard Gossage, a famous ad person from the 1950s, said, "People read what interests them, and sometimes it's an ad."

Try not to look like an ad.

People don't buy magazines to look at ads. So why look like one? This doesn't mean you should make it look like nonsense. Just try not to look like an ad. An ad says, "Turn the page."

Perhaps you don't need to stick a logo in the lower right-hand corner. Can you find another way to sign off? Can your TV spot look like documentary footage? Or a soap opera?

Try not to sound like an ad.

Don't let your concept get in the way of the product. Bernbach said, "Our job is to sell our clients' merchandise . . . not ourselves. To kill the cleverness that makes us shine instead of the product." This can happen, and when clients kill an ad for this reason they may be right.

From more than one client, I've heard this dreaded phrase: "Your concept is a 'Visual Vampire.' " What they mean is the concept's execution is so busy it sucks the life out of their commercial message. Be ready for this one. Sometimes clients use the phrase as a bludgeon to kill something unusual they don't like. But sometimes, a few of them are right.*

This usually happens when the product bores you. Which means you haven't dug deep enough to find the thing about it that's exciting or interesting. You settle for doing some sort of conceptual gymnastics up front and tacking your boring old product on the back side, hoping the interest from the opening will somehow bleed over to your sales message. But the interesting part of an ad shouldn't be a device that points to the sales message, it should be the sales message.

To understand what it means to make your whole ad or commercial be the sales message, consider the analogy of giving your dog a pill. Dogs hate pills, right? So what do you do? You wrap the pill in a piece of baloney.

Well, same thing with your commercial's message. Customers

---

*I'm reminded of a garage-sale sign I saw tacked to a neighborhood phone pole. To attract attention to the sign they'd decorated it with balloons. But the wind blew the balloons across the sign and obscured the information. See? Kinda like that.

hate sales pitches. So you wrap your pitch in an interesting bit, and they're more likely to bite.

Unfortunately, most students take this to mean, "Oh, I see. All I have to do is show something interesting and funny for the first 25 seconds and then cut to the product." The answer is no. Because the customer will eat up the 25 seconds of interesting baloney and then walk away, leaving the pill in the dog dish.

You gotta wrap that baby right into the *middle* of the baloney. The two have to be one. Your interesting device cannot just point to the sales message; it must *be* the sales message.

Remember Bernbach's advice: "The product, the product, the product. Stay with the product." Don't get tangled up in unrelated ideas, however fanciful.

David Ogilvy used a classical reference to make this same point: "When Aeschines spoke, they said, 'How well he speaks.' But when Demosthenes spoke, they said, 'Let us march against Philip.'"

SIMPLE = GOOD, PART II.

If you take away one thing from this book, let it be this advice: Simple is almost always better.

Maurice Saatchi, of London's M&C Saatchi, on simplicity: "Simplicity is all. Simple logic, simple arguments, simple visual images. If you can't reduce your argument to a few crisp words and phrases, there's something wrong with your argument."

"Simplicity, simplicity, simplicity!"

Henry David Thoreau, sitting in his shack by the famous pond, penned this oft-quoted line. Seems to me Hank needs a dose of his own medicine:

"~~Simplicity, simplicity,~~ simplicity!"

There. That's better. Well, do the same with your ads. Look at this simple Nike piece (Figure 3.20). Every extraneous thing has been shaved away.

That reminds me. There's an old axiom called *Occam's razor:* When you have two correct answers that both solve the problem, the more correct answer is the simplest one. Because it solves the problem with fewer moving parts. It solves the problem more elegantly.

Figure 3.20   Michelangelo *said: "Beauty is the purgation of superfluities."*
I think Michelangelo would have dug this ad, big-time.

How difficult it is to be simple.

—Vincent van Gogh

Simple is hard to miss.

I've always thought a stop sign is a perfect metaphor for a good ad.
It makes me stop. It is relevant. It has one word. And most of all, it
is simple. It says, "STOP."

There is no introduction to "stop." No asterisks are needed to
understand "stop." And "stop" needs no snappy wrap-up.

So how is a stop sign different from a good ad in a magazine? I'm
turning the pages and suddenly right in my face is a big, simple, relevant message. How can I ignore it? This Japanese ad touting the
safety of Volvo cars stopped me (Figure 3.21).

Simple is bigger.

On May 7, 1915, a German U-boat sank a passenger ship, the
Lusitania, killing some 1,190 civilians, many of them women and
children. America was finally too angry to stay out of the Great
War, and enlistment posters began to appear in shop windows, one
of which is reprinted here (Figure 3.22).

Most other World War I posters were not as visual and instead
used headlines like "Irishmen, Avenge the Lusitania!" and "Take
Up the Sword of Justice." Seems to me, all these decades later,

Figure 3.21 An ad produced in Japan by two guys named Masakazu Sawa and Minoru Kawase. The translation to English is perfect.

they're not nearly as powerful as this one simple image, this one word.

Look at Google (Figure 3.23). One of the biggest brands in the world and perhaps the best search engine out there. Yet the simplicity of their home page could hardly be scrubbed down any further; in fact, it hasn't changed much since they first went online. Its very simplicity makes it easy to approach, easy to use. If they ever start adding stuff to the home page *("To see more links to YOUR favorite activities, click here!"),* I'll probably search somewhere else.

Remember, in a cluttered TV or print environment, less is truly more. So have your radio spot be one guy saying 40 words. Have your print ad be all one color. Lock the camera down and do your whole TV spot on a tabletop. Show a scorpion walking up a baby's arm, I don't know. Just do something simple. Simple is big.

The artist Cezanne said, "With an apple, I will astonish Paris."

Simple is easier to remember.

On a rainy November day in 1863, a U.S. senator named Edward Everett walked up to a podium and gave a two-and-one-half-hour speech consecrating a new cemetery. It was an impassioned speech,

Figure 3.22   Simple graphic images are powerful. Even decades later, this World War I recruitment poster still works.

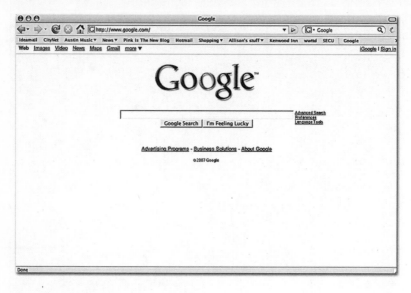

Figure 3.23   Google links to billions of sites—
all from this simple home page.

I'm sure, but I have been having trouble finding a transcript of this speech at the library.

The speaker that followed gave a 273-word speech, beginning with the words "Four score and seven years ago . . ."

Which of the two Gettysburg addresses given that day are you more familiar with?

Simple breaks through advertising clutter.

As we noted earlier, the only effective antidote to clutter is simplicity. How can anything else but simplicity break out of clutter?

Even the Super Bowl, with its annual collection of eye-popping TV commercials, has its own brand of clutter. Call it "pretty good clutter" if you will. But it's clutter just the same, and you have to find a way to improve what a scientist might call its "signal-to-noise ratio." You have to break out. You can do that only with an idea of sparkling simplicity.

The One Show recently honored a commercial created overseas that was sparkling in its simplicity, and inexpensive as well. The camera opens on a woman in a small, dingy room seen from behind glass. She's wearing orange overalls and is tired and dirty— probably a prisoner just getting off work detail. Appearing on the other side of the glass is her daughter, who asks, "When are you going to get out of here?" The exhausted mother shakes her head dispiritedly; all she can say for sure is, "In a while." Their hands come to the glass in between and touch tenderly. "I love you, Momma," says the girl before leaving. Mother replies, "I love you, too." The camera pulls back and we see the glass is just a shower door and that Mom is in the middle of a long, dirty job of cleaning the tiles in their family shower. The voice-over comes in to conclude this simple tableau with: "Spend less time cleaning. Vim Cream. Cleans the tough stuff. Easily."

Keep paring away until you have the essence of your ad.

Let's start with three observations from three different men: one dead, one British, and one crazy.

Robert Louis Stevenson said, "The only art is to omit."

Tony Cox, a fabulous British writer: "Inside every fat ad there's a thinner and better one trying to get out."

And then there's Neil French, one of my heroes and an absolutely stellar writer from Singapore. I was lucky enough to meet him one day, and he walked me through a wonderful exercise in in the art of omitting, of reductionism.

He started by drawing a thumbnail sketch of a typical ad (number one in Figure 3.24). You have your headline, your visual, some body copy, a tagline, and a logo.

Okay, he asked, can we make this ad work without the body copy? Maybe we could do that by making the headline work a little harder. We can? Good, let's take out the body copy. That leaves the slightly cleaner layout of number two.

What about that tagline? Is it bringing any new information to the ad? No? Then let's broom it. Look, the third layout's even better.

Now, about that headline. Is it doing something the visual can't do? And that logo—isn't there some way we can incorporate it into the visual?

Ultimately, Neil reduced his ad to one thing. He suggested I do the same with my next ad. Get it down to one thing. Sometimes it's just a headline. Sometimes a picture. Either way, he said, the math always works out the same. Every element you add to a layout reduces the importance of all the other elements. And conversely, every item you subtract raises the visibility and importance of what's left.

Figure 3.24   Neil's cool idea: reductionism. Ad number five is almost always going to be better than ad number one.

I admit, this kind of draconian reductionism is hard to pull off, especially when you have a client wanting to put more in an ad, not less. In my career I've done it only once. But to this day, that ad remains one of my favorites. It's the one you see here, reminding store buyers to stock Lee jeans (Figure 3.25). No logo. No headline.

The less you have to put in the ad, the better. The writer Saki said, "When baiting a trap with cheese, always leave room for the mouse."

LET'S START WITH OUTDOOR.

Billboards force you to be simple.

In all of advertising, billboards are the best place to practice the art of simplicity. In fact, my first mentor, Tom McElligott, told me if you have outdoor in the media mix for the campaign you're about to do, start there first. Nothing focuses you on a problem like this medium.

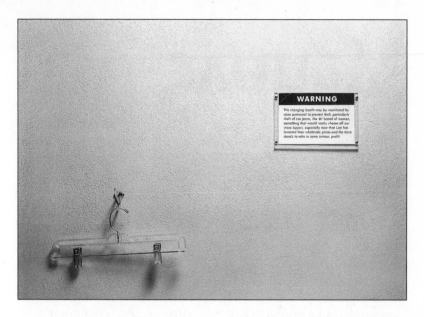

Figure 3.25   It's hard to read as it's reprinted here, but the little warning sign says: "This changing booth is monitored by store personnel to prevent theft, particularly theft of Lee jeans, the #1 brand of women, something that would really cheese off our store buyers, especially now that Lee has lowered their wholesale prices and the store stands to rake in some serious profit."

It's been said that a board should have no more than seven words. Any more and a passing driver can't read it. But then you add the client's logo. One or two words. Now you're up to nine. And if your visual is something that takes one or two beats to understand, well, in my opinion, you've already got too much on your plate.

I suggest draconian measures. Shoot for three words, tops. It doesn't mean you'll be able to keep it to three. But start with three as your goal. The board from the 1960s pictured here (Figure 3.26) works with just one word.

Here's a great way to test whether your outdoor ad is simple enough and works fast. It's also a great way to present it to the client. Walk up to your client, holding the layout of the idea with its back to your audience. Say, "Okay, here's a billboard we were thinking about" and then flip it around and show them the idea for two seconds.

*Figure 3.26   This old 1960s billboard for Pan Am Airlines
does its job with one word.*

Just two seconds—one Mississippi, two Mississippi—then flip it
back around again.

Check out this wonderful billboard for a new flavor of Altoid's
Curiously Strong Mints (Figure 3.27). It's marvelous. And it's fast.
Two words and a product shot. You hardly have to count past "one
Mississippi" to get it. Same thing for the great board for the JFK
museum (Figure 3.28). One visual, three words. Elegant and very
fast.

Your outdoor ideas will have to work just as quickly. Visualize
precisely how your idea is going to be viewed by the customer. Car
approaches, billboard whizzes by, and it's gone. If the idea you're
showing is as fast as these, I've found this presentation technique
can be persuasive. Remember, the rule is your board has to go at
least 65 miles an hour.

*Figure 3.27   An example of a billboard so simple you
could actually present it to a client in two seconds.
(Reprinted with permission of Callard & Bowser-Suchard, Inc.)*

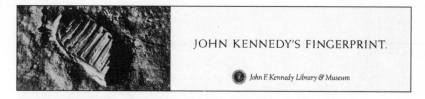

*Figure 3.28   Three beautifully chosen words that make the
reader reinterpret the visual.*

Outdoor is a great place to get outrageous.

Big as they are on the landscape, outdoor boards are an event, not
just an ad. In fact, what makes for a good print advertisement
doesn't necessarily make for a good billboard. Whatever you do,
don't create something just okay. The final size of a billboard out
there in the world only magnifies how an idea is just

OKAY.

You don't wanna be just okay.

Check this board out; it's way better than okay. Adidas brought to
life its "Impossible is nothing" tagline with a live-action board in
New Zealand. To launch the Fifa World Cup games there, the agency
(TBWA/Whybin) created a reverse bungee "Sky Screamer" ride
that looked like a giant soccerball, setting it up in front of a large
image of a popular player, Steven Gerrard. Fans who purchased a
ball were given the chance to "Be the Ball" and were strapped in on
seats inside. A sportscaster gave commentary on a match and at the
exact second they described Gerrard kicking the ball, the Sky
Screamer launched, reaching 105 mph in two seconds (Figure 3.29).

Outdoor begs for the ostentatious. Go for broke. Remember,
you're in "made-you-look, made-you-look" territory here. Outdoor
companies, prop makers, and tech firms can help bring just about
any wild idea to life. And now with the confluence of the Web and
mobile phones, people on the street can interact with boards, sending either video or text for all the world to see.

Figure 3.29   An example of "outdoor as event."

Your outdoor must delight people.

Except for the handful of great ideas in the One Show every year, most of the outdoor I see really sucks. When an ad in a magazine isn't good, I can turn the page. But if I live across the street from a bad billboard, there's nothing I can do about it except close my curtains.

Copywriter Howard Gossage didn't believe outdoor boards were a true advertising medium: "An advertising medium is a medium that incidentally carries advertising but whose primary function is to provide something else: entertainment, news, etc. . . . Your exposure to television commercials is conditional on their being accompanied by entertainment that is not otherwise available. No such parity or tit-for-tat or fair exchange exists in outdoor advertising. . . . I'm afraid the poor old billboard doesn't qualify as a medium at all; its medium, if any, is the scenery around it and that is not its to give away."[16]

The city of Sao Paulo, Brazil, has already outlawed billboards, and here in America several states are weighing similar bans. Well, until the day billboards are outlawed altogether (either as "corporate littering" or perhaps "retinal trespassing"), you owe the citizens of the town where your outdoor appears—you owe them your very best work. You must *delight* them.

———

A FEW THINGS BEFORE WE
BREAK FOR LUNCH.

Learn to recognize big ideas when you have them.

There will come a time when you see a great idea in a One Show annual, a campaign that'll make you go, "Damn! I thought of that once!" It's a hard thing to see, "your" idea done, and done well. That's why you have to be smart enough to pursue a promising idea once you've stumbled onto it. I'm reminded of a line by Ralph Waldo Emerson: "In every work of genius we recognize our own rejected thoughts."

See that one idea you have up on the wall? The one that's so much better than the others? Investigate why. There may be oil under that small patch of land. A big idea is almost always incredibly simple. So simple, you wonder why nobody's thought of it before. It has "legs" and can work in a lot of different executions in all kinds of media.

Coming up with a big idea is one skill. Recognizing a big idea is another skill. Develop both.

Big ideas transcend strategy.

When you finally come upon a big idea, you may look up from your pad to discover that you've wandered off strategy.

That's okay. The gold isn't always in them hills. But gold is gold, and good account people will understand this and help you retool the strategy to get the client past this unexpected turn in the road.

My friend Mike Lescarbeau compares a big idea to a nuclear bomb. Does it really *have* to land precisely on target to work?

Don't keep runnin' after you catch the bus.

After you've covered the walls with ideas and you've identified some concepts you really like, stop. And I mean covered the walls. This isn't permission to stop because you're tired or you have a few things that aren't half-bad. It's a reminder to keep one eye on the deadline.

Blue-skying is great. You have to do it. But there comes a time (and you'll get better at recognizing it) when you'll have to cut bait and start working on the really good ones. You have a fixed amount of time, so you'll need to devote some of it to making what's good great.

How to do a
Volkswagen ad.

1. Look at the car.

2. Look harder. You'll find enough advantages to fill a lot of ads. Like the air-cooled engine, the economy, the design that never goes out of date.

3. Don't exaggerate. For instance, some people have gotten 50 m.p.g. and more from a VW. But others have only managed 28. Average: 32. Don't promise more.

4. Call a spade a spade. And a suspension a suspension. Not something like "orbital cushioning."

5. Speak to the reader. Don't shout. He can hear you. Especially if you talk sense.

6. Pencil sharp? You're on your own.

Figure 4.1   A short course in copywriting from one of the best teachers in the world: Volkswagen.

4

Write When You Get Work

Making an ad—some finer touches

BEFORE WE BEGIN, A QUICK NOTE. The first edition of this book came out in 1998—last century, basically. At the time, the possibilities of advertising online were just starting to be realized, and since then the number of other media used to deliver advertising has gone kaleidoscopic.

That said, to begin our discussion of advertising ideas we still have to start somewhere. And for the purposes of this book, we'll make the humble print ad our starting point. No, it's not interactive and it doesn't link to other print ads. You don't have to go to L.A. to make a print ad, and it usually ends life under a puppy or a bird. But in its simple two dimensions and blank white space, it contains all the challenges we need in order to discuss the creative process.

So let's begin.

Come up with a lot of ideas. Cover the wall.

It's tempting to think that the best advertising people just peel off great campaigns 10 minutes before they're due. But that is perception, not reality.

In fact, "Perception/Reality" (the famous *Rolling Stone* campaign) is a perfect case in point. Those great ads that you may have seen in all the awards annuals are only the tip of the iceberg. The rest of it, a four-foot-high pile of other layouts, sat in writer Bill Miller's office for years. So massive was the pile of ideas that what he didn't use as ads actually served as a small table.

As a creative person, you will discover your brain has a built-in tendency to want to reach closure, even rush to it. Evolution has left us with circuitry that doesn't like ambiguity or unsolved problems. Its pattern-recognition wiring evolved for keeping us out of the jaws of lions, tigers, and bears—not for making lateral jumps to discover unexpected solutions. But in order to get to a great idea, which is usually about the 500th one to come along, you'll need to resist the temptation to give in to the anxiety and sign off on the first passable idea that shows up.

Linus Pauling: "The best way to get a good idea is to get a lot of ideas.... At first, ideas seem as hard to find as crumbs on an oriental rug. Then they start coming in bunches. When they do, don't stop to analyze them; if you do you'll stop the flow, the rhythm, the magic. Write them down and go on to the next one."

Which leads to our next point.

Quick sketches of your ideas are all you need during the creative process.

Don't curb your creativity by stopping the car and getting out every time you have an idea you want to work out. Just put the concept on paper and continue moving forward. You'll cover more ground this way.

Tack the best ideas on the wall.

Seeing them up there all in a bunch helps you determine whether there are campaigns forming and where there are holes that need to be filled.

You keep working on the details on your pad. But up there on the wall the big picture begins to take shape.

Write. Don't talk. Write.

Don't talk about the concepts you're working on. Talking turns energy you could use to be creative into talking about being creative.

It's also likely to send your poor listener looking for the nearest espresso machine because an idea talked about is never as exciting as the idea itself. If you don't believe me, call me up sometime and I'll describe the movie *The Matrix* to you.

There's an old saying: "A manuscript, like a fetus, is never improved by showing it to somebody before it is completed." Work. Just work. The time will come to unveil. For now, just work. The best ad people I know are the silent-but-deadly kind. You never hear them out in the hallways talking about their ideas. They're working.

Write hot. Edit cold.

Get it on paper, fast and furious. Be hot. Let it pour out. Don't edit anything when you're coming up with the ads.

Then, later, be ruthless. Cut everything that is not A-plus work. Put all the A-minus and B-plus stuff off in another pile you'll revisit later. Everything that's B-minus on down, put on the shelf for emergencies.

The wastepaper basket is the writer's best friend.

—*Novelist Isaac Singer*

Once you get on a streak, ride it.

When the words finally start coming, stay on it. Don't break for lunch. Don't put it off till Monday. You'd be surprised how cold some trails get once you leave them for a few minutes.

Athletes call this place (where everything is working, where all the pistons are firing) "the Zone." Some artists call it "the White Moment." I call it "that Brief Moment each week when I Don't Suck."

The moral: Never walk away from a hot keyboard (or a drawing pad).

If it makes you laugh out loud, make it work. Somehow.

You know those really funny ideas you get that make you laugh and say, "Wouldn't it be great if we could really do that?" Those are often the very best ideas, and it is only your superego/parent/internalized client saying you can't do it. You've stumbled on a mischievous idea. Something you shouldn't do. That's a good sign you're on to something you should do. Revisit it.

———

HOW TO WRITE HEADLINES BETTER THAN THIS ONE.

Get puns out of your system right away.

Puns, in addition to being the lowest thing on the joke food chain, have no persuasive value. It's okay to think them. It's okay to write them down. Just make sure you toss them.

Don't just start writing headlines willy-nilly. Break it down. Do willy first. Then move on to nilly.

If you have an assignment that calls for a more verbal solution, don't just start spitting out the headlines. Instead, methodically explore different attributes and benefits of your product as you write.

Here's an example from my files. The project is a bourbon.

The client can afford only a small-space newspaper campaign and a billboard or two. They've said they want to see their bottle, so the finished ads will likely be just a bottle and a headline. After some discussion with the account folks about tone ("thoughtful, intellectual"), the art director and I consider several avenues for exploration.

The bourbon's age might be one way to go. Bourbon, by law, is aged a minimum of two years, often up to eight, sometimes longer. So we start there to see what happens. We put our feet up and immediately begin discussing the movie *The Terminator*. Sometime after lunch we take a crack at the "aging" thing.

AGE IDEAS

Order a drink that takes nine years to get.

Like to hear how it's made? Do you have nine years?

(Note: On the pages from the actual file, there are about five false starts for each one of these headlines. Tons of scratch-outs and half-witted ideas that go nowhere.)

Nine years inside an oak barrel in an ugly warehouse. Our idea of quality time.

After nine years of trickle-down economics, it's ready just in time.

Nine long years in a barrel. One glorious hour in a glass.

Okay, nine years. What else happens in nine years? What about the feeling of the slow passage of time?

Continental drift happens faster than this bourbon.

Mother Nature made it whiskey. Father Time made it bourbon.

We can't make it slow enough.

What wind does to mountains, time does to this bourbon.

On May 15th, we"ll be rotating Barrel #1394 one-quarter turn to the left. Just thought you'd like to know.

Tree rings multiply. Glaciers speed by. And still the bourbon waits.

Maybe one of these might work. There's another take on age we might try—namely, how long the label's been on the market. Not the age of the whiskey, but of the brand.

HISTORY OF BRAND IDEAS

First bottled when other bourbons were knee-high to a swizzle stick.

First bottled back when American History was an easy course.

First bottled when American History was called Current Events.

First bottled when the Wild West meant Kentucky.

Smoother than those young whippersnapper bourbons.

Back in 1796, this bourbon was the best available form of central heating.

The recipe for this bourbon has survived since 1796.

Please don't bury it in a mint julep.

Write us for free information on what you can do with wine coolers.

We've been making it continuously since 1796. (Not counting that brief unpleasantness in the 1920s.)

If you can't remember the name, just ask for the bourbon first bottled when Chester A. Arthur was president.

110 years old and still in the bars every night.

If we could get any further behind the times, we would.

Are we behind the tymes?

A blast from the past.

First bottled before billboards.

This premium bourbon was first marketed via ox.

Introduced 50 years before ice cubes.

Okay, maybe there's some stuff we could use from that list. Maybe not. So far we've played with aging and brand history. What about where it's made?

KENTUCKY IDEAS

Kind of like great Canadian whiskey. Only it's bourbon. And from Kentucky.

Kind of like an old Kentucky mule. Classic, stubborn, and plenty of kick.

From the third floor of an old warehouse in Kentucky, heaven.

Warming trend expected out of Kentucky.

Now available to city folk.

If this ad had a jingle, it'd be "Dueling Banjos."

What the Clampetts would serve the Trumps.

This bourbon is the real McCoy. Even the Hatfields agreed.

It's not just named after a creek in Kentucky. It's made from it.

This is a beautiful picture of a tiny creek that flows through the back hills of Kentucky. (Picture of bottle.)

Old as the hills it's from.

Smooth. Deep. Hard to find. Kind of like the creek we get the water from.

Hand-bottled straight from a barrel in Kentucky. Strap in.

Tastes like a Kentucky sunset looks.

Its Old Kentucky Home was a barrel.

Maybe those last two might also make for good outdoor, given how short they are. We make a note. Remember, the point here isn't, hey, let's see how many headlines can we write, but rather how many different doors can we go through? How many different ways can we look at the same problem?

Okay, now let's see what can be done with the way some people drink bourbon—straight. Or perhaps the time of day it's drunk. (Wait a minute. Bad word.)

HOW-YOU-DRINK-IT IDEAS

With a bourbon this good, you don't need to show breasts in the ice cubes. In fact, you don't need ice cubes.

Neither good bourbons nor bad arguments hold water.

Water ruins baseball games and bourbon.

For a quiet night, try it without all the noisy ice.

Great after the kids are in bed. Perfect after they're in college.

Mixes superbly with a rocking chair and a dog.

You don't need water to enjoy this premium bourbon.

A fire might be nice.

Perfect for those quiet times. Like between marriages.

As you can see, each one of these doors we went through—age, history, Kentucky—led to another hallway, full of other doors to try. Which is one of the marvelous things about writing. It's not simply a way of getting things down on paper. Writing is a way of thinking— thinking with your pencil, your wrist, and your spine and just seeing where a thing goes.

Clearly, a few of the bourbon ideas presented here aren't very good. (Lord knows, you may think they all suck.) But like Pickett's Charge at Gettysburg, with 15,000 soldiers, one or two are going to make it over the wall.

One more little case study, this one for one of the nation's largest airlines. They had just purchased a whole bunch of new 777s and A320s (read: "roomier wide-body jets"), and they wanted print ads to promote the benefits to business travelers.

Well, if we break it down, perhaps some of the concepts could focus on more personal space and some on the comfort of the seat itself. We could further break it down into ideas that are headline driven and ideas that are visually driven.

PERSONAL-SPACE IDEAS, HEADLINE DRIVEN

Maybe we could try some headlines that would work by themselves (or perhaps with a "flat" visual like a shot of a wide aisle or a roomy seat).

Most passengers would give their right arm for more room for their right arm.

Everyone who'd like more personal space, raise your hand, if possible. (✔)

Getting incredibly close to people is fine for encounter groups, not planes.

Now even luggage has more elbow room.

You can use a camera lens to make your planes look big. Or you can buy big planes.

Wouldn't it be great if an airline advertised wider planes instead of wider smiles?

Choose one: Bigger bags of peanuts. Bigger smiles. Bigger planes. We thought so.

Airline math: The wider the plane, the shorter the flight feels.

PERSONAL-SPACE IDEAS, A LITTLE MORE VISUALLY DRIVEN

This, only higher.
(VISUAL: A well-worn La-Z-Boy recliner.)

There are two places you can stretch out and let someone solve your problems. With ours, you get miles.
(VISUAL: Shrink's office.)

Which one would you take on a long trip? Exactly. Now let's move on to planes.
(VISUAL: Small car versus big SUV.)

We put it in our planes.
(VISUAL: Man in his living room, football game on TV, quizzically looking at flattened area of shag rug where his La-Z-Boy recliner used to be.)

Traveling has always been easier when you have room to yourself.
(VISUAL: Old family photo of three kids fussing at each other in the backseat of station wagon.)

Da Vinci never designed a plane that worked, but he had this cool idea about personal space.
(VISUAL: Da Vinci drawings of the body showing the arc of the arms, motion of legs.)

EMOTIONAL BENEFITS, A LITTLE MORE VISUALLY-DRIVEN

What would happen if we concentrated more on the emotional benefits of a wider more comfortable seat?

If our new seat doesn't put you to sleep, try reading the whole ad.
(VISUAL: Airline seat with long copy and lots of callouts.)

It doesn't matter how roomy a seat is if you don't like the service.
(VISUAL: Little boy dwarfed in a big dentist's chair.)

Almost every passenger arrives feeling human.
(VISUAL: Dog getting out of airline pet carrier.) (✔)

"Some settling may occur during shipment."
   (VISUAL: Seat shot with sleeping passenger.)

With our new seats, you won't have to count for long.
   (VISUAL: A single sheep with caption under it: "One.") (✔)

When you fly with us, never promise "I'll work on the plane."
   (VISUAL: Close-up shot of computer screen with menu button of "Sleep" backlit.) (✔)

Have you always done your best thinking way up high somewhere?
   (VISUAL: A kid's treehouse seen from way at bottom of ladder, two sneakered feet sticking out of the door.)

After I've finished writing a list about this long, I'll go back over it and make a little mark (✔) next to my favorites. Then I transfer those few ideas over to a clean sheet of paper and start all over.

I mean, start *all* over. Pretend you have nothing so far. The fact is, there are only 22 airline ideas in the preceding list—22. We cannot seriously believe we'll have crafted a ticket-selling, brand-building, One Show–winning ad after 22 stinking tries. We'll need hundreds. If that sounds daunting, get ready for a long and hard career. This is the way it's done.

Remember, the wastepaper basket is the writer's best friend.

If the ad needs a headline, write 100.

Sorry, but there's no shortcut. Write 100 of them. And don't confuse this with Tom Monahan's exercise of 100-Mile-an-Hour Thinking.[1] (That's a pretty good exercise, too, but better for the very beginning of the creative process. In that exercise, Tom advises creative people to turn on the fire hydrant for 20 minutes and catch every single first thought that comes out. Each idea goes on a separate Post-it Note, with absolutely no editing.) Nope, here I'm not talkin' about 100-mile-per-hour writing. This is sitting down and slowly cranking out 100 workable lines—100 lines that range from decent, to hey-not-bad, to whoa-that-rocks. The key is they *all* have to be pretty good.

To prove this very point, Sally Hogshead bravely posted all of the BMW motorcycle headlines she came up with to get to her final five ads featured in the One Show and *Communication Arts* (Figure 4.2). Read the list and you'll see a copywriter really thinking it through, rattling different doorknobs up and down the conceptual hallway, sometimes writing about the union of rider and bike, sometimes

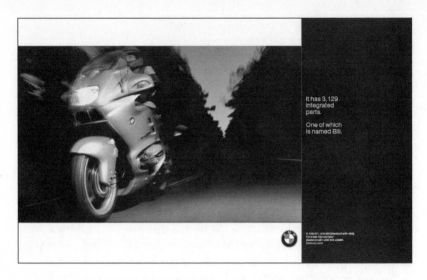

*Figure 4.2   The headline reads: "It has 3,129 integrated parts.
One of which is named Bill."*

about goose bumps. They're all pretty darn good. (She's good at other stuff, too—particularly career advice for creatives. Check out her web site at sallyhogshead.com.)

Even atheists kneel on a BMW. • Some burn candles when praying. Others, rubber. • There are basilicas, cathedrals, mosques. And then there"s Route 66. • Buy one before the Church bans such marriages. • People take vows of chastity to feel this way. • More Westminster Abbey than Cal Tech. • Runners get a high from jogging around a track at 8 miles per hour. Pathetic. • This is exactly the sort of intimacy that would frighten Jesse Helms. • Fits like a glove. A metallic silver, fuel-injected, 150-horsepower glove. • You don't get off a BMW so much as take it off. • Relationships this intimate are illegal in some states. • Usually, this kind of connection requires surgery. • Didn't George Orwell predict man and machine would eventually become one? • The Church has yet to comment on such a marriage of man and machine. • Somebody call Ray Bradbury. We've combined man and machine. • Do you become more machine, or does it become more human? • And then there were two. • "Oh look, honey. What a sweet looking couple." • If you ever connect like this with a person, marry them. • Fits tighter than OJ's glove. ☺ • Why some men won't stop and ask directions. • "Darling, is that . . . a smudge of motor oil on your collar?" •

The road is calling. Don't get its message by voicemail. • The feeling is more permanent than any tattoo. • "Yippee! I'm off to my root canal!" • Your inner child is fluent in German. • The last day of school, any day of the year. • Your heart races, your senses tingle. Then you turn it on. • There is no known antidote once it gets into your blood. • There are no words to describe it. Unless "Wooohoo!" counts. • No amusement park ride can give this feeling. • If he had a mood ring on, it'd be bright green. • Never has a raccoon baking in the sun smelled sweeter. • How "joie de vivre" translates into German. • Put as much distance as possible between you and the strip mall. • Off, off, off, off-road. • If it had a rearview mirror, you'd see your troubles in it. • There's something worth racing towards at the end of this road: another 25 miles. • The best psychotherapy doesn't happen lying on a couch. • A remote control is a more dangerous machine. • A carnivore in the food chain of bikes. • If you're trying to find yourself, you sure as hell won't find it on the sofa. • If you had eight hours, alone, no radio, imagine what you could think about. • Where is it written the love for your motorcycle must be platonic? • Seems preoccupied. Comes home later than usual. Always wanting to get out of the house. • You possess a motorcycle. You're possessed by a BMW. • Let's see. You're either riding it, or wishing you were riding it, or thinking about the last time you rode it. • Men who own a BMW have something else to think about every 22 seconds. • You've got just one companion on the road. Find one you can get along with. • What you're seeing is his soul. His body's in a meeting in Cincinnati right now. • Merge with traffic. Not every other motorcycle owner. • Your estimated time of arrival just got bumped up. • Where do you drive when you daydream? • And together they rode off into the sunset. • What walking on air actually looks like. • The invitation said to bring your significant other. She thinks it's her. • Lust fueled by gasoline. • The bike, the girlfriend. Guess which model he'll trade in first. • She wonders why she sometimes feels like a third wheel. • Room for luggage. None for baggage.

The point here is both quantity *and* quality. You don't get to great until you do a whole bunch of good.

Save the operative part of the headline for the very end.

You know that single part of a headline where the concept comes to life? That key word or phrase where the idea is unveiled? Save that unveiling for the end of your headline.

Take, for example, this headline from the preceding list of airline ideas.

Almost every passenger arrives feeling human.
  (VISUAL: Dog getting out of airline pet carrier.)
The line could have been constructed other ways:

You'll feel human when you arrive, thanks to our new seats.

When the seats let you sleep, almost everybody feels human on
  arrival.

Some of the punch is missing, isn't it? It feels better when you save your wrap-up punch for the end of your sentence. It has more surprise and power.

Never use fake names in a headline.
(Or copy. Or anywhere else for that matter.)

"Little Billy's friends at school call him different." Lines like this drive me nuts.

"Little Billy will never know his real father."

Hey, little Billy, c'mere. Go back and tell your copywriter that a strange man in the park said to tell him he's a *hack*. Anybody reading this kind of crap knows these ad names are fake. And an irritating kind of fake at that. Like those manufactured relatives they put inside of picture frames at stores.

Avoid fake people.

Avoid fake names.

There are times, however, when using a person's name is the only way the concept *will* work. And in the hands of a seasoned team, as in this Vitro-Robertson ad for client Taylor guitars (Figure 4.3), it can be done beautifully. It comes down to style. To how gracefully and believably you pull it off.

Don't let the headline flex any muscles
when the visual is doing the heavy lifting.

As it is in dancing, one should lead, one should follow. If your visual is a hardworking idea, let your headline quietly clean up the work left to it. And if the headline is brilliant, well-crafted, and covers all the bases, the visual (if one exists at all) should be merely icing on the cake.

Remember, the rule of thumb is never show what you're saying and never say what you're showing. This ad for Harley-Davidson

Figure 4.3   When you have a wild visual, the headline should be straight. When the headline's doing all the work, like this one, the visual should not try to take center stage. It should just "be there."

motorcycles is a perfect example (Figure 4.4). By itself, the visual is fairly tame. By itself, the headline is dull and almost meaningless. But together, they make one of the best ads I've ever seen.

When it's just a headline, it'd better be a pretty good headline.

One of the best campaigns of all time (in this writer's opinion) is Abbott Meade Vickers's work for the *Economist* (Figure 4.5). This campaign was basically an outdoor campaign of brilliant headlines against a backdrop of the color red (lifted from the magazine's masthead). Several of the finished ads are pictured throughout this book, but the lines all by themselves are also great lessons in brilliant copywriting. I include my favorites here.

Think someone under the table.

If you're already a reader, ask your chauffeur to hoot as you pass this poster.

"Can I phone an Economist reader, please, Chris?"

Don't be a vacancy on the board.

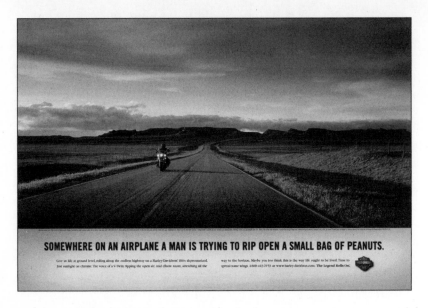

Figure 4.4   A perfect marriage of word and picture.

If your assistant reads The Economist, don't play too much golf.

Retire early with a good read.

Look forward to school reunions.

It's lonely at the top, but at least there's something to read.

$E = iq^2$

If they did brain transplants, would you be a donor or a recipient?

In opinion polls, 100% of Economist readers had one.

If someone gave you a penny for your thoughts, would they get change?

Would you like to sit next to you at dinner?

Think outside the dodecahedron.

Ever go blank at the crucial . . . thingy?

Cures itchy scalps.

"Is it me, or is quantum physics easier these days?"

Certain headlines are currently checked out. You may use them when they are returned.

Lines like "Contrary to popular belief . . ." or "Something is wrong when . . ." are pretty much used up. Get over it. Do something new.

Lose the ability to slip out of meetings unnoticed.

The Economist

Figure 4.5   What an elegant way to say that reading the Economist *can help make your business thinking indispensable.*

Remember, anything that you even think you've seen, forget about. The stuff you've never seen? You'll know that when you see it, too. It raises the hair on the back of your neck.

Don't use a model number in the headline.

Client numbers like "TX-17" may seem familiar to you. But you're used to it; you work on the account. In a headline, they serve only as a speed bump. They're not words, they're numerals, so they force readers to switch gears in their heads to 17, x45, 13z42 to get through your sentence.

SOME NOTES ON DESIGN (FROM A WRITER).

Something has to dominate the ad.

Whether it's a big headline, a large visual, or a single word floating in white space, somebody's got to be the boss.

It's easy to spot ads where the art director (or perhaps client) couldn't decide what was most important. The ads are usually in three big pieces. The visual takes up a third of the page. A headline takes up the next third. And a combination of body copy–logo–tagline brings up the rear. And the whole thing has about as much cohesion as a cookie in the rain.

Your ad needs a boss, as well as an overall visual hierarchy. The late Roy Grace, one of the famous art directors from Doyle Dane Bernbach, spoke to this issue:

> There has to be a point on every page where the art director and the writer want you to start. Whether that is the center of the page, the top right-hand corner, or the left-hand corner, there has to be an understanding, an agreement, and a logical reason where you want people to look first.[2]

Avoid trends in execution.

Don't take your cues from design trends you see in the awards books. (For one thing, if they're in the books, they're already two years old. The One Show book arrives, literally, on a slow boat from China, where it's printed.) But this is about more than being up-to-date. It's about concentrating on the soul of an ad instead of the width of its lapels. Do as you wish, by all means, but I'll warn you of two things. Riding the wave of every passing fad will make your portfolio look trendy and derivative. Also, when you enter your piece in a show, the judges (who've seen just about every trend come and go) will likely deep-six it in a heartbeat.

Develop a look no one else has.

You've got to find something your client can call their own: a shape, a color, a design, something that is unique.

Helmut Krone: "I was working on Avis and looking for a page style. That's very important to me, a page style. I feel that you should be able to tell who's running that ad at a distance of twenty feet."[3]

What's interesting about Krone's statement is that he's not talking about billboards but print ads. And if you look at his two most famous campaigns, they stand up to the test. You could identify his Volkswagen and Avis ads from across a street (Figure 4.6).

The longer I'm in this business, the more I'm convinced art direction is where the major battle for brand building happens. Once you establish a look, once you stake out a design territory, no one else can use it without looking like your brand. The *Economist* practically *owns* the color red. IBM continues to letterbox its television with those iconic blue bars. And Apple Computer's signature color

Avis is only No.2 in rent a cars. So why go with us?

We try harder.
(When you're not the biggest, you have to.)
We just can't afford dirty ashtrays. Or half-empty gas tanks. Or worn wipers. Or unwashed cars. Or low tires. Or anything less than seat-adjusters that adjust. Heaters that heat. Defrosters that defrost.

Obviously, the thing we try hardest for is just to be nice. To start you out right with a new car, like a lively, super-torque Ford, and a pleasant smile. To know, say, where you get a good pastrami sandwich in Duluth.
Why?
Because we can't afford to take you for granted.
Go with us next time.
The line at our counter is shorter.

Figure 4.6   In an interview, art director Helmut Krone said that the Avis look came from a deliberate reversal of the VW look. VW had large pictures; Avis, small. VW had small body type; Avis, large. Note the absence of a logo.

of a clean white screams "Apple" before the first word of copy is read.

Own something visual.

Always do ads with babies or children.

Oh, and another thing. Always, *always* write the headline in the script of a child's handwriting. It's very cute, don't you think? ☺ And don't forget to have at least two of the letters be adorably backward. Backward Ǝ's are best. Backward O's don't work. Here's a regular O and here's a backward O. See? Not as adorable as a backward Ǝ.

(Just checking to see if you're awake.)

WRITING BODY COPY.

Writing well, rule #1: Write well.

I don't think people read body copy. I think we've entered a frenzied era of coffee-guzzling, e-mail-sending channel surfers who honk the nanosecond the light turns green and have the attention span of a flashbulb. If the first nine words of body copy aren't "May we send you beer and money for free?," word 10 isn't read. Just my opinion, mind you.

Raymond McKinney at The Martin Agency had it right when he wrote a line for those condensed-book study aids: "Cliff Notes. When you don't have time to see the movie."

Yet when I write body copy, long or short, I work hard at making it as smart and persuasive and readable as I can. I suggest you do the same. Because a few people are going to read it. And the ones who do, you want. They're interested. They're peering in your shop window.

So as much as I hammer away on the importance of visual solutions, when you have to write, write smartly. With passion, intelligence, and honesty. And when you've said what you need to say, stop.

Five rules for effective speechwriting from Winston Churchill.

1. Begin strongly.
2. Have one theme.

3. Use simple language.

4. Leave a picture in the listener's mind.

5. End dramatically.

Write like you talk.

In copy for ads, in letters to clients, and in memos to colleagues, write like you talk. For some reason, when handed a pen and asked to write something that will be seen by others, 9 out of 10 people decide an authoritarian tone is somehow more persuasive than clear English.

Consider this memo from my files. It was written by a man about whom, were you to meet him, you'd say, "Sharp guy, that Bob. I want him on my account." Yet Bob wrote the following memo. (What he was trying to say was the program was killed because it was too costly.)

> Effective late last week the Flavor-iffic® project was shelved by the Flavor-Master Consumer Products Division Management. The reasoning had to do with funding generated covering cost of entry, not cost of entry as it would relate to test market in '95, but as it would relate to expansion, if judged successful across major pieces of geography in '96 and beyond. In sum, the way Flavor-Master new products division served up Flavor-iffic® to Consumer Products Division Management was that if Flavor-Master were to relax financial parameters for Flavor-iffic® in '95, '96 and '97, in effect have Corporate fund the program, Consumer Products Division could recommend to Corporate to proceed with the program. The decision was made at the Consumer Products Division Management level that Corporate would most probably not accept that and the subject was taken no further.

Except for the name "Flavor-iffic," I swear, every word of this memo is real.

The program was killed because it was too costly. That's nine words. Bob, in 143 words, was not only unable to get that nine-word message across, he effectively lobotomized his audience with a torrent of corporate nonsense that said nothing. It couldn't be decoded.

Bob proudly dictated this Rosetta stone, snapped his suspenders, and took the elevator down to the lobby, thinking he'd done his bit to turn the wheels of capitalism for the day.

Yet when he got home, he probably didn't talk that way to his wife.

> Honey, RE: supper. It has come to my attention, and the concurrent attention of the other family members (i.e., Janice, Bill, and Bob Jr.), that your gravy has inconsistencies of viscosity (popularly known as "lumps"), itself not a disturbing event were it not for the recent disappearance of the family dog.

Write like you talk.

Write with a smooth, easy rhythm that sounds natural. Obey the rules of grammar and go easy on the adjectives. Short sentences are best. One-word sentences? Fine. End with a preposition if you want to. And if it feels right, begin a sentence with "and." Just be clear.

Through it all, remember, you are selling something. Easy to forget when you start slinging words.

Write like you would talk if you were the brand.

Every brand has a personality. You could describe Apple Computer's personality perhaps as "benevolent intelligence." Read any piece of copy in any Apple ad from the last 10 years—doesn't matter if it's an old ad for an Apple Lisa, or an iMac, or an iPhone. No matter what Apple work you read, you'll feel like you're listening to the same smart big brother, one who wants to sit in the chair with you in front of the keyboard and show you how easy and smart and cool technology can be. Successful brands discover their own distinct voices and then stick with them year after year.

If you're inheriting an established voice, you can learn its cadences by reading their previous advertising.

If you have a new brand or you're creating a new voice for an old brand, consider yourself lucky. It's one of the most creative and rewarding things you can do in this business—discovering "who" a brand is and giving it shape and form and voice.

This isn't done to create stylish writing. What you're doing is creating a brand personality, an important point in a marketplace where the physical differences between products are getting smaller and smaller.

Let's say, for example, you're working on a car account. Most of the time, it's likely you'll have to show the car. Your ad may feel half art-directed already, and in a sense it is. So if it comes down to showing just a headline and a picture of a car, your headline ought to have a voice no one else does.

Here are three car headlines:

If you run out of gas, it's easy to push.

We'll never make it big.

It's ugly, but it gets you there.

Here are three more:

In a fuel-obsessed society, is it blasphemy to suggest that a car should be fun to drive?

A luxury sedan based on the belief that all of the rich are not idle.

The people with money are still spending it, but with infinitely more wisdom.

Can you tell which ones are from Volkswagen and which from BMW? It's pretty easy. Which is as it should be.

Before you start writing copy, have the basic structure of your argument in mind.

Know where you're going to go. "Okay, I've got to come off that headline, then hit A, B, and then end on C." If you neglect this preparation, you will buzz about in a meaningless pattern, like a fly on a summer screen.

Don't have what they call a "pre-ramble" in your body copy.

The first paragraph of copy in many ads is usually a waste of the reader's time, a repetition of what's already been said in the headline. Consider the analogy of a door-to-door salesman. Your headline is what he says through the crack in the door: his name, what he is selling, and why it's better than the other guy's stuff.

Okay, the reader has let you in. And now you're in the foyer. Don't waste time in your first paragraph being reintroductory. "Hi. Remember me? I'm the guy who was out in front of your door two seconds ago. Remember? Said my name, what I'm selling, and why it's better than that other guy's stuff?"

Get to the point. It's time for the details. Put your most interesting, surprising, or persuasive point in the first line if you can. You're lucky if people read your headline and luckier yet if they let you into the foyer by reading your copy.

Your body copy should reflect the overall concept of the ad.

When you start writing, borrow from your concept's imagery, lift colors from its palette. This advice isn't given for stylistic reasons. It helps keep the ad simple. One concept, one voice, one style.

Don't overdo this, a common mistake that leaves copy looking amateurish. Use it as you would a spice. In particular, resist the urge to do a "snappy" last line. I suggest ending with the client's address and phone number.

"It's not fair to inflict your own style on a strategy."

This is from Ed McCabe, one of the great writers of the 1970s. Your job is to present the client's case as memorably as you can, not to come up with another great piece for your portfolio. You want to do both. But you aren't likely to do both if you're concentrating on style. Don't worry about style. It will be expressed no matter what you do. Style is part of the way your brain is wired. Just concentrate on solving the client's problem well. The rest will just happen.

Eschew obfuscation.

My point exactly. Those words say what I mean to say, but they aren't as clear as they could be. This doesn't mean your writing has to be flat-footed, just understandable.

E.B. White said, "Be obscure clearly."

Pretend you're writing a letter.

Why write to the masses? It's one person reading your ad, isn't it? So write to one person.

Write a letter. It's a good voice to use when you're writing copy. It's intimate. It keeps you from lecturing. The best copy feels like a conversation, not a speech. One person talking to another. Not a corporate press release typed in the PR department by some guy named Higgs.

Visualize this person you're writing the letter to. She's not a

"Female, 18 to 34, household income of blah-blah." She's a woman named Jill who's been thinking about getting a newer, smaller car. She's in an airport, bored, trying to get a Gummi Bear out of her back tooth, and reading *Time* magazine backward.

Provide detail.

In headlines, in body copy, anywhere you can say something specific and concrete, do it. It will make your argument more persuasive and your ad more interesting.

Here's an example of the power of detail. The headline read: "It began 400 years before Christ. It is visible from Mars. You can touch it this spring." Punctuated by a small picture of the Great Wall of China, the details in this headline made me keep reading about Royal Viking's cruises to China.

Once you lay your sentences down, spackle between the joints.

Use transitions to flow seamlessly from one benefit to the next. Each sentence should come naturally out of the one that precedes it. When you've done it well, you shouldn't be able to take out any sentence without disrupting the flow and structure of the entire piece. (This fragile coherence of beautiful writing is lost on many clients and is one of the reasons copywriters are often seen mumbling to themselves at bus stops.)

Break your copy into as many short paragraphs as you can.

Short paragraphs are less daunting. I've never read William Faulkner's classic *Intruder in the Dust* for this very reason. Those eight-page paragraphs look like work to me. Remember, nobody ever had to read *People* magazine with a bookmark. This isn't an argument for dumbing down your work. Be as smart as you can be. Just don't write paragraphs the size of shower curtains, okay?

When you're done writing the copy, read it aloud.

I discovered this one the hard way. I had to present some copy to a group of five clients. I read it to them aloud. It was only during the act of reading it this way I discovered how wretched my copy was.

Just hearing the words hanging out there in the air with their grade-school mistakes, seeing the flat reaction of the clients' faces, hearing my voice crack, feeling the flop sweat, it's all coming back to me.

When you're done writing, read it aloud. Awkward constructions and wire-thin segues have a way of revealing themselves when read aloud.

When you're done ~~writing your body copy~~, go back and cut it by a third.

Proofread your own work.

Don't depend on Spell-Check. First of all, that's lazy writing. Second, Spell-Check can't tell the difference between *your* and *you're*. (If you have to use any computer program on your writing, use Suck-Check.®)

If you have to have one, make your tagline an anthem.

If you have to craft a tagline, work on it first. Do it early in the process of creating a campaign idea. Try to write about something bigger than just the client's product. Own some high ground.

In my opinion, the best ever written was for Nike: "Just Do It." That's not about shoes. It's not just about sports, either; it's about life. But it sold a lot of shoes.

In addition to being cool because it's about more than just some product, an anthem allows you executional freedom later on when you may have to go in new tactical directions and still work off the same campaign.

But do you really *have* to have a tagline? A slogan?

It's just one more thing to cram in an ad. One more element to clamor for attention. From what I've seen, few taglines bring any new information to an ad. They're usually piffle.

"Looking Backward, but Poised Toward the Future . . . Today."

"A Century of Excellence for Over 50 Years."

Should your client insist on a tagline, I refer you to this piffle-generation device John Lyons included in his book *Guts*. "Simply pick one word from each column," he wrote, "string them together, and you've created a terrific corporate slogan."[4]

Systems	Confidence	Excellence
Commitment	Tomorrow	Trust
Spirit	Achievement	Technology
Research	Science	Future
Soaring	Understanding	Quality
Mankind	Helping	Today
People	Winning	Innovations

"Commitment to an Understanding of Excellence." "The Spirit of Winning through Quality." Ultimately, they're all the same.

In my opinion, unless you've penned a "Just Do It," just don't.

I once saw a tagline tragically misfire, injuring several. The line was for Stouffer's frozen entrées. The way Stouffer's wanted you to read it was: "People *Expect* Us to Be Better." But if you read "People Expect Us to Be *Better*," it left a bad taste in your mouth.

Sweat the details.

Go to any length to get it right. Don't let even the smallest thing slide. If it bothers you even a little bit, work on it till it doesn't.

Poet Paul Valery said, "A poem is never finished, only abandoned."

Be objective.

Once you've put some good ideas on paper and had time to polish them to your satisfaction, maybe it's time to cart them around the hallways a little bit, even before you take them to your creative director. You're not looking for consensus here, just a disaster check.

This may not be your style, and if you're not comfortable doing this, don't. But it can give you a quick reality check, identify holes that need filling, and point out directions that deserve further exploration.

Be objective. Listen to what people have to say about your work. If a couple of people have a problem with something, chances are it's real. Keep in mind that when you're showing an ad around the agency, you're showing it to people who *want* to like it. Once your ad's out the door, it's quite the opposite. People will approach your ad thinking it's going to be as bad as everything else they see.

So listen to them. There's the old maxim: "When 10 people say you have a tail, sooner or later you oughta turn around and look."

Kill off the weak sister.

If your campaign has even one weak ad in it, replace that okay ad with one that is as great as the others.

I have often talked myself into presenting campaigns that include weak sisters because time was running out. But readers don't care if most of your ads are great. They see them one at a time, so they all should be excellent.

There's a saying the Japanese use regarding the strict quality control in their best companies: "How many times a year is it acceptable for the birthing nurse to drop a baby on its head?" Is even one time okay?

There's another famous line. I don't know who wrote it. "Good is the enemy of great." It's true. Good is easy to like. Good throws its arm around you and says, "Hey, I'm not so bad, am I?" You talk yourself into it. Next thing you know you have a campaign that goes great—great—good. And that's bad.

WHAT TO DO IF YOU'RE STUCK.

First of all, being stuck is a good sign. Really.

Being stuck means you have moved through all the easy stuff. You've waded through all the crappy ideas, through the okay ideas, passed the low-hanging fruit, and are entering the outlying area of big, new thoughts. Being stuck is not only not unusual, it's what you want.

So don't be creeped out by those long silences that can happen during creative sessions. You can spend whole days, even weeks, trying very hard, and come up with diddly. But I've found it's only after you've suffered these excruciating days of meat-loaf brain that the shiny and beautiful finally presents itself to you. The trick is to stay with it. Suffer through it. Remember, the only way out is through.

Leave the room and go work somewhere else.

A conference room maybe. Or leave the agency. Work in a public place. Some restaurants are close to empty between one and five in the afternoon. Hotel lobbies are great, especially those lobbies on the second floor that looked really "sharp and modern" on the architect's drawing but nobody *ever* uses. And as Sally Hogshead reminds us, "Domino's delivers to Starbucks."

There are other things you can do. If the print isn't coming, work on the radio. If you can't write the headline, write the body copy. And if it's not happening during office hours, stop in the middle of dinner and write.

> If you are in difficulties with a book, try the element of surprise: attack it at an hour when it isn't expecting it.
> —*H.G. Wells*

Get off the stinking computer.

If your keyboard freezes up, get a pen and paper. In fact, you may find handwriting brings an altogether different part of your brain into play. David Fowler agrees: "Try it. . . . It's just different. The connection between your hand and the page via a tiny strand of ink imparts something that's somehow closer to your heart."[5]

Ignore the little voice that says, "I'm just a hack on crack from Hackensack."

We all feel that way. Even the superstars in this business secretly believe they're hacks at least twice a day. The difference is they get better about ignoring it. In their book *Pick Me,* Vonk and Kestin give advice on making the evil little voice shut up.

> You have to learn to mute the voice. Or just use it to spur you on to do better. The painful truth is that all the awards in the world don't take away the tyranny of the blank page. The only thing that does is making a mark on it. Somehow, just getting those first few thoughts out is helpful, even if they genuinely do suck. The act of moving the pen across the paper is the antidote to the belief that you can't do it.[6]

Go to the store where they sell the stuff.

There is demographic data typed neatly on paper. And then there's the stark reality of a customer standing in front of a store shelf looking at your brand and at Brand X. I'm not saying you should start bothering strangers in store aisles with questions. Go ahead if you like. I find it inspiring just to soak in the vibes of the marketplace. Just watch. Think. I guarantee you'll come back with some ideas.

Ask your creative director for help.

That's what they're there for. There is no dishonor in throwing up your hands and saying, "I'm in a dark and terrible place. Help me or I shall perish."

Your CD may be able to see things you can't. She hasn't had her nose two inches away from the problem for the last two weeks like you have. She knows the client, knows the market, and can give you more than an educated guess on what's jamming up your creative process. Sometimes all it takes is a little push, two inches to the left, to get you back on track.

Get more product information.

You may not know enough about the problem yet, or you may not have enough information on the market. So ask your account folks or planners to go deeper into their files and bring you new stuff. It's likely they edited their pile of information and gleaned what they thought most important. Get to the original material if you can.

If you're stuck, relax.

Most of the books that I've read on creativity keep bringing up the subject of relaxation. You can't be creative and be tense. The two events are never in the same room together. Stay loose. Breathe from the stomach. If you're not relaxed, stop until you are. Just the simple act of physical relaxation will bring on new ideas. I promise.

But remember, you do need a certain amount of pressure to be creative. Creativity rarely happens when things are perfectly under control. To make the kettle boil, a little fire is necessary, and a deadline that's a month and a half away isn't always a good thing. I find that if I have too much time to complete a project, I'll put off working on it until two or three weeks before it's due just so I can dial up the pressure a little bit.

The trick is to control the pressure, not let it control you. Relax.

Read an old *Far Side* collection by Gary Larson.

The man is an absolute screaming genius. The cartoons are always funny. But look at the economy of his ideas. Look how simple they are. How few moving parts there are.

At the very least, with a trip to Larson's sick little world you get a break from the tension. But you might get that small nudge you need. I know I have.

I also get that nudge by leafing through magazines from different categories. I'll be working on an insurance campaign, but if there's a snowboarding magazine on the conference room table, I'll pick it up and go through it.

Leafing through the awards annuals is okay, too. The shows are a good learning tool, early in the business; they're a good starting point, early in the ideation process. But at some point, they will begin to steer your thinking. (I know plenty of absolutely stellar advertising people who don't own a single *CA* or One Show.) They realize, sooner or later, they're going to have to unmoor and sail into the unknown.

Go to a bookstore and page through books on your subject.

Say you're doing an ad on outboard engines. Go to a bookstore and page through books on lakes, oceans, submarines, vacation spots, fish, pistons, hydraulics, whatever. Just let your brain soak up those molecular building blocks of future concepts.

You might get the ideas flowing right there in the store. And even if you don't, what's to risk except maybe getting the hairy eyeball from the clerk who thinks you ought to be buying something. *("Hey, whattaya think this is? A li-berry?")*

Sometimes it's good to work on three projects at once.

You may find that the ideas come faster if you move between projects every hour or so. Designer Milton Glaser said, "Working on one thing at a time is like facing a rhinoceros; working on ten things at a time is like playing badminton."

Don't burn up too much energy trying to make something work.

Follow the first rule of holes: If you are in one, stop digging. There's a book called *Lateral Thinking*, by Edward DeBono. His metaphor:

Don't dig one hole and keep digging down until you hit oil; dig lots of shallow holes first, all over the yard.

Even when you do manage to force a decent idea onto paper, after hours of wrestling with it, it usually bears the earmarks of a fight. You can count the dents where you pounded on the poor thing to force it into the shape you wanted. There's none of the spontaneous elegance of an idea born in a moment of illumination.

Be patient.

Tell yourself it will come. Don't keep swinging at the ball when your arms hurt. Maybe today's not the day. Give up. Go see a movie. Come back tomorrow. Pick up the bat and keep trying. Be patient.

Learn to enjoy the process. Not just the finished ad.

I used to hate the long process of writing an ad. I simply wanted the reprint in my hands. I wanted to be in L.A. editing the spot. But thinking like this made my job harder than it had to be. The fact is, most of your time in this business will be spent in some cluttered, just-slightly-too-warm room, thinking, not admiring your finished work.

Even if you have an award-winning career, only 0.00000002 percent of it will be spent walking up to the podium to accept an award at the One Show. You will spend most of your career trying to decide whether *crisp* or *flaky* is the right word to use. Keep reminding yourself: Let the fun be in the chase.

Remember you aren't saving lives.

When you get stressed and the walls are closing in and you're going nuts trying to crack a problem and you find yourself getting depressed, try to remember that you're just doing an ad. That is all. An ad. A stupid piece of paper. It's not even a whole piece of paper you're working on. It's just a half of a piece of paper in a magazine, and somebody else is buying the other side. Remember, advertising is powerful, and even a "pretty okay" ad can increase sales. (I know, I know. Don't tell my clients I said this. But we're talking those times when it feels like your mental health is at stake.) Don't kill the goose trying to get a golden egg on demand.

Bertrand Russell said: "One of the symptoms of an approaching nervous breakdown is the belief that one's work is terribly important"

INSANITY, OFFICE POLITICS, AND AWARDS SHOWS.

"Be orderly in your normal life so you can be violent and original in your work."

I don't know much about novelist Gustave Flaubert, except he said the cool line you just read, and it seems to fit in right about here.

Many creative people find that a dash of ritual in their lives provides just the structure they need to let go creatively. I happen to prefer an extremely clean and empty room in which to write. That may sound weird, but I've heard of stranger things.

In *The Art and Science of Creativity*, George Kneller wrote: "Schiller [the German poet] filled his desk with rotten apples; Proust worked in a cork-lined room. . . . While [Kant was] writing *The Critique of Pure Reason*, he would concentrate on a tower visible from his window. When some trees grew up to hide the tower, [he had] authorities cut down the trees so that he could continue his work."[7]

Your office manager may not like it, but if some trees are bugging you, hack those suckers down.

Be buttoned-up.

This is a business. The whole chaos-is-good, whiskey-and-cigarettes, showing-up-late-for-work thing is fine for artists and rock stars. But advertising is only half art. It's also half business. The thing is, both halves are on the deadline.

So don't be sloppy. Don't be late. Meet your deadlines. Don't lose your writer's headlines. Don't leave your art director's layouts at home. Don't forget to do the outdoor because the print is more fun.

This also applies to expense reports and time sheets. Learn how to do them early on, do them impeccably, and turn them in on time. Be a grown-up. Sure, they're boring. But, like watching an episode of *The Brady Bunch*, if you just sit down and apply yourself, the whole unpleasant thing will be over in a half hour.

Don't drink or do drugs.

You may think that drinking, smoking pot, or doing coke makes you more creative. I used to think so.

I was only fooling myself. I bought into that myth of the tortured creative person, struggling against uncaring clients and blind product managers. With a bottle next to his typewriter and his wastebasket filling ever higher with rejected brilliance, this poor, misunderstood soul constantly looks for that next fantastic idea to rocket him into happiness.

In a business where we all try to avoid clichés, a lot of people buy into this cliché-as-lifestyle. I can assure you it is illusion.

Identify your most productive working hours and use them for nothing but idea generation.

I happen to be a morning person. By three in the afternoon, my brain is meat loaf and a TV campaign featuring a grocer named Whipple doesn't seem like such a bad idea. But you might be sharper in the afternoon. Just strike while your iron is hot. And save those down hours for the busywork of advertising. What I call "phone calls and arguments."

Keep your eye on the ball, not on the players.

Don't get into office politics. Not all offices have them. If yours does, remember your priority—doing ads. Keep your eye on the ad on your desk.

You are a member of a team.

Don't ever forget that. Never get into that "I did the visual" or "I did the headline" thing. You work as a team; you lose as a team; you win as a team.

You are not genetically superior to account executives.

During my first years in the business I was trained to look down on account executives. At the time, it seemed kind of cool to have a bad guy to make fun of. (*"Oh, he couldn't sell a joint at Woodstock." "She couldn't sell a compass to Amelia Earhart."*) But I was an idiot.

It's wrong to think that way. They are on my side. Make sure they are on yours.

Stay in touch with the real world.

> Young creative people start out hungry. They're off the street; they know how people think. And their work is great. Then they get successful. They make more and more money, spend their time in restaurants they never dreamed of, fly back and forth between New York and Los Angeles. Pretty soon, the real world isn't people. It's just a bunch of lights off the right side of the plane. You have to stay in touch if you're going to write advertising that works.[8]
>
> —*Jerry Della Femina*

Stay in touch with the world. Read. Listen. Go places. One of my personal favorites is to watch TV all the time. (Is this a great business or what?)

"What are you doing, honey?"

"Oh, I'm in here analyzing the psyche of my culture—absorbing the zeitgeist, as it were. I can't be bothered."

Read books and magazines. See all the movies. Go to the weird new exhibits at the museums. Know what's out there, good and bad. It's called keeping your finger on the pulse of the culture, all of which has direct bearing on your craft.

On the value of awards shows.

I shouldn't talk. In my younger days, I was a pathetic awards hound. Just around April, you'd find me lurking in the mail room pining for "the letter" from the One Show announcing accepted entries. "Is it here yet? . . . Well, check againnnnnn."

But I won't be too hard on myself. Our work isn't signed. And when you're new in the business, there's no better way to make a name for yourself than getting into "the books. Awards shows allow tiny agencies to compete with the behemoths. They serve as great recruiting tools for agencies. And they expose us to all kinds of work we'd not see otherwise. So I recommend them. With some caveats.

Don't make the wrong name for yourself by entering too many campaigns for easy, microscopic, or public service clients. They might get *in*.

Don't talk about awards shows around clients or account executives. You'll devalue yourself in their eyes and make your work suspect. *("Is that last ad she did on strategy or is it just another entry into Clever-Fest?")*

Don't enter every show. As of this writing, I count 39 different national awards shows in this industry. No kidding—*39*. It's pathetic how much this industry awards itself. (Remember, we aren't saving lives. Even Hollywood isn't this award-crazy.) *Thirty-nine*, and that's not even counting the local shows.

Here's the deal. Only three of them have any merit. In my opinion, the best are the One Show and *Communication Arts*. And, in England, D&AD.

One last thing. If awards are why you want to get into the business, don't get into the business.

Awards are candy. They're fun. But by nature of their exclusivity, they represent about 0.000002 percent of all the work being created every year. If you hang your self-esteem on such odds, you're likely to be disappointed.

Here's the other thing. If winning awards becomes true north on your compass, you'll warp your understanding of what this business is about: building brands and increasing sales.

Yes, I want you to win all kinds of awards by hitting that sweet spot we talked about in Chapter 3—doing ads that are great for your book and great for the client's sales. But when you sit down to work on an ad, make sure you're trying to get into a customer's head and not into the award books.

I remember a long, interesting talk with my former boss, Mike Hughes, of The Martin Agency. Over lunch one day, we wondered what it would be like if there were no award shows. Or barring that, what if our respective agencies actually banned creatives from entering their work in them?

What would the creative teams come up with if we took away the gravitational pull of the shows? Where would creatives go if all constraints, all presuppositions, and every bit of influence were removed, *including* the influence of the design and advertising trends being lauded in the latest awards annuals? Our opinion was that the teams would probably start experimenting in some fresh and entirely unexplored areas.

As it turns out, neither of us had the guts to stop our agencies from entering work in the award shows. We understood that peer recognition is an important part of any endeavor. Still, we looked at each other and wondered, "What if?"

Open on the coast of Scotland. Pan to Sigourney Weaver mohawked and saddled on a breaching whale. Using only a blowgun and a flare, she takes out every Russian whaling ship in the Atlantic. It's action. It's 90's. It's Eco-Aliens with a Gorillas In The Mist twist. Of course, there'll be shark-related casualties and heavy gunfire.

[All locations for this blockbuster can be found in Oregon. Call David Woolson at the Film & Video Office, 503-373-1232.]
Oregon. Things look different here.

Figure 5.1   *If print advertising is the book, television is the movie.*

5

In the Future, Everyone Will Be Famous for 30 Seconds

Some advice on making television commercials

———

SOMEWHERE IN AMERICA IS THE WORST DENTIST; he's out there somewhere.

We don't know where he is, but he's out there right now, probably accidentally sticking a novocaine needle in somebody's nose or putting a filling in their dentures. He is the worst dentist in the entire country.

And here's the rub: No one knows who he is.

That's right. He's the worst dentist in all of America, and he does his horrible work in anonymity. You don't hear people gathered in the company kitchen goin', *"Oh, man, did you see that piece of crap bridgework Dr. Hansen did last week? Teeth made outta old paperback books and Bubble Yum? Guy's a complete idiot."*

On the other hand, where is the worst commercial in all of America?

It's right there on national TV, playing night after night. Unlike the anonymity the worst dentist enjoys, our failures here in the ad industry are very public. The worst commercials from the worst agencies (and the worst clients) are all right up there on the big screen, in all their digital horror, seen by tens of millions every night. And people *do* talk about them at the office.

Here's my point: You don't wanna suck in this business of advertising, and you *really* don't want to suck at TV. Even your mom's gonna see it.

People generally get into this business learning their craft on print ads. But you'll find as you grow, you need to start doing more and more TV. To advance, you'll have to do it well. The medium remains a powerful way to sell stuff despite all the inroads made by alternative media like the Internet, digital video recorders, cell phones, DVD players, and video on demand.

Many of the suggestions from the chapters on general concepting apply to this medium, the virtues of simplicity being perhaps the most important. Here are a few other things I've learned from my colleagues along the way.

CREATING THE COMMERCIAL.

Rule #1 in producing a great TV commercial:
First, you must write one.

It takes exactly as much work to produce a bad TV spot as a good one. If you have a so-so storyboard approved, you're going to put in the same hours producing it that they put in making Apple's famous "1984" commercial (Figure 5.2).

The writer's job on a TV spot doesn't end with coming up with the idea. That's just the beginning of a long process—a process you'll play a part in all along the way. Sell a so-so print idea and at least you'll have the thing out of your hair relatively quickly. A so-so TV spot will haunt you for weeks. You'll have the same long casting sessions as you would producing a great spot, the same boring hours on the set during prelighting, and the same cold coffee in the editing suites. But when you're done, you'll have a ho-hum commercial.

Put in the hours now, during the creative process. Make the concept great. Otherwise, you will have a long time to wish you did.

Make sure you know what kind of money is available
for your project before you start.

It's no fun to waste time coming up with a great campaign the client can't afford. So ask your account people to provide a real production

Figure 5.2   1/1,440th of Chiat/Day's famous "1984" commercial for Apple Computers. *A recent customer survey named it the best commercial of all time. For a few more frames, as well as all the copy, see the One Show, volume 6.*

estimate. Don't let them tell you the client doesn't really know. That's like walking into a Mercedes dealership and telling the salesperson you "don't really know" how much you have to spend. *("I might have $70,000 . . . I might not. I don't really know.")*

Typically, production estimates are 10 percent of the total TV buy. Getting this figure is sometimes difficult, but *somebody somewhere* at the client has a dollar amount in his head, and it's best you find out what it is now.

Remember, just because you can think it up doesn't mean you can shoot it.

Before you get too excited about selling an idea, make sure your idea can be executed within your budget. Even the simplest effects can be surprisingly expensive, and some are hard to pull off regardless of the money available—particularly if they involve animals, children, or water.

Study the reels.

There's nothing like seeing a great commercial on a real television screen. They just don't make the transition to the printed page very well. (That's why I've included only a few stills from favorite spots in this chapter.) You need to see the reels.

There are a lot of them out there. There's the annual Cannes reel. There are the reels from the One Show and *Communication Arts*. You can also get reels from directors and effects houses, and, of course, there's tons of stuff online. Ask your producers to help keep you up on what's new. Stay abreast, too, of who's shooting the hottest music videos. There's a lot of churn in this industry, with new people coming in all the time: independent filmmakers, students out of school, still photographers moving into film. A sharp producer can help keep you up-to-date.

Most of the commercials mentioned in this book are viewable online somewhere. With a few prudently chosen search words you should be able to see all the spots (and the web sites) that are covered here.

Solve the problem visually.

TV is a visual medium, and it begs for visual solutions. Try to avoid verbal approaches. Don't talk at customers. Tell them a story with pictures. Start with images. Stay with images.

There is a saying: "The eye will remember what the ear will forget." Remember the last time you tried to tell somebody about a great commercial you'd seen? Did you recite the script? Or paint a picture?

Can you make the picture do all the work?

Let your TV concept be so visually powerful that a viewer would get it with the sound turned off. This isn't a rule; it doesn't always work. But when it does, it's great. It means you have a very simple, very visual idea.

This famous old Maxell audiotape commercial from the 1970s said it all with one image (Figure 5.3). A guy listening to music on a Maxell tape is literally blown away by the fidelity and power of the sound. You could have been vacuuming your living room when this spot came on and you still understood it.

Figure 5.3   One image tells the story without words.
Maxell's still using this image to sell digital products.

Think in terms of story.

There's a great book I recommend to ad students. It's not about advertising but about screenwriting: Robert McKee's *Story: Substance, Structure, Style and the Principles of Screenwriting*. McKee makes a convincing case that the human brain is wired to hunger for story—that a structure of three acts, taking us from problem to unexpected solution, is something our brains crave. Story just sucks us in. Even when we know how a story's going to end, we stay up later than we ought to just to watch an old movie play out on TV.

Theorists suggest that story is actually a cognitive structure our brains use to encode information. So in addition to its drawing power, story has lasting power—it helps us remember things. *("Did you see that spot last night? The one where the ...")*

Find one great image and build a story around it.

Try looking at your TV assignment as a print job. If you had to settle on a single image to convey your point, what would it be? Once you've found that image, try spinning a story into or out of it. If you try this, make sure you move far enough off that one image to develop some real story, some beginning, middle, and end. If you don't, you may end up with what's often called "a print idea on TV"—a spot with one moving part. The viewer can see it coming, and once they've seen it . . . *feh*. Print ads on TV are a mistake to the degree that they don't take full advantage of the medium.

Be simple.

The advice about staying simple applies to TV as it does to print. And nowhere does it apply more than in low-budget commercials.

If you've been assigned a cheapo TV spot, congratulations. It's going to force you to pare away the dross and get to the essence of the client's marketing problem. So valuable is this kind of thinking, you should start here even if your client has a large budget.

The Martin Agency's John Mahoney and Hal Tench did a great (and very simple) commercial for an agricultural pesticide using two hammers set on a white tabletop (Figure 5.4). One hammer appears to be forged out of gold; the other, iron. Next to the hammers, two

Figure 5.4   If the creative team had five times the budget, they couldn't have improved on this simple, wonderful commercial.

bugs. A voice-over says, "You have your expensive insecticide." (Hand comes in, picks up gold hammer, smashes bug.) "And your cheap insecticide." (Hand comes in, picks up iron hammer, smashes bug.) "So," concludes the voice-over, "which worm is more dead? Ammo. Guaranteed worm control. Cheap."

Even if you have a normal-size budget, start with a clean slate. Empty the stage in your mind; dress it with just a ladder and a chair, like Thornton Wilder did in *Our Town*. This intellectual challenge of working with a small budget (or any constraint) is one of the best mental reset buttons there is. It's such a fruitful place to begin that Ernie Schenck wrote an entire book about it. Pick up a copy of *The Houdini Solution: Put Creativity and Innovation to Work by Thinking Inside the Box.*

It's okay to think big, too.

Even if you've landed a TV job with a sizable budget, your final spot will be better if your idea is simple. When you have a simple idea *and* a good budget, all the money ends up on the screen, as they say in Hollywood. You can put the production dollars into amplifying an already cool idea instead of depending on money to give your idea some oomph. The ideas behind these two Cannes-winning commercials were, on paper, simple.

In Wieden + Kennedy's famous "Cog" commercial for Honda (Figure 5.5), it's this: *"Let's dramatize how well a Honda is built by showing all the parts working together sorta like dominos."* The idea might have been charming on a small scale, but the spot was planned as a two-minute commercial using real car parts and without any special effects—it would be one single, long camera pan along a stylized room as parts of an Accord roll, trip, bump, and set each other off in Rube Goldberg fashion. Ultimately, the action ends in front of an assembled vehicle as a voice-over concludes, "Isn't it nice when things just work?" It took five months of design and preproduction before they could even roll film, and then the real test began. Over the course of one hairy week in a Paris studio, the crew did 605 takes. It's likely you can view the spot today on any of a hundred sites that archive incredible advertising.

Another Cannes-winning high-production-value spot that comes to mind is one for Guinness Draught beer called "noitulovE" (Figure 5.6). People who enjoy this Irish brew know it takes a bit longer to draw a Guinness beer from the tap; thus, their tagline: "Good things come to those who wait." AMV BBDO's spot sug-

*Figure 5.5   When they filmed "Cog," only six hand-built
pre-mass-production Accords existed. And they had to completely
disassemble one of them for this spot.*

gests evolution has really just been one long, long wait for a
Guinness beer. A trio of guys at a pub drinking Guinness beer takes
a journey backward through eons, devolving through cavemen and
monkeys, and finally ends up in the primordial muck as three pop-
eyed mudskippers who look like they could use a beer.

*Figure 5.6   Guinness brand's big-budget spot showed evolution
backward; hence, the name "noitulovE," itself a
memorable little handle to use in the PR.*

The spot could have been smaller in scale and still would have worked. But you could see the money on the screen, and the wow factor was part of the fun as well as the staying power. Yeah, big can be good. But remember, it's the same with commercials as in Hollywood. If you don't have a good story, you don't have a good commercial or a good movie.

If you can make the first two seconds of your spot visually unusual, do so.

Think about it. Your viewer's watching TV. His eyes are glued to it. The cop shoots the bad guy. The camera closes in. Oh, no! He shot his partner. Fade to black. You now have two seconds to keep the viewer's eyes on the screen before he heads to the kitchen to eat chili out of a can over the sink.

Competition with Funyuns and bathroom breaks isn't the only reason to open strong. When you open with something that's inherently interesting or dramatic, you create what George Lowenstein called a "curiosity gap." He says we feel curiosity when there's a gap between what we know and what we want to know, and describes curiosity as an itch. When you set up your spot with something that opens this gap, it creates an itch, and watching the rest of your commercial is the only way to scratch it.

As an example, a well-known spot by Jamie Barrett and Mark Wenneker for Saturn automobiles (Figure 5.7) starts with a very curious image: a man running backward out of his garage. It's hard to see that image and not wonder "What's next?" Eventually we understand that the man's just "backing out" of his garage into a world without cars. They illustrated Saturn's value of "People First" by showing a world of human beings on the road without their cars wrapped around them. (The voice-over explains: "When we design our cars, we don't see sheet metal. We see the people who may one day drive them. Introducing the redesigned L, the VUE, and the all-new ION. It's different in a Saturn.") Here on paper, the spot sounds almost simplistic, but it was elegantly shot, set to an understated piano score, and was a thing of beauty.

Solve the last five seconds.

There's an old Hollywood axiom that says "Movies are all about their last twenty minutes." Writer/creative director David Fowler reiterates that advice in *The Creative Companion:*

Figure 5.7   Open strong. You're competing against getting a second bag of Cheetos or going to the bathroom—sometimes both, sadly.

The most important part of any television advertisement is its conclusion, the last five seconds. That's the part that resolves, explains, summarizes, or excuses the preceding twenty-five seconds. If you're not clear about the last five seconds, you're not clear about anything, because that's where your premise gets pounded home. Try to write the last five seconds first. If you can't, you don't need to write a spot, you need to develop a premise for a spot.[1]

A television commercial should entertain throughout the entire spot.

Avoid a long buildup to an "unexpected" conclusion, or what I call a "waw-waw" ending. (Remember that muted pair of trumpet notes on shows like *Leave It to Beaver*?) Once you know a commercial's unexpected ending, how many times will you really enjoy watching it? A great spot is a joy to watch from beginning to end, over and over. There's something new to look for in each frame.

Please don't take this to mean I'm against surprise in a TV spot— just gimmicky little switcheroos at the back of a spot. Those suck. Real surprise, the gasp you hear when you move a viewer's whole mind-set from one place to another and in doing so, create insight and a fresh new way of seeing—well, that's pretty cool.

Don't force your TV to look like your print.

A lot of the bigger clients insist on this, saying that identical print and TV executions will give them "synergy." If your print also happens to work as great TV, fine. But if it doesn't, don't let them force you to drag an idea kicking and screaming from one medium into another.

All you should promise the client is the campaign will have one voice, one message, across all media—not an unfair request, not an unfulfillable promise. But if your TV sounds like David Letterman and your print reads like the *Wall Street Journal*, your campaign isn't holding together.

Write sparely.

Don't carpet your spot with wall-to-wall copy. Leave breathing room. Lots of it. After you've written your script, get out a really big, scary knife. Like the one in *Halloween 4*.

You'll be glad you did, come editing time. You'll find you need space to let those wonderful moments on film just happen by themselves, quietly, without a voice-over jabbering in your ear.

Author Sydney Smith suggested, "In composing, as a general rule, run your pen through every other word you have written; you have no idea what vigor it will give to your style."

For 15-second spots, write very, very sparely.

Ten- or fifteen-second TV spots are a different animal from a 30. You have no time for a slow build. With four to five seconds already set aside for the wrap-up and client logo, you're looking at 10 very skinny seconds to unpack your show, put it on, and hit the showers.

So strip your 15-second TV spots down to the bones. And then strip again down to the marrow. Lock off the camera and keep it to one scene if you can. Even two cuts can make a 15 look choppy.

I remember a Toyota 15 that was this simple. The camera is locked down on an empty red Toyota parked on a quiet suburban street. Suddenly a barking dog comes rushing down the driveway of the house behind it and careens into the back of the car. Type comes up to silently explain: "Looks Fast." A pause. Then: "The New Celica Action Package."

Avoid showing what you're saying or saying what you're showing.

This idea, discussed in print advertising, has a counterpart here in broadcast, with a few twists.

You have two tracks of information in a TV spot occurring simultaneously: audio and visual. To some degree, they have to match up. If either track wanders too far afield of the other, viewers will not know which to attend to; they'll lose interest and begin feeling around in the couch for change. On the other hand, you don't want to have the voice-over and video so joined at the hip that viewers hear again what they've already seen on screen.

It's better to have one track complete the other, or play off the other, just as you do in print. That $1 + 1 = 3$ thing works to great effect here in television. The words and the visuals can supply slightly different pieces of information, tracks that viewers can integrate in their heads.

Sometimes you can add creative tension between what is seen and what is heard by giving the copy an unexpected tone, perhaps of irony or understatement. For instance, I remember a Reebok spot featuring a popular Dallas Cowboy running back crashing into defensive players. What you heard, though, was the player quietly musing about how football "allows you to meet so many people."

━━━━━

TV'S JUST GONNA KEEP GETTING WEIRDER.

I hope these few pieces of advice will be enough to help frame your thinking as you begin working in this cool medium. Its high visibility and public forum make it one of the most exciting media you can work in—the most exciting and most public part being, perhaps, the Super Bowl. There's nothing quite like settling in with a group of friends at the big game to see your cool idea along with a billion other people.

Things are going to get *really* interesting when Internet Protocol TV (IPTV) is fully rolled out and in every home. Basically, IPTV is television provided over the Internet. When it arrives, it'll mean the convergence of all things digital in the home: computers, TV sets, digital recorders—pretty much all of it will be on one device and fed through one pipe.

Actually, all the technology exists now, but broadband speeds are going to have to go up and the price come down before IPTV really takes off. Once it does, though, it'll be a new landscape for customers as well as advertisers. The biggest advantage to your clients is that they can customize a TV commercial not just to a zip code, not just to a neighborhood, but to a customer.

You know how Amazon.com sometimes sends a message that says, "Hey, Bob, because of your last purchase, we thought these new titles might interest you"? Well, it's now the same thing on TV but with commercials. Say Bob lives in Chicago. And your client is a cruise line out of Miami. Maybe they co-op with the Weather Channel. So when Chicago's temp goes below freezing, Bob gets a commercial extolling the virtues of Caribbean sailing intercut with the frozen silhouette of Chicago's skyline. The spot ends with a special offer for snowbirds freezing their asses off in Chi-town with a cruise price that includes the exact airfare out of Midway. Bob clicks "Select" on his remote, his TV goes from the Weather Channel to Travelocity.com, and he books the trip.

Man, it's a new world. When I was a kid, we had three channels. And we *liked* it.

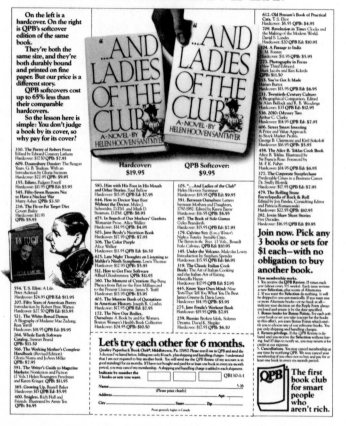

Figure 6.1   Just because an ad has to have a coupon in it doesn't
mean it has to suck. I think this is an elegant ad, perfect for
budget-minded book readers.

6

But Wait, There's More!

*Does direct-response TV
have to suck?*

THE DARK AGES PRODUCED A THING called the Iron Maiden—a coffin with spikes on the inside that slowly skewered the victim as its lid was closed. Yet even the Dark Ages—that period of superstitious insanity and violence—never came up with a torture as horrifying as Suzanne Somers telling me about all the great benefits of the ThighMaster.

The direct-response TV (DRTV) part of our industry has traditionally produced some of the most horrible blather in the history of television. Richard Simmons and his Deal-A-Meal cards. The old lady in the First Alert spots who said, "I've fallen and I can't get up!" And most recently, the plague of ab workout machines: the Ab-Ripper, the Ab-inator, the Ab-Whatever. George Orwell must've foreseen the state of modern infomercials when he referred to advertising as "the rattling of a stick inside a swill bucket."

But here's the deal. The guy who did that ThighMaster thing? He's a multimillionaire. So are Richard Simmons and Ron Popeil. (Popeil sold his company in 2005 for $55 million.) And all those commercials you hate? They sell products by the Mall-of-America load.

Given this, it would seem we've come back around to Mr. Whipple and the main question we started with: To be effective, do DRTV spots and infomercials *have* to suck?

I like selling things. I think it's cool. But when I look at the Home Shopping Network and the geeky way they honk that horn when people call in, well, I throw up in my mouth a little bit. (Is it just me?) Yeah, I know they're makin' money hand over fist and the people who own it could buy and sell me a thousand times. But, again, it comes down to this: For me to actually work in this field of DRTV and infomercials, I need to be able to look my kids in the eyes and say, "Yeah, you should see this thing I worked on today. It's pretty cool."

So, in spite of evidence to the contrary, I don't believe DRTV spots and infomercials *have* to suck to be effective.

While we're not in the majority, there are some of us who believe DRTV can do the heavy lifting required of it, and do it without tossing taste, intelligence, and common decency under the treads of capitalism's tanks. Yes, DRTV has some special considerations—rules, if you will—that help yield better results. And results are why your client comes to work every morning. Results are why more and more blue-chip clients are adding DRTV to their marketing mix. Results are why the big agency holding companies are buying up direct-response agencies left and right. But does getting results mean DRTV has to make us feel so urpy?

Well, remember the two overlapping circles in Figure 3.3? Pretend for a minute that one circle represents all the rules the DRTV specialists know about how to make the phone ring and the other circle represents Things That Don't Suck. Isn't it possible the two circles could sometimes overlap?

Perhaps the best way to begin is by exorcising some of the horrible things associated with this industry.

SPRAY-PAINT TOUPEES AND PSYCHIC FRIENDS.

The entire DRTV industry was created by entrepreneurs solely for the purpose of selling widgets on TV. None of these gadgets had a brand—or, at least, not a brand with a purpose beyond making money. Things like the Salad Shooter and the ever-creepy GLH (bald-spot spray paint) were created solely to be promoted on TV. Many of these items weren't even manufactured until after the infomercials ran and the marketers had the customers lined up. There was simply no brand to protect, build, or polish; it was all about getting people to call now and cough up $19.95 to get an Inside-The-Shell Scrambler. Since the marketers weren't looking for any long-term relationship, they had no scruples about trying every carnival trick in the book. *("Now how much would you pay?")* According to an industry magazine,* the top 25 products being sold via DRTV this very month include three male enhancement creams, four weight-loss supplements, two power wheelchairs, and Urine Gone, an odor elimination spray. Not exactly an august lineup of blue-chip clients. God, next they'll be selling lawyers. *(They what? They do already? Never mind.)*

Because of this pedigree, DRTV has remained advertising's mutant stepchild, kept in a box under the basement stairs. Creative people still walk across the street to avoid saying hello. I don't blame them. I ordered copies of the top 20 all-time moneymakers in DRTV, and after some study I can testify that it looks as bad up close as it did from across the street. Most of these infomercials plugged their made-for-TV product into a prefabricated format: the fake talk show format, the fake news show, and fake rallies (where hundreds of supposed brand advocates filled the studio just to cheer on a can of spray-paint hair). I noted an almost complete absence of production values. Every actor was horrible, reading from a transparent sales script, saying things no human being would say. Then there's the wall-to-wall voice-over of the Constantly Talking Man, as well as the nonstop graphics. The overall feeling one gets watching these shows is of being cornered by a salesman in an elevator at a crack convention. They are exhausting. I also note the music, most of which has the cheap synthesized sound that—a friend of a friend tells me—sounds like porn. And finally, DRTV is frequently used to sell products that people are too embarrassed to buy from an actual human being: male enhancement creams, spray-paint hair-in-a-can, psychic friends.

Almost every spot I reviewed was dreadful. So it's not surprising that mainstream creatives and good directors avoid DRTV. Its reputation is deserved. The whole category should be torched and rebuilt. But on our way out, let's grab a few of the good things that seem to work, and then set a lighter to the rest.

Electronic Retailer magazine, April 2007, page 26, retail rankings for February 2007 of Short-Form Products Sold on TV.

IF IMAGE = EMOTION, THEN DRTV = REASON.

Recently, marketers have begun to use DRTV to sell real main-stream products such as computers and brokerage services; it's no longer all about kitchen widgets.

Part of the reason for this surge is that stations charge a lot less to air DRTV. (There are a couple of reasons for this, but suffice it to say that it costs clients a lot less.)

The main reason marketers like DRTV isn't cost anyway, but accountability. Clients can track exactly what they're getting for their money. If brand TV is a shotgun, DRTV is a sniper. My friend Richard Apel is a DRTV expert and explained it to me this way: "To use a bad analogy, God in his infinite beneficence lets the sun shine on the just and the unjust alike, right? Which is kinda like brand advertising. But in DRTV, we're not as benevolent. We want the sun to shine only on the just—you know, those *exact* people most likely to respond to our spot. The unjust?" he concluded with a smile, "They can go to hell."

The ability to pinpoint a client's message to just the right audi-ence and then to track that data in nearly real time has incredible marketing power. Today, customer data is easier, cheaper, and faster than ever to obtain and analyze. My buddy Richard says, "Once clients have had the taste of raw, segmented or analyzed response data, I swear, it becomes like an addiction."

Because of this power, DRTV has started to move from late-night into the more respectable hours of daytime and prime-time TV. Along the way, the discipline has attracted lots of blue-chip companies like Apple and Nokia. These are companies that want a revenue-building vehicle like DRTV in their portfolio but aren't willing to cheapen the brand just to make a sale. These brands con-tinue their regular image advertising, which helps give customers a certain feeling about their brand, and then use DRTV to make them act on those feelings. Brand provides the air cover; the troops of retail and direct response do the rest.

DRTV takes several forms. Any ad with a consumer response that can be specifically tracked is technically DRTV, but for our purposes we're talking about long form and short form. Long form is any commercial longer than two minutes (the infamous infomer-cial), and the short form, anything two minutes or under.

My friend Jim Warren is a specialist in direct-response TV and he sees DRTV existing along a spectrum (Figure 6.2). On one side

| Brand | "25/05" | Transactional |

Figure 6.2   On the left, pure image advertising. In the middle, a little of both. And on the right, pure transaction.

there's pure brand advertising; on the other is hard-core DRTV. But, he continues,

> ROI and accountability pressures are requiring agencies to move away from both extremes and instead find sweet spots along the spectrum that satisfy *both* of the objectives most important to their clients: 1) building a brand that people love, and 2) selling the products to those people. In other words, all advertisements should have at least some of both components, and there's only limited reason for ads on the extreme ends of the brand-demand spectrum.[1]

Here's another way to think of the brand-to-direct spectrum. (It's creepy, but bear with me.) If image advertising is kinda like a first date, DRTV is the second.

On a second date, you're done trying to get someone's attention, right? You have it, obviously. They seem to like you and now they just wanna know more about you. Your relationship with the customer has moved from catching their eye from across the room to having a nice, long conversation. It's moved from a chemistry check to looking for rational reasons to buy. (And get married.)

Okay, enough with the creepy metaphor. The point is, DRTV is all about providing information, and lots of it. This is your opportunity to remove any objection that could keep a customer from buying your product. It means answering all the questions customers might ask if they were standing in front of you. "The more you tell, the more you sell," says my friend Jim, and if he tells me one more time, I'm gonna barf.

But the guy's right. Let's go back to that brand-demand spectrum again. On the left side, it's pure brand image stuff. Cool, we've covered that in Chapter 5. On the right is DRTV, purely expository and full of facts. (And *way* over on the right is the hard-sell "Call right now!" kind of spot—the kind this book will not touch, even with Ronco's new Ten-Foot Pole®. (*"The new Ten-Foot Pole® lets you touch all kinds of skeevy stuff with no muss, no fuss!!"*)

But in between those two extremes, there's a variety of hybrids that allow an advertiser to dial up or down the amount of information and the call to action.

With creatives on the general advertising side, the most popular is the *lead generation* format, which is usually in the shape of a "25/5." It's more on the brand side of the spectrum because here you have 25 seconds of what amounts to brand image advertising followed up with a 5-second call to action. The brilliant GEICO campaign is a perfect example. In the first 25 seconds, GEICO says that it's so easy to lower the cost of your car insurance "even a caveman could do it." (At which point we see modern, well-dressed Neanderthals taking offense at the insult.) The spots all end with a simple call to action: With the phone number up on the screen, the voice-over says, "Fifteen minutes could save you 15 percent on your car insurance."

Lead generation spots like this don't need to answer all of a customer's questions, only enough to get them to call. And in GEICO's case, the calls came in. According to Mike Hughes at The Martin Agency, the long-running caveman series is one of GEICO's biggest successes.

Now, as we push farther to the right on the spectrum, we dial up the amount of information. Typically, as the amount of information goes up, you move from buying 30-second spots to 60s, and even two-minute spots. It's here where the challenge lies. The more you tell may well mean the more you sell, but it could also mean the more you suck—*if* you don't find a graceful and intelligent way of telling your story.

SHORT- AND LONG-FORM DRTV.

Short-form DRTV works best for products that sell themselves quickly because they can be explained in under a minute or two. GEICO's lead generation is a good example of a quick get. But let's say you have a bit more of a story to tell.

Well, here's where DRTV differs somewhat from brand image work. You've got a lot of information to impart. You need to present it in a way that makes sense and doesn't bore people. You need a structure. In a great article on DRTV, OgilvyOne's Bruce Lee put it this way:

> Structure comes down to how you want to organize your information, and since most DRTV spots carry a lot of information (the better to convince you to act), the easier you can present that information, the easier the viewer can absorb it. And I've never met an organizing method more viewer-friendly than linear storytelling.[2]

To make his point, Lee sites a 60-second DRTV commercial, one I like every bit as much as any brand image commercial. It tells a marvelous story, has two great characters, and is fun to watch from beginning to end.

Here's the entire script of the Ameritrade DRTV commercial:

> *(We open on a staid office setting, where we see a goofy-lookin' twentysomething lying on the copier, photocopying his face. A much older man brusquely motions the kid into his office.)*
>
> MR. P.: Stuart, can I see you in my office, please?
>
> OLDER WOMAN STANDING NEARBY: That kid is sick. Very sick.
>
> MR. P.: Stuart, get in here.
>
> STUART: Sure thing, Mr. P.
>
> *(Stuart enters, closes door. The smile on Mr. P's face tells us quickly that Stuart's not in trouble. Something else is going on.)*
>
> MR. P.: Stuart, I just opened my Ameritrade account.
>
> STUART: *(Conspiratorially.)* Let's *light* this candle. Let's go to Ameritrade-dot-com. It's easier than fallin' in love. What do you feel like buying today, Mr. P?
>
> MR. P.: Kmart.
>
> *(Phone number comes up and stays up in lower left-hand corner.)*
>
> STUART: So research it. All this stuff is provided for you free of charge.
>
> *(As Mr. P. types, the camera shows us the easy-to-navigate web page.)*

MR. P.: No charge?

STUART: Yeah, that's synonymous with free.

MR. P.: Looks like a good stock.

STUART: Let's buy!

MR. P.: Let's buy a hundred shares.

STUART: All right, click it in there! How about *five* hundred?

MR. P.: *One* hundred, Stuart.

(Stuart imitates the sound of a chicken squawking.)

STUART: You feel the excitement? You're about to buy a stock *online.*

(Stuart writhes in a victory dance while Mr. P. makes his buy.)

MR. P.: Fabulous! I'm thrilled! What did it cost me?

STUART: Eight dollars, my man.

MR. P.: Eight? My broker charges me *two hundred* dollars.

STUART: You're riding the wave of the future, my man. I've got to get a soda, Mr. P. Hey, I'm having a party on Saturday night. *(He hands Mr. P. an invitation.)* If you really want to go . . .

MR. P.: I'm gonna try to get there.

STUART: Happy trading.

(Mr. P. sees Stuart to his office door.)

MR. P.: Thank you.

STUART: Rock on.

MR. P.: All right, Stuart.

(Graphics with phone number, URL, and logo.)

ANNOUNCER VOICE-OVER: Call toll-free, 800–573–9914, or visit Ameritrade-dot-com. Ameritrade. The way to trade. Period.

Wow. In that 60 seconds I learned Ameritrade is an online brokerage where I can do it myself. I learned it costs $8, or $192 less than what a broker charges. I learned that I can research a buy before I make it and that the information is free. I learned that it's fast and that the site is easy to navigate. I learned this is not only a new product but a whole new category. I learned where to go to get this cool new thing. And not for one second was I bored.

This script observes the one ironclad rule for any form of advertising—do something interesting—but it also observes several important DRTV guidelines.

Have a crystal clear call to action.

Along with imparting a lot of information, the other big difference about DRTV is the call to action (the CTA). DRTV isn't embarrassed about asking for the sale. The advertiser has to move a viewer from "Hey, that's pretty cool" to "I have to get that right *now*." Talk about pressure to perform. Just slapping a phone number on the back of a brand image spot probably won't do it. The CTA is a big deal, and in DRTV it's generally the first thing you create.

In the very first part of the CTA it's a good idea to quickly revisit all the main highlights of your product, probably in both voice-over and a super. (But please don't blink or spin the words at me, okay?) It's also a good idea to have your voice-over say the phone number, URL, or mailing address a couple of times. Number and address supers should stay up about twice the time it takes to actually read them.

Don't shortchange the time on any of this. This isn't brand image TV. If you cut the CTA too short, it'll mean fewer calls and that means a higher cost per response or cost per sale, which are the main metrics used to measure the effectiveness of DRTV. On the other hand, if you try to pack too much stuff in your CTA, it'll sound rushed and your credibility will suffer. Instead, try to include all the information you can while maintaining an unhurried, assured voice.

Find a structure that allows you to impart a lot of information in an entertaining way.

In the case of Ameritrade, the story is two unlikely characters—the older boss and the office knucklehead—buying stocks online. That's it. The entire structure is a conversation—the vessel into which all the other information is poured.

But other structures can work equally well, including some of the ones that work in brand image TV; the basic problem-solution architecture, for example. All I'm asking here is *please* don't use the structures so common in this industry now: the fake game show, the fake call-in show, the fake news show, the fake pep rally. Yes, folks, I know we're in advertising. But as Bill Bernbach showed us, we can sell things and have our dignity, too.

Logically map out the main reasons your product or service rocks.

If you organize your information in a logical flow and pace it well, you'll be surprised how many benefits you can impart in a one- or two-minute format. Yes, this is different from the advice everywhere else in this book (say one thing, stay focused, etc.). But this is different—it's DRTV. It's advertising to people who are nearing the end of the purchase process and are about to buy. They might be at home watching TV, but they may as well be in the dealer showroom kickin' tires. Does this give us license to wear a plaid coat and bark at them? No, not if we want them to like our brand. But we *can* point out to them some cool features they probably didn't know about. We *can* give them that one last push.

Bruce Lee put it this way:

> While information is critical to breaking down a prospect's barriers and getting him to act, you cannot tell everything. A DRTV commercial is not a brochure. It is a movie. It has to move. So you must be selective and pick your . . . strongest points. You are trying to persuade and persuasion takes time. So take your time. Unfold your selling proposition lovingly. But don't forget to hurry.[3]

Be passionate.

This advice isn't about pushing the talk button in the recording studio and telling your voice-over to "be passionate." It's about how you pace the entire spot. Passion can come through in your cut.

I like how Lee says, "Unfold your selling proposition lovingly." DRTV is not afraid to brag on its products a bit. Be front and center with what's cool about your product. Look at the Ameritrade TV spot. They're using the product and talking about it for almost the entire length of the spot. Remember, you're not asking someone to *think* about buying something. You're not asking them to form an opinion. You're asking them to buy it right now. That means tooting your own horn a bit. Just don't lean on the horn, okay? Most of the

DRTV literature out there will tell you to not only lean on the horn, but spot weld the horn in an on position and park it on top of the customer's head. Almost every author on the subject has a chapter on how important it is to use "magic" words like *free* and *new* and *announcing* and *revolutionary*. I'm not an expert, but I have two thoughts here. The first is that you can yell at customers only so long before they start to hate you. We're trying to sell our brand's products here without throwing the brand under the bus. And second, my guess is that for many of these marketers of male enhancement creams and psychic friends, magic words are all they have—they don't have a bona fide product because it's all tommyrot and flim-flam. (I love sayin' "tommyrot" and "flimflam.") They have no steak to sell, only sizzle. (*"Are you tired of steak?!?* ANNOUNCING REVOLUTIONARY NEW *Sizzle!"*)

That said, let's not throw out the baby with the bathwater, either. If you have a free offer, great, say so. Unfold your selling proposition passionately. If you can say it twice, do so. It will increase sales. But do you have to scream it? Probably not.

Be clear.

Nowhere in advertising is it more important to make perfect sense than in DRTV. There's no room for ambiguity here. Yes, you need to be interesting, but it cannot be at the expense of being crystal clear about what your product or service does. You need to point out as many benefits as is prudent while you move the viewer along a logic trail from Reason A to Reason B and C and D, and then end on "Call this number." Remember, we're working the rational side of the room now, removing barriers to purchase. We're giving people logical support for what is an emotional decision.

Say the product's name.

I read somewhere that you're supposed to say the product's name three times every minute. I assume they suggest this so that people tuning in late will know what's going on. While there's no evidence that constantly repeating a client's name will increase sales, DRTV isn't the place to be coy.

Get a good director, fer cry-eye.

Over the years, the DRTV category has developed its own list of go-to directors and production houses. Meanwhile, all the good directors have stayed away from DRTV because of its reputation for male enhancement creams and psychic friends. The DRTV marketers didn't seem to care, either, given the higher costs charged by the fraternity of mainstream directors and production houses. But now that DRTV is coming in from the cold and we care as much about the brand as about the sale, it's time to get a decent director.

LONG-FORM DRTV: "NOW *THAT'S* BASS!"

Long-form TV has been so bad for so long that the infomercial has become one of the most parodied communication forms on the planet. *Saturday Night Live*'s "Bass-O-Matic" fish blender was a memorable skewering. More recently, Crispin Porter + Bogusky parodied the long form by manufacturing and selling silly made-for-TV accessories for the MINI Cooper. Interestingly, they made the MINI infomercials so delightfully dreadful, there was no loss of points to the brand. Viewers *knew*.

Okay, so what if you have to create an infomercial and you can't suck, even on purpose? Here are a few things I've learned from some of the smart DRTV folks I've come to know.

Before you get to the concept, write the CTA.

Again, writing the CTA comes first. It's the most important part of the infomercial. All the same CTA advice from short form applies here. How long it is depends on the product or service, but boiling your offer down is a good exercise in clarity. You'll be forced to think through the most logical and compelling way to express it.

Have a unique TV offer in your CTA.

When what's being sold on TV is also available in stores, DRTV specialists know that fewer phone orders will come in. (Customers say, *"Feh! We'll buy it at the store."*) Therefore, it pays to make your TV offer unique. It builds in urgency and makes the proposition of calling more logical. Anything else you can do to add to the uniqueness of the offer and its urgency, do so. If it's a limited-time offer, say so. Anything that overcomes couch inertia is good.

Add an incentive on top of the offer.

First you lay out the basic offer. Then when you get to the CTA, you sweeten the deal with an incentive of some kind. (Yes, this is the genesis of that tired old line: *"But wait! There's more."*) Yet it's here where the real science of DRTV comes in. Experienced direct-response marketers have found that by rotating different incentives and measuring the difference in sales they can, as James Twitchell says, "readjust the pitch until they find the point of harmonic convergence." Since 75 to 95 percent of all phone calls are made within 30 minutes of broadcast, the marketer can tell exactly which offers and incentives are working best; then they readjust. They fiddle with the media buy, the offer, the incentive, the edit, always comparing the new results against a control.

Bring in the phone number at just the right time.

If you put your client's phone number up on screen in the first two seconds and then leave it up till the end, you may end up actually losing your client money instead of making them money. Think it through. If you put up the phone number before you've fully explained what it is that you're selling, you're likely to get thousands of phone calls from people who ultimately reject the offer because they haven't heard the whole offer or they don't know the details. Let the show be its own self-selecting mechanism. Let your story play out. Putting up an 800 number after the offer is spelled out will net a higher rate of *sales* even though the number of calls will be lower. (Plus you won't tie up your client's call center with people who happen to have a cool new cell phone, but all their friends are asleep.)

You've got 30 minutes of time. Find a big stage to play on.

The infomercial writer's primary goal is to motivate an immediate response. The secondary goal, and nearly as important, is to keep viewers watching as long as possible.

Once you've boiled down your offer in your call to action, it's time to draw a concept out of it. And now, for a little while, you can think the same way you do when you concept for brand print or TV. You're searching for the story and the emotion in the product. You might find it in the product or it may come out of what you know

*Figure 6.3   Jean Van de Velde walks through the March cold of
Scotland's Carnoustie golf course in Fenske's fascinating
long-form spot for Never Compromise putters.*

about the customer. You may find it in problem-solution architecture or in simple storytelling. And long form is a great place to tell a
story. Remember Ken Burns's *Civil War*—just a voice-over and
black-and-white photographs, yet it was riveting.

In the 30-second brand image world, we try to reward our viewers
for staying with us by entertaining them. DRTV is no different. Long
form can reward viewers with interesting content above and beyond
the sell copy. As an example, I refer to a long-form show done by
Mark Fenske for a brand of golf club, a putter called Never
Compromise (Figure 6.3). The show had an interesting story at its
core: A famous golfer named Jean Van de Velde used a putter to play
the entire course at a famous Scottish golf course, a course where
he'd failed the previous summer in a world-cup sort of game. I'm not
even a golfer and it was fascinating. They'd cut between scenes of the
golf pro whacking long fairway shots with a putter, and then cut to
detailed product information segments where the VO explained the
special way the putter was made. Viewers who stayed with it got to
watch a famous golf pro talk about a difficult game he played on a
famous course in Scotland, all while playing 18 holes with a putter.

Build your idea out in segments.

The average unit of TV time that American couch potatoes eat in
one sitting is 8 to 10 minutes. With network programming, that's

what they're used to anyway—8 to 10 minutes of sitcom, then a pod of commercials. So it may make sense to build your infomercial the same way, perhaps in three self-contained segments.

8 to 10 minutes of selling

Call to Action #1

8 to 10 minutes of selling

Call to Action #2

Final 8- to 10-minute segment

Final Call to Action #3

Network viewing habits aren't the only reason this format seems to work. Marketers have found that half of an infomercial's viewers watch for 20 minutes or more and the other half watch for 20 minutes or less. By completing a selling cycle in 10 minutes, you're ensuring that most people who watch will have an opportunity to place an order.

Do not suck.

What? We covered it? Never mind.

Move back and forth between rational and emotional.

Don't stay too long in either place. After you've rolled out two or three rational benefits, swing over to the emotional side and remind the viewer of the higher emotional state the product appeals to. Is it joy or security? Safety or vanity? Whatever that higher-level emotion is, connect to it; connect what you're selling to that stuff which really drives us as people. Then go back to laying out rational support for buying now. You'll find that going back and forth recharges each side.

Testimonials can work.

When done correctly, seeing and hearing a real person talk about a product or service can be compelling. Doing it correctly means you have to interview hundreds of customers to find those few, that handful of people who are both comfortable on camera and come across as real people. There's nothing like a true believer to extol the virtues of a brand.

Currently, most infomercials shoot fakey testimonials in fake sets that feel like the fake lobby of a fake hotel. Shooting on site seems more credible. The U.S. Navy's recruiting DRTV did this particularly well, showing real people talking about their service on the aircraft carriers, submarines, and other really cool locations. Bose speakers also went on location for their show, and instead of testimonials, they used third-party experts. To tout the value of their sound quality for home entertainment systems, they did long interviews with sound engineers in Hollywood, audio experts who talked at length about how much work they put into creating sound effects for movies. It was interesting content and, to audiophiles, relevant.

CAN WE TAKE THE EXCLAMATION POINT OUT OF DIRECT RESPONSE?

I'm not an expert in DRTV. Far from it. In fact, I'm so far from being an expert that you'd have to use some of your airline miles to get from DRTV expertise to my house. Also, I don't have the sales figures on the DRTV ideas I've included in this chapter. For all I know, they had miserable cost-per-sale figures.

Still, I stand by what I said.

I don't think DRTV has to suck in order to sell.

My friend Jim Warren *is* an expert and he thinks only 1 in a 100 infomercials or DRTV spots breaks even. Given those numbers, it seems fair to posit that many of the tried-and-true ham-fisted formulas espoused by traditional DRTV marketers may simply not be valid. And that DRTV may ultimately be subject to some of the same things that make or break brand image TV. Perhaps simply being interesting and doing something really cool is the answer.

If you decide the direct-response side is for you, good. DRTV is a growing field. And even if you're on the brand advertising side of the business, it's likely that fortune may bring you a client who doesn't have a direct agency and needs a commercial that has to make the phone ring. If so, good for you, too. Make something cool happen.

My friends in Canada, Nancy Vonk and Janet Westin, seem to feel the same way. In *Pick Me*, they wrote:

At the top direct marketing agencies, many of the writers are refugees from general agencies. And the work they do is clever, idea-driven, surprising, exciting, and every bit as good as the work they did in their previous agencies. The lines are blurring everywhere. Today's best strategy may be to learn to write for a broader number of media channels.[4]

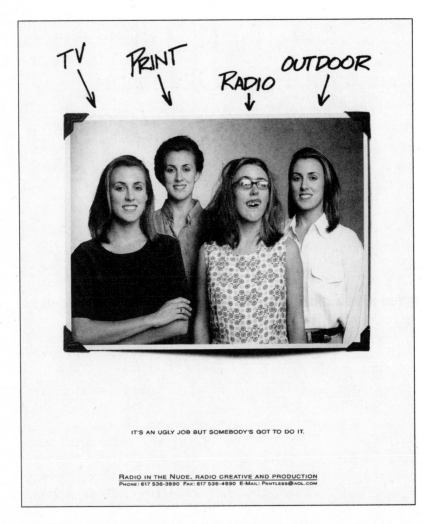

Figure 7.1   Everybody fights to get on a TV account. Everybody wants to do the color magazine spreads. And then there's radio.

7

Radio Is Hell.
But It's a Dry Heat.
Some advice on working in a tough medium

IF YOU HAVE A CHILD AGE FIVE OR UNDER, you already understand the basic problem that the radio writer faces.

"Put that down. No, do not *draw on the dog. Do not draw on the dog! Didn't you hear me? I said do not stick that crayon in the dog's . . . NO! Put that down."*

Both the parent and the radio writer are talking to someone who is not listening.

In the end, parents have a slight edge. They can send their children to their room, but the poor radio writer is left to figure out a way to get customers to listen.

If you think about it, the whole radio medium is used differently than print or TV. In print, you have readers actively holding the magazine or newspaper up to their face; they're engaged, as is the TV watcher or the Web surfer. But radio is typically on in the background while people are busy doing other things. It's just sort of *there.* People tune in to and out of it depending on how interesting the material being broadcast is.

And so we're back to our old problem. We must be interesting.

First rule: Do not suck.

It is one of the great mysteries of advertising. Most radio is . . . well, it's not very good.

Over the years, I've judged many awards shows. In every show I can remember, the judges loved poring over the print. Looking at the TV was fun. But when the time came to sit down and listen to several hours of radio commercials, the room thinned out. Nobody wanted to judge it because most of it sucked. It wasn't interesting.

Senior writers at agencies often turn radio jobs over to the juniors. Great. Here's your chance. Knock it out of the park. It pays to learn to write radio; not many people know how. Ed McCabe once advised young writers, "Quick, do something good on radio before someone catches on and makes it as difficult as it is everywhere else."

———

WRITING THE COMMERCIAL.

Radio is visual.

It's a tired old cliché, but there's truth in it. Radio has been called "theater of the mind." The good commercials out there capitalize on this perception. In radio you can do things you can't in any other medium.

You can make listeners see the impossible image of a cactus man in a werewolf mask pour through the keyhole and eat your cat. (Actually, I *did* see this once in college, but I . . . never mind.)

The point is, in radio the canvas is large, stretching off in every direction. Radio lets you do impossible things—things way too expensive to make into TV commercials. *"Hey! Let's have the entire Third U.S. Armored Division go crashing through the mall to get to our client's brunch."* In radio, you can.

Lewis Carroll wrote, "Sometimes I've believed as many as six impossible things before breakfast." So should you.

Cover the wall with scripts.

When you're working in radio, come up with a lot of ideas, just like you do when you write for print. You don't have to write the whole script; for now, just scribble down the general concept on a Post-it Note.

Come up with radio ideas you can describe in a sentence.

With a stirring musical score, Bud Light raises its glass and extols the virtues of unsung American heroes: "Here's to you, Mr. Giant Foam Finger Maker." (It closes with: "So crack open an ice-cold Bud Light and know we speak for sports fans everywhere when we say . . . *you're* number one.")

Hollywood Video stores open their commercials with this simple explanation: "Hollywood Video presents Sixty Second Theatre, where we try (unsuccessfully) to pack all the drama and suspense of a two-hour Hollywood production into 60 seconds."

These two concepts can be summed up in a sentence. They're funny just as sentences. Writing them out to a 60 makes them even funnier. (You can read the full scripts in *Communication Arts* #41.)

Figure out the right tone for your commercial.

I can assure you that humor is the first fork in the road taken by every copywriter in the nation on every radio job they get. I don't blame them. It's fun to laugh, and radio seems to beg for it.

But do the math. According to the American Association of Advertising Agencies, there are 12,489 U.S. agencies as of this writing. Even if they're all producing just one radio spot a week, by the end of the year you're looking at nearly three-quarters of a million commercials all vying to be the funniest. I don't like the odds.

So before you rush to the keyboard to start being funny, first figure out what you want your listeners' response to be. What emotion do you want them to feel after hearing your spot? This is a decision you should make early in the process, and it should be based partly on your product, partly on what the competition is doing, and partly on what you know about the customer. Once you get a feeling for the general tone your finished commercials should have, avenues will open up to you.

I can hear some of you saying, "Oh come on! This isn't Shakespeare. I've got a car client and they need a spot for their spring sale. It's gonna be humor!" I agree. Humor sounds perfect for that. All I'm saying is, think it through. There may be approaches other than humor that are not only more effective but *cooler* as well.

Here's an example. It's a very straightforward, very sober-minded radio spot for a bank, written by my friends Phil Hanft and Pat Burnham when they were at Fallon McElligott. I doubt this spot (or any of the following commercials) will come off as well on paper as they do on the radio. Broadcast advertising rarely makes the translation to print very gracefully. On this page you can't hear the nostalgic instrumental rendition of "Stand By Me" playing quietly underneath this 90-second script. And you can't hear the simplicity and honesty in the actor's voice.

> MAN: I guess you could say I'm kinda slow to do the big things in life. I mean, there's some stuff I think we'd all agree you just shouldn't rush into. Like buying a house. Took me a long time to do that. Some might say too long. Now when I tell friends who are younger about the benefits of buying a house, I can see that familiar doubt. That look behind the eyes that says "Yeah, I hear you and yeah I know you're right and that's true and I agree, but you know I can't tell you this because I know you won't understand, but it's a big deal and I'm just not sure it's going to go the same way for me as it did for you because I haven't *done* it." I guess somebody could say that's fear, but I don't think so. That's fear, like, like jumping off a building is courage. Forget that. All I can say now is what everybody said to me back then. It's the best thing to do. I did it. You should do it. 'Cept I would also add . . . I know how you feel right now. And it's okay.
>
> ANNOUNCER VOICE-OVER: A reminder from First Tennessee that whatever stage of life you're in, it's far less difficult when you have money in the bank. First Tennessee. Member FDIC.

Maybe it's one of those you-had-be-there things, but this radio spot stands out in my mind as one of the best I've ever heard. Partly because of its incredible production values. And partly because it isn't another Yuk-Fest, Laff-A-Minit radio script cranked out by a frustrated stand-up comedian doing time in an ad agency until his agent calls. It was real.

Two more reasons not to be funny.

Hey, what if *you* aren't funny? It's possible to be a really good writer and still not be particularly adept at comedic dialogue. Hey, I'm just sayin'. Here's another reason. What if your product or service doesn't call for a funny treatment?

Don't get me wrong. I am not against comedy. But I am against assuming all radio spots should be funny. They don't. They need to be interesting.

Okay. Okay. If you *are* gonna be funny, at least avoid these comedic clichés.

My friend Clay Hudson is a terrific writer and particularly good at radio. He came back from judging the radio for the One Show and wrote me this e-mail: "Everything I heard was pretty good. But as I listened to all of it what kept going through my head was, 'Heard it, heard it, heard it.' There were so many tired, overused formats in radio I found myself waiting for something really different."

Clay concluded his e-mail with a list of tired clichés to avoid, which I pass on to you, word for word.

Anything that sounds like Don Pardo

Spots that start with, "I'm here at . . ."

Just about anything that starts with "(Client name) presents . . ."

Fake game shows

Fake call-in shows

Fake newscasts

Bleeping out the dirty words to show how edgy you are

Using the NFL Films voice-over guy

Way over-the-top, abrasive, cartoon voices

Answering machine messages

Spots that start off all warm and fuzzy and then turn out to be for something—gasp!—totally edgy!!!

Spots where there's no idea but they rip off Dennis Miller's style and throw in 15-word hyphenated phrases full of equestrian-jock-itch-monkey-pimples to show us they can write weird crap even if they don't have an idea

Voices that age or get younger during the spot

Soap opera parodies (organ music and bad actors playing bad actors)

Morphing several voices together during the spot

Jingle parodies

Neanderthal spots that border on misogyny because they're for "guys"

Movie ad parodies ("In a world where . . .")

And did I mention parodies?

Funny isn't enough. You must have an idea.

Should you do something humorous, don't mistake a good joke for a good idea. Funny is fine. But set out to be <u>interesting first</u>. You <u>must have an idea</u>.

Here's an example of an interesting premise, written by my friend, the late Craig Weise.

> ANNOUNCER: Recently, Jim Paul of Valley Olds-Pontiac-GMC was driving to work when . . . (MAN: "Gee, look at that.") . . . he noticed a large inflatable gorilla floating above another dealership. He'd noticed several of these inflatable devices floating above car dealerships lately and he asked himself some questions. Did anybody ever go into that dealership and say, "Great gorilla. Makes me feel like buying a car." Why don't other businesses use gorillas? Would people be more likely to buy, say, a new home with a gorilla tethered to the chimney? "Three bedrooms, two-and-a-half baths, sun porch . . . gorilla." Would people have more confidence in the doctors if a medical clinic featured a gorilla on the roof? Without car dealers, would there even be an inflatable gorilla business? Right then, Jim Paul made an important, courageous decision on behalf of his fine dealership. (MAN: "I don't think I'll get a gorilla.") Just 8 miles south of the Met Center on Cedar Avenue, Jim Paul's Valley Olds-Pontiac-GMC. A car dealership for the times.

Over lunch one day, Craig pointed out that there are no gags in this spot, no goofy-sounding voice-over. Just a guy reading about 160 words. And although radio is often described as a visual medium, Craig called this an example of radio as print. I think he's right. This commercial is simply an essay. Yet I think it's an incredibly funny spot. So did a lot of listeners. This commercial made a bunch of money for Mr. Paul.

Make sure your radio spot is important or scary or funny or interesting within the first five seconds.

Your spot just interrupted your listener's music. It's like interrupting people having sex. If you're going to lean in the bedroom door to say something, make it good: "Hey, your car's on fire."

If your spot's not interrupting music, it's probably following on the heels of a bad commercial. Your listener is already bored. There's no reason for him to believe your commercial's going to be any better. Not a good time to bet on a slow build.

Also, awards show judges, like consumers, are very harsh. They'll grumble "fast-forward" in about five seconds if your spot isn't striking their fancy.

The following spot has an interesting opening line. (I include it for more reasons than just the setup: It's a simple premise, 130 words long, with no sound effects, and it entertains the whole way through.) It's a British spot and it may help to hear it read with a droll English accent.

> MALE VOICE-OVER: My life. By an ordinary HP grade battery.
>
> Monday. Bought by the Snoads of Jackson Road, Balham. Placed in their torch. At last. A career.
>
> Tuesday. How can I describe the cupboard under the stairs? After much thought, I've come up with . . ."dark."
>
> Wednesday. The Snoads' hamster goes walkabout. After nearly five hours of continuous blazing torchlight, we track it down on Clapham Common.
>
> Thursday. Oh dear. I'm dead. They swapped me for Duracell. It can power a torch nonstop for 39 hours. Which is nearly a full eight hamsters.
>
> Friday. How can I describe the [garbage can]? After much thought, I've come up with . . ."rank." Still, I've led an interesting life. It's just been a bit . . ."short."
>
> ANNOUNCER: Duracell. No ordinary battery looks like it. Or lasts like it.

Find your voice.

Imagine how a novelist's fingers must start to fly over the keys once she discovers her character. Finding your voice in radio can be just as liberating.

Think about who your character is. What's his take on your client's product or on the category? Is he thoughtful or sarcastic? Cynical or wry? Once you find this voice, you will see the material unfold before you, see all the possibilities for future executions, and your pen will start to move. Some of the best radio out there is just one voice reading 10 sentences. But it's that attitude the voice has, its take on the material, that makes it so compelling.

Write radio sparely.

Unless your concept demands a lot of words and fast action, write sparely. This allows your voice talent to read your script slowly. . . . Quietly. One word at a time.

You'll be surprised at how this kind of bare-bones execution leaps out of the radio. There is a remarkable power in silence. It is to radio what white space is to print. Silence enlarges the idea it surrounds.

But even if your idea isn't a bare-bones kind of idea, write sparely. There's nothing worse than showing up at the studio with a fat script. You'll be forced to edit under pressure and without client approval.

Another safeguard you can use against overwriting is to get the mandatories done and timed out first. For instance, if your bank commercial has to end with a bunch of legal mumbo jumbo, write it as sparely as you can and then time it. What you have left over is where your commercial has to fit.

Overwriting is the most common mistake people make in radio. Be a genius. Underwrite.

If a 60-second spot is a house, a 30 is a tent.

Thirties are a different animal. If you think you're writing sparely for a 60-second commercial, for a 30 we're talking maybe 60 words. Thirties call for a different brand of thinking. It's a lot like writing a 10-second TV spot. If your 30 is to be a funny spot, the comedy has to be fast. A quick pie in the face.

Here's an example of a very simple premise that rolls itself out very quickly.

> ANNOUNCER: We're here on the street getting consumer reaction to the leading brand of dog food.
>
> VARIOUS VOICES ON STREET: Yelllllchh! Aaaarrrrrgh! Gross! This tastes awful!
>
> ANNOUNCER: If you're presently a buyer of this brand, may we suggest Tuffy's dry dog food. Tuffy's is nutritionally complete

and balanced and it has a taste your dog will love. And at a dollar less per bag, it comes with a price you can swallow.

VOICES ON STREET: Yellllch! Aaaarrrrrgh!

ANNOUNCER: Tuffy's dry dog food.

One other thing to keep in mind: Most radio spots are promotional in nature, and many clients will have different promotional tags they'll want to add on at the end. This, too, cuts into your total time. So remember, write sparely.

Another way commercials can be tagged is in the middle of the spot, in a place called a *donut*. As you can see, the metaphor describes a hole in the middle, and it's for this reason that I urge you to avoid putting promotional material in a donut—it creates a hole in the middle of your spot and hurts continuity and flow. In my opinion, it's generally better to add promotional stuff at the very end.

Get a stopwatch and time it.

Read it slowly while you do. Sometimes I'll find myself cheating the clock in order to convince myself there's time to include a favorite bit. I'll read it fast but pretend I'm reading it slowly. I know, it's pathetic, but it happens. Read your script s-l-o-w-l-y.

If you're doing a dialogue, do it extremely well.

Write it exactly as people actually speak. This can be tough.

One of the problems you face with dialogue is weaving a sales message into the natural flow of conversation. "Can I have another one of those Flavor-rific® brownies, now with one-third larger chocolate bits, Mom?" Always hard. Better to let a straight voice-over do the heavy lifting. Remember also that real people often speak in sentence fragments. Little bits of talk. That start, but go nowhere. Then restart. Also note that two people will often step on each other's lines or complete each other's thoughts.

Remember, just as the eye isn't fooled by cheap special effects, the ear picks up even slight divergences from real speech. Be careful with dialogue.

This next spot is a good example of dialogue and a personal favorite. It's written by London's Tim Delaney, and if it's a bit politically incorrect, well, that's partly because it was written in the

1980s . . . and it was written by Tim Delaney. (Again, if you can read this copy with an English accent, all the better.)

> SFX: *Shop door with bell, opening and closing.*
>
> CUSTOMER *(clearly an idiot)*: Morning, squire.
>
> CLERK *(patient and wise)*: Morning, sire.
>
> CUSTOMER: I'd like a videocaster, please.
>
> CLERK: A video *recorder*. Any one in particular?
>
> CUSTOMER: Well, I'd like to have some specifications. . . .
>
> CLERK: Yes?
>
> CUSTOMER: . . . and functions. I *must* have some functions.
>
> CLERK: I see. Did you have any model in mind?
>
> CUSTOMER: Well, a friend mentioned the Airee-Keeri-Kabuki-uh-Kasumi-uh watchamacallit. You know, the Japanese one, the 2000. 'Cause I'm very technically minded, you see.
>
> CLERK: I can see that.
>
> CUSTOMER: So I want mine with all the little bits on it. All the Japanese bits. You know, the 2000.
>
> CLERK: What system?
>
> CUSTOMER: Uh, uh, well, electrical, I think, because I'd like to be able to plug it into the television. You see, I've got a Japanese television.
>
> CLERK: Have you?
>
> CUSTOMER: Yeah, I thought you'd be impressed. Yeah, the 2000, the Oki-Koki 2000.
>
> CLERK: Well, sir, there is this model.
>
> CUSTOMER: Yeah, looks smart, yeah.
>
> CLERK: Eight hours per cassette, all the functions that the others have, and I know this will be of interest. A lot of scientific research has gone into making it easy to operate . . .
>
> CUSTOMER: Good, yeah.
>
> CLERK: . . . even by a comp*lete* idiot like you.

CUSTOMER: Pardon?

CLERK: It's a Phillips.

CUSTOMER: Doesn't sound very Japanese.

CLERK: No, a *Phirrips*. I mean, a Phirrips. It's a Phirrips.

CUSTOMER: Yeah, it's a 2000, is it?

CLERK: Oh, in fact it's the 2022.

CUSTOMER: Hmmmm . . . no. Hasn't got enough knobs on it. Nope. What's that one over there?

CLERK: That's a washing machine.

CUSTOMER: Yeah? What? It's a Japanese? *(Fade out.)*

ANNOUNCER VOICE-OVER: The VR 2022. Video you can understand. From Phirrips.

It's obvious from the get-go in the "Phirrips" spot that the advertiser is being funny. It's very broad humor at that. Here's another bit of great dialogue by Aaron Allen of BlackRocket—very funny, but much more tongue-in-cheek. Picture it over a soundtrack of a running shower.

SFX: *Shower.*

MAN: *(from the living room)* Hey, honey?

WOMAN: *(Speaking a little loud, over the running water of her shower)* Hi, sweetie.

MAN: Were you doing something to the lawn?

WOMAN: Yeah, I put in a sprinkler system.

(Pause.)

MAN: What?

WOMAN: I put in a sprinkler system.

MAN: When did you do that?

WOMAN: Today.

MAN: But how di . . . *really*?

WOMAN: Yep.

MAN: I would've done that.

WOMAN: Oh, that's okay. It was kind of fun.

MAN: Does it *work*?

WOMAN: What?

MAN: Nothing. *(Pause.)* You know those trenches have to be at least ten inches deep or the pipes will freeze.

WOMAN: Yeah, I know. They're seventeen.

(Long pause.)

MAN: Don't use my conditioner, okay?

WOMAN: I'm not.

ANNOUNCER: Tools. Materials. Advice. Sanity. OurHouse-dot-com. We're here to help. Partnered with Ace.

Read your radio out loud.

You'll hear things to improve that you won't pick up just by scanning the script. The written and spoken word are different. Make sure your writing sounds like everyday speech. Read it aloud.

Avoid the formula of "shtick—serious sales part— shtick reprise."

You've heard them. The spots begin with some comic situation tangentially related to the product benefit. Then, about 40 seconds into the spot, an announcer comes in to "get serious" and sell you something. After which there's a happy little visit back to the joke.

One of the problems with this structure is that ungraceful moment when the salesman pops out of the closet in his plaid coat. This shtick-sales-shtick structure can work, but make sure you don't jar your listeners too much when you switch over to sales mode.

Personally, I think it's better to construct a comic situation that you don't have to leave in order to come around to the sale. Remember our earlier metaphor of the dog and the pill? How it's best to wrap the baloney all around the pill? Well, same thing here. Here's a great example of premise flowing seamlessly into sale, written by Mike Renfro of The Richards Group.

MAN *(in a very straightforward, monotone voice)*: Ever had the feeling when you're driving that idiots just seem to follow you wherever you go? Well, it's true. I should know. You see, I am an idiot and I've been assigned to you. Actually, I'm only one of three idiots assigned to you. We each work eight-hour shifts. This month, I happen to be on days. So it's my job to dog you relentlessly. Today, I might be the guy in the blue Nova who cuts you off. Tomorrow, the guy in the orange Pacer who runs a light. Next week, who knows? Which is why you might want to be certain you're properly insured. With me and my colleagues out here, you need to call Great American Insurance Company. They're a company that's been around since 1872. And since they don't cover guys like me, they can save good drivers money. Just tell 'em some idiot on the radio sent you.*

ANNOUNCER: Great American®. Call 1–800–555-XXXX.

Here's another example of what I mean when I say bake your sales idea right *into* the concept.

(This spot was recorded in environment, all one continuous single take—breaths, ambient noise, warts, and all. The read begins at a natural pace and builds.)

KID: Tobacco companies make a product that's responsible for one death every eight seconds. Which means another person will probably die in the time it takes me to tell you that tobacco companies make a product that's responsible for about one death every eight seconds. And that means *another* person probably just died while I was telling you that another person will probably die in the time it takes me to tell you that tobacco companies make a product that's responsible for about one death every eight seconds. And that would also mean that about *two* people probably just died in the time it took me to tell you that another person probably died while I was telling you that another person probably died in the time takes me to tell you that tobacco companies make a product that's responsible for about one death every eight seconds. And you know what? *Another* two people probably just died in the time it took me to

---

*Used by permission of Great American Insurance Company, Cincinnati, Ohio.

tell you that about two people probably died in the time it took me to tell you that another person probably died while I was telling you that another person will probably die in the time it takes me to tell you that tobacco companies make a product that's responsible for about one death every eight seconds. And that means that during this commercial somewhere in the world, tobacco companies' products killed about eight people. This message brought to you by truth.

Make your spot entertaining all the way to the end, particularly when you get to the sell.

I've heard many radio spots that start out great, but when they get to the selling message, they sputter out and fail. You can't just write the sell off as "the announcer stuff." It is part and parcel of the spot. It's the hardest part to make palatable but also the most important.

A humorous radio spot is like a good stand-up comedy routine. You need to open funny and end funny. And in the middle, you need to pulse the funny bits, to keep 'em coming. Do a funny line and then allow some breathing room, another funny bit, then more mortar, then another brick, more mortar, brick, mortar. Actually, such a structure can serve a commercial of any tone—just keep reeling out something interesting every couple of feet.

This commercial from BBDO West sells all the way through. But the way it's written, you are entertained all the way along. It's just one guy, a very straight-laced voice-over reading 189 words without a trace of irony.

ANNOUNCER: Fire ants are not loveable. People do not want fire-ant plush toys. They aren't cuddly. They don't do little tricks. They just bite you and leave red, stinging welts that make you want to cry. That's why they have to die. And they have to die right now. You don't want them to have a long, lingering illness. You want death. A quick, excruciating, see-you-in-hell kind of death. You don't want to lug a bag of chemicals and a garden hose around the yard. It takes too long. And baits can take up to a week. No, my friend, what you want is Ant-Stop Orthene Fire Ant Killer from Ortho. You put two teaspoons of Ant-Stop around the mound and you're done. You don't even water it in. The scout ants bring it back into the mound. And this is the really good part. Everybody dies. Even the queen. It's that fast. And that's good. Because killing fire ants shouldn't be a full-time job. Even if it is pretty fun. Ant-Stop Orthene Fire-Ant Killer from Ortho. Kick fire-ant butt.*

Once you get an idea you like, write the entire spot before you decide it doesn't work.

Tell your internal editor to put a sock in it. Just get that raw material on paper. You may find that in the writing you fix what was bothering you about the commercial.

Avoid the temptation to use any sort of brand name or other copyrighted material.

As an example, I once wrote a script where I referred to The Beatles. They weren't the focus of the spot; their name was used in an offhand sort of aside. The spot was approved, but one week before we recorded the script, the lawyers landed on it like a ton of hair spray and cell phones. When I tried to rewrite it, days after the original heat of the creative moment had cooled, I found myself unable to replace the line without repair marks showing.

Lesson: Don't even touch copyrighted stuff. Famous people, brand names, even dead guys who've been taking a dirt nap for 50 years—their lawyers are all still alive and slithering about, full of grim reptilian vigor. Stay generic.

Don't do jingles.

Do I have to say this? Jingles are a boring, corny, horrible, and sad thing left over from Eisenhower's 1950s—a time, actually, when *everything* was boring, corny, horrible, and sad. Avoid jingles as you would a poisonous toad. They are death.

———

THE JOY OF SFX.

A sound effect can lead to a concept.

It's an interesting place to start. Find a sound that has something to do with your product or category and play with it.

———

*Used by permission of © Monsanto Company.

Here's an example of a sound effect, set inside a good comic premise and used to great effect.

SFX: *Telephone ring.*

MAN: Hello.

CALLER: Oh. I'm sorry. I was looking for another number.

MAN: 976-EDEN?

CALLER: Well . . . yeah.

MAN: You got it.

CALLER: The flyer said to ask for Eve.

MAN: Yeah, well she's not here. I can help you.

CALLER: Oh . . . no. That's okay, I'll just . . .

MAN: Hold on, hold on. Let me get the apple.

CALLER: The apple?

MAN: You ready? Here goes . . .

SFX: *Big juicy crunch of an apple.*

CALLER: That's . . . you're eating an apple. That's the "little bit of paradise" you advertised?

MAN: Well, that's a "little bite of paradise." The printer made a mistake.

CALLER: I'm supposed to sit here and listen to you eat an apple?

MAN: Well, it is a Washington apple.

SFX: *Crunch.*

CALLER: Look, I'm not going to pay three dollars a minute just to sit here while you . . .

MAN: Nice, big, Red Delicious Washington apple.

SFX: *Crunch.*

CALLER: . . . eat an apple. . . . It does sound good.

MAN: It's nice and crisp, you know.

CALLER: Sounds good.

MAN: Kinda sweet.

CALLER: Uh-huh.

MAN: Fresh.

CALLER: I shouldn't . . . this is silly . . .

SFX: *Crunch.*

CALLER: What are you wearing?

MAN: Well, a flannel shirt and a paisley ascot.

CALLER: Oh. Describe the apple again.

MAN: Mmmmm-hmmmm.

ANNOUNCER: Washington apple.

SFX: *Crunch.*

ANNOUNCER: They're as good as you've heard.

You can also base a spot on a sound effect that doesn't even exist. To get to this spot for a technical school in Minneapolis, I first started by thinking about what sound effect said "all alone." I settled on the classic sound effect of a cricket, which I thought ably represented the loneliness of a person living in their parents' basement, a liberal arts graduate waiting by the phone for a job offer that would never come. Once I got the script done, the fun part was messing around at the controls with the engineer, Andre, trying to morph the sound of a cricket into the sound of a ringing phone and then into a hallucination. It was fun.

MALE VOICE-OVER: After graduation, as you sit in your parent's basement waiting for the phone to ring with job offers that will *never* come, you'll begin to hear them. The crickets.

SFX: *Crickets.*

VOICE-OVER: That lonely sound. The theme song of the disenfranchised. Sometimes you think you hear the phone ringing, with a job offer.

SFX: *Telephone ring, which then becomes crickets again.*

VOICE-OVER: But it's just them—the crickets. Soon you start to hear what they're *really* saying.

SFX: *Cricket sound morphs into a teasing, high-pitched, vibrating voice that says, "Looooser. Looooser."*

VOICE-OVER: Now's probably not a good time to hear about the graduates of Dunwoody Institute,

SFX: *A few regular cricket chirps. then a few saying "Loooooser."*

VOICE-OVER: How there's an average of four job offers waiting for every Dunwoody graduate. No, you're going to hold out. For a call that will never come.

SFX: *Actual real phone, ringing loud. phone is picked up.*

GUY: Hello????

SFX: *Cricket, heard through phone speaker, says, "Looooser." Laughs and hangs up. . . . One last little cricket chirp.*

VOICE-OVER: Call Dunwoody Institute and get training in one of sixteen interesting careers. Call 374–5800. 374–5800.

Radio is where you can think of six impossible things before breakfast and then actually do them.

Don't overdo sound effects.

Sound effects can be great tools for radio. They can help tell a story. They can be the story. But don't overuse them or expect them to do things they can't.

Since 90 percent of radio listening is done in the car (to and from work, during what media buyers call *drive time*), minute subtleties are going to be lost. The buttoning of a shirt does indeed make a sound, but it probably isn't enough to communicate somebody getting dressed.

My friend, Mike Lescarbeau, says that any day now he expects a client to ask him to open a radio spot with "the sound effect of somebody getting a great value."

Don't waste time explaining things.

Screenwriter William Goldman advised, "Cut into a scene as late as you possibly can." Good advice. Crisp self-editing like this keeps your story moving along with a minimum of moving parts. His advice has a classical precedent. In Greek plays, this technique was called *in media res*—in the middle of things.

Cut right to the important part of a scene. For instance, in your radio spot, we hear the sound effect of a knock at the door. Does the next line really have to be "Hey, someone's at the door"? Probably not. Let the sound effects tell your story for you. People are smart. They'll fill in the blanks if you provide the structure.

Avoid cacaphony.

You might as well learn now that you can't put sirens in a radio spot. At least not in my market. I can see why. It confuses drivers. They hear a siren sound effect on their radio and pull over to let an ice cream truck pass by.

While we're on the subject of irritating noises, keep any kind of cacophony out of your spot. That includes yelling—even "comedic" yelling. It grates on the listener. Especially on the third and fourth airing.

I've always thought of radio as the best medium to target carpenters. These guys have their radios on all day. They're not just going to hear your spot, they're going to hear the entire radio buy. One carpenter told me he actually changes stations to avoid hearing an irritating spot played over and over again.

Keep carpenters in mind when you write. Remember, these guys have hammers.

———

CASTING: BORING, TEDIOUS, ESSENTIAL.

Cast and cast and cast.

Casting is everything. In radio, the voice-over you choose is the star, the wardrobe, the set design, everything all rolled into one. It's the most important decision you make during production.

Start casting as soon as possible. Send your script to as many casting houses in as many major cities as you can. I strongly suggest that two of those cities be Los Angeles and New York. Along with the scripts, send your casting specs: some description of the quality of voice you have in mind.

About a week later, the auditions will turn up, usually via a link on the Internet. Listen to all of them (at my agency, 60 to 100 auditions for one voice is normal). Make your selections and then make a short list of the best voices back-to-back so you can zero in on those nuances that make a real difference. Your final short list should be your top three. You'll also have a second and third choice to return to if your client has a problem with the one you recommend. (Also, you can pick one voice from New York, another from Los Angeles. It doesn't matter; you digitally patch them into your local recording studio.)

One last note: Consider using the voice of just "some guy"— a friend, the babysitter, or somebody in the media department. A modicum of talent is necessary, but it can work and be really fresh sounding.

Cast people who have some edge to them.

Spielberg is alleged to have responded to the question "What is the key to making great movies?" with "Eccentric casting."

This is good advice. Most of the auditions you'll be listening to during casting are going to be vanilla. That's because you're hearing a lot of highly skilled voice people doing reads they think will keep them on the short list. They'll be taking their edges off, moving toward the middle, and going white-bread on you.

Listen for authenticity. Listen for grist. Don't listen for a great voice talent who will read your fake script for money. Listen for real.

As you listen to the casting, keep an open mind about the voice you're looking for.

You may discover someone who brings a whole new approach to your script. Sometimes it comes from an ad-lib or from an actor who doesn't understand the soul of the spot. These fresh approaches to your material may open up new possibilities for how you might produce the final commercial.

Rewrite based on what you learn from the casting.

You'll have one last chance to make your radio spot better. When you're listening to the actors read your lines, keep an ear cocked for those sentences where the actors stumble.

If more than one actor has a problem with a line, it's likely it's the line that's the problem, not the actors.

I usually discover that if I have a dialogue, one or two of the lines I have given the actors are too long. The dialogue is flowing along and suddenly it's a monologue. So as you listen to the casting tapes, listen for the general flow. Is it entertaining in the first 10 seconds? In the second 10? The last? Are you saying the same thing twice?

Are you saying the same thing twice? If you can take something out, do it now. It's your last chance to make a change and have the client sign off before you go into the studio.

Sometimes the best way to present a spot is to do a demo.

Ask your producer if there's a couple hundred in the budget you could use for this purpose. If your spot depends on the unique presentation of a particular actor's voice, this may be the way to go.

PRODUCING A RADIO COMMERCIAL.

Production is where 90 percent of all radio spots fail.

For some reason I don't quite get, radio is an all-or-nothing medium. It works or it doesn't. There is no in-between. I urge you to learn how and learn well all the elements of production.

Copywriter Tom Monahan on radio:

> In radio, there's simply no place to hide anything. No place for the mistakes, the poor judgment, the weaknesses. Everything is right there in front for all 30 or 60 seconds. Everything must be good for the spot to be good. The concept, copy, casting, acting, production— everything. One of them goes wrong, sorry, but it's tune-out time.[1]

So, start with a good idea. Craft it into a great script. Congratulations, you are 10 percent of the way there.

Develop a good working relationship with a local audio engineer.

My friend, copywriter Phil Hanft, reminded me of the importance of finding a good recording engineer in your town—a technician with a great ear who will add to the process. One who understands timing, and the importance of the right sound effects and the right music. Not someone who wants to get you in and out as fast as possible or someone who agrees with everything you do. As William Wrigley Jr. said, "When two people in business always agree, one of them is unnecessary."

Keep the studio entourage to a minimum.

Try to produce your spot alone. Well, just you and the engineer, I mean. No clients. No account executives. Not that they're bad people and you, you *alone*, are a Radio God. It's just that large crowds bring tension into those small rooms. Your spot will have more focus if it isn't produced by a committee of six.

Provide your talent with scripts that are easy to read.

Unless your actor really needs to see the cues of sound effects (or the lines of another actor), cut out everything except what he or she has to read. Set the type in something like 14 point and double-space it so there's room for the talent to scribble in any coaching advice or last-minute changes.

Don't worry about proper punctuation. Write for the flow of speech. And underline or italicize words you know you want the voice-over to hit. But don't OVERdo *it* or your *final* read IS going *to* SUCK.

Also, come to the session prepared to cut certain lines, in the event your script runs long. Know in advance what to cut, or you'll find yourself rewriting under pressure at the studio. Not good.

When you're in the recording studio, tell the voice-over to read it straight.

Most of them have been trained by years of copywriters telling them to "put a smile in your voice" or hit the word "tomorrow" in the line "So come on in *tomorrow*." People don't talk like that. Have your voice-over talk like you talk. I find a flat read is best.

When directing talent, be precise.

My engineer friend Andre Bergeron says he often sees writers directing with flabby, inarticulate language that leaves the talent clueless and uncomfortable. "Can you make that read more . . . more green?"

Try not to be so . . . so . . . what's the word? . . . *irritating*.

My advice: For the first few takes, let the talent read it the way she wants. Some of them are very experienced. If your script is great, she may pick up on what you want right at the outset. If she doesn't, fine; you've involved the talent up front and now you both have a baseline from which to work.

Also, don't wear out your talent by making them start from the top for every take. If you've got a good opening on tape, do what's called a *pickup* and start the read further into the script. Then do a quick edit to see if it cuts together. It usually does.

Don't let the talent steamroll you.

If you're a young writer on your first studio session, let your engineer in on this fact, but not the talent. The engineer, if he's a good soul, will show you the ropes and teach what you need to know. But if the voice-over catches a whiff of "junior meat" in the studio, they'll take over the session, particularly if you're working with some of the higher-priced Hollywood or New York talent. Don't let it happen.

TV shoots are controlled by the director. Radio, by the writer. Stay in charge of the room. Give-and-take is fine, but ultimately you're the one who has to show up back at the agency with a spot. If you're new to the business, it's probably not a bad idea to ask a senior writer if you can observe a few recording sessions before you tackle one alone.

Don't be afraid to stray from the script.

It's just the architecture. Get the client-approved script in the can, but if something else seems to be working, explore it. Record those other ideas and come back to experiment with them later.

Spread your production over a couple of days.

Record voices on the first day, review all the takes, and make your selections of the best tracks. Maybe get a rough cut done. But save the music, sound effects, and final mix for the next day. That second day gives you a chance to react to your spot more objectively.

Don't overproduce.

I've seen it happen a million times. You get into that tiny room with all the knobs and buttons. You drink too much coffee. You start messing with the "s" on the end of the word *prices*, borrowing the "s" from take 17 and putting it on *price* from 22. You start taking a breath out here and adding it there. By the time you're done, you have a slick, surgically perfect piece of rubbish that sounds as natural as Michael Jackson.

When painting a picture, never put your nose closer than six inches to the canvas.

If your client can afford it, always produce one more radio spot than you need.

It's the darnedest thing. But the script you thought was the hilarious one turns out to be the least funny. It happens every time I go into the studio. One or two spots are simply going to be better than the others. The more you have to choose from, the better.

One way to get a few more spots out of the session is to record your alternate scripts at what they call *demo* rates and then upgrade the talent (pay the full rate) if the client approves the commercials.

Keep a digital master of every spot you record.

Compile your own master reel and keep it current. I store each new radio spot on my Apple. It beats having a hundred CDs clutter up your office, and when you need to send out a reel, you can put your best five or six spots on one CD. It doesn't cost a lot, and it looks cool.

CAN WE HIT "PAUSE" FOR A SEC?

So we've talked about creating ideas in a variety of different media—how to think in print, outdoor, TV, and now a bit in radio. Okay, if those were like beginning lessons in each of the instruments, now it's time to think orchestra. This is where it gets pretty cool.

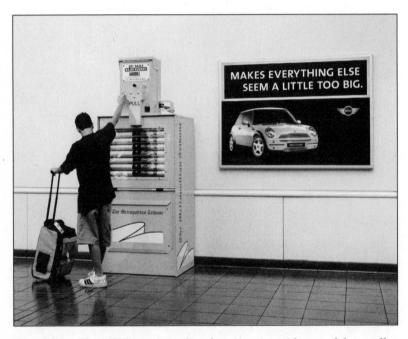

*Figure 8.1   The MINI was introduced to America with one of the smallest
TV budgets ever—fortunately.*

© 2007 MINI, a division of BMW of North America, LLC. All rights reserved. The MINI
and BMW trademark, model names, and logo are registered trademarks.

8

Big Honkin' Ideas

Hitting on every cylinder

BECAUSE I AM FREQUENTLY ACCUSED OF BEING OLD, I feel the need to point out that I was not a winner in—nor even *in attendance at*—the 1902 award ceremonies for the One Show. However, since you brought it up, I believe it was a very short program. They announced winners in just two media categories—best newspaper ad and best sandwich board—and pretty much called it a night.

Times have changed, haven't they?

The other day I found myself in a meeting where somebody actually kept a straight face as he proposed making a "blog-isode." He also wanted to create a few "content-mercials," and a "web-inar."

I can wrinkle my patrician Merriam-Webster nose at it all I want, but we may actually have to start inventing words for some of the new media fragments created since the whole grid reached critical mass in the late 1990s. A truncated list of what's called the new media might include banners, blogs, branded entertainment, blue-casting, buzz marketing, consumer-generated content, experiential marketing, gaming tie-ins, interactive billboards and kiosks, intranets and extranets, mobile phone texting, mobile video, PDA downloads, public relations and earned media, rich media, screen savers, video on demand, widgets, and those funny viral videos you e-mail to friends even though their company firewalls will probably block them.

This list doesn't count all the odd nooks and crannies now for sale as paid media. You can print your client's good name on the stripes in between car spaces in parking lots. You can paste it under diving boards, stick it on the skins of fruit at the grocery store, and by wearing shoes soled with a client's logo, impress their name into beaches everywhere. Citizens are even selling the space on their foreheads. And now that urinal deodorizing pucks are a hot media opportunity, it's no longer considered curmudgeonly to grumble how a guy can't even take a piss around here without seeing an ad. It's crazy.

I'm reminded of a headline in the *Onion* that read "Area 14-Year-Old Collapses Under Weight of Corporate Logos." Everything is branding, ladies and gents. It's all for sale. We can either bemoan how we've become the dystopia once imagined in the opening scene of *Blade Runner* or we can decide to fill all these new spaces with stuff that's cool, stuff that's interesting. (Come to think of it, that *Blade Runner* scene was actually pretty interesting.) One of Wikipedia's contributors nicely summed up the draw of new media: "Within the advertising business there is a blurring of the distinction between creative (content) and the media (the delivery of this content). New media *itself* is considered to be creative and the medium has indeed become the message."[1]

This is where the clients are spending more and more of their marketing dollars. The shift is clear; it's away from huge TV buys and toward the new media. Roy Spence of GSD&M says we should do more than just welcome all these new opportunities; he says, "Kiss change on the lips." I'm pretty sure he's right. But before we start filming a "webi-sitcom" or writing ads for every flat surface we can see from our office windows, it'll pay to first sit down and figure out a few things.

Imagine a day in the life of your customer.

Let's put our ad-writing pencils down for a minute and think way upstream about our client and their customer.

How does our client's typical customer spend a day? What does he or she do in the morning? Is the radio on while he fixes breakfast or does he grab something on the go? Does he drive to work? Does he have an iPod? Does he recycle? What blogs does he read when he's supposed to be working? Does he run at a gym or on the streets, or does he run like me . . . into the kitchen for another Krispy Kreme?

This thinking doesn't have to be guesswork. It's likely that your agency colleagues have gathered all kinds of good research about the customer. So before you start work on a campaign, it's time to sit down with the account, planning, and media team and map out a day in the life. (*I read the news today, oh boy.*) Newspapers may indeed play a part in this person's life, as will other common media, like television and radio. But those are the easy ones. And we're not making a media checklist here anyway. What we're doing is looking for insight. It's kinda like we're trying to see the aquarium from the inside out, to move through our customers' world. We're looking for contact points with customers that are unexplored. We're looking for places where customers might even welcome a cool message from our brand. Places where the right message could be less of an ad and more like information or entertainment.

A day in the life of a real estate agent is gonna be different than a corporate executive's day. A real estate agent practically lives online and his cell phone rings constantly. The executive probably has people to answer her phone and gets information by listening to podcasts at the gym or reading business pubs on the plane.

While all this different-strokes-for-different-folks stuff may seem a little obvious, it's surprising how many agencies use the same media plan to reach every audience (*"We'll buy TV for reach, magazines for frequency, and throw in a little radio for promotions."*)

Okay, now before we start writing, there's one other mental exercise that may be helpful.

Imagine the buying process.

After you've mapped a day in the life with your customer, switch gears. Now think through how a customer decides to buy your client's product. Here again, agency research and insights from your colleagues can help you see the entire buying process through a customer's eyes.

Some folks call this the *purchase funnel*, though that's a little creepy for my money. I guess any number of visual metaphors might be helpful in visualizing the buying process. Whatever image you settle on, scribble it on a big pad and start visualizing what happens to your customer as he or she moves toward actually buying your client's product. Think it through. How is it that a normal person can move from a state of being perfectly happy without, say, your client's fabulous flat-screen TV—to noticing the flat screen in the sports bar—to thinking, "Geez, my old TV does kinda suck"—to swooning in front of all the brands on display at the mall—to checkin' prices online—to triumphantly swiping their VISA card through the machine at Circuit City (or swallowing hard and hitting "Buy now with one click"). As you go through the process, jot down the contact points that pop up—those times a customer might have occasion to think about a flat-screen TV, or about the whole home entertainment category in general.

As you might imagine, the consideration process is different for a flat-screen TV than, say, buying a pack of gum, or a car, or insurance. Depending on the product, the process can be short or long; the longer ones typically consist of phases. I'm sort of making up some phases here for a nonexistent product, but a customer could move from (pardon my punctuation) general awareness > short-listing > comparison > store contact > trial. Phases such as these may be useful to keep in mind as you work on your overall idea. Different media will be in play at different parts of the purchase cycle, and each of them has its strengths.

Here's the thing to remember about this whole exercise: *Your main idea may come out of one of these contact points—an idea you can then spread sideways and backward to fill in the whole campaign.*

Pick a small customer contact point and then think big.

We're ready to sit down and start coming up with big honkin' ideas. Oh, one last thing. You can't do any TV or print.

When you sit down to begin work, start by imagining there are no TV commercials and no print ads. Anywhere. They're all gone.

Here's where it gets interesting. You still have to sell your client's product or service, but you have to find a new way of doing it.

What are you going to do?

Now don't get me wrong. I'm not saying TV and print are passé. What I'm saying is that when you start with TV (and its usual side orders of print-'n'-radio) you're solving problems in a prepackaged way. Ultimately, you may very well end up airing a TV spot. Great. But you don't have to start there. This advice may at first seem kinda weird, since most of this book so far has been about coming up with print ads and TV, right? Well, yes and no. We've used print and TV as starting points to talk about the craft, yes. But what we've really been talking about is thinking creatively. And now it's time to apply that creative thinking free of form.

Start with a blank piece of paper. In fact, let's not even think paper. How would you tell your brand's story around a campfire? How would you tell the story if Blackberry PDAs were your only medium? Or vending machines? What if all you had to work with was the way the store operators answered the phone? What if you made it a free download from iTunes? How would you start bloggers talking about your product? How about those flyers placed under windshield wipers? (Uh, on second thought, I hate those things. Never mind.)

As you can see, I'm exhorting you to start somewhere. You have to, obviously, but I urge you to pick one of the more intriguing customer contact points and then begin. It's sort of like that bumper sticker: "Act Locally, Think Globally." Go over the two lists you just made: a day in the life and the purchase process. What opportunities jump out at you?

In Laurence Minksy's book (*How to Succeed in Advertising When All You Have Is Talent*), Weiden's Susan Hoffman put it this way:

> Think holistically. . . . [What] would you do in the store? How can you pull the iconography of the campaign right into the clothing hang tag? A coupon? Online? The best work has legs to go everywhere and puts a strong, consistent, visual imprint on every consumer touch point. It's important to bring this kind of thinking to your work. . . . Take this inventiveness and apply it to the business. But do more than just ads. Produce an album, experiment with graffiti, invent a new product, shoot a film, or write a book.[2]

Think creatively about different media where your message can appear. Play out that day in the life of your customer, see where it matches up with the world of your product, and then just start screwing around with it.

For instance, the inside bottom of a paper coffee cup might be a good place to put a message about sweeteners. (Nahhh . . . the ink printing inside the cup would creep the drinker out. Anyway, you see my point.) Maybe a dingy subway car is just the place to tell a glassy-eyed commuter she needs a cruise to St. Thomas. If your client is an organization for some social issue, why not paint your idea all over the building across from city hall? (I heard an agency actually projected a provocative ad *directly onto* a government

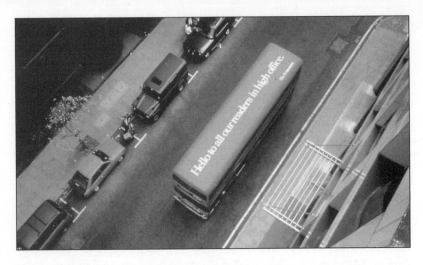

*Figure 8.2   Your ad doesn't have to appear in a magazine.
Some of the best ones don't.*

building.) Just go for it; maybe you can do it, maybe you can't, but until someone makes a phone call, you don't know.

Abbott Mead Vickers put a message from the business magazine *The Economist* on top of a bus that rolled through London's financial district, the Square Mile. (See Figure 8.2.)

As for finding a startlingly effective place to put a client's message, the most brilliant I've ever seen was a spot that ran on the porn channel in hotels. Virgin Atlantic wanted to tell business travelers about the nice new seats in their transatlantic flights. The team figured—cynically and correctly—that a day in the life of a traveling businessman might include a quick visit to the in-room "adult" channel. So that's where they placed their commercial, smartly labeling it "Free Movie." When you pressed "Play" you saw a 12-minute video that looked and sounded like porn but was really just a long, raunchy infomercial full of double entendres about the pleasures of flying across the Atlantic in a seat that goes all the way back. The idea was so naughty, its very existence drew tons of free media coverage.

To fully realize the possibilities of a multimedia campaign, you're going to need to drag your main idea through each medium and start from scratch when you get there. What works in outdoor may suck as print. The challenge is to make your product look totally cool in each medium and then, at the end of the day, have your overall campaign hang together with one consistent look, one consistent message.

Bring your idea to life in one medium and then go on to the next.

Okay, we've talked about taking in the big picture before you write, thinking through a day in the life, considering a product's purchase cycle, and putting a typical media buy into the blender and hitting purée. Any one of these mental exercises should help free up your thinking and take you to some new places.

Now it's time to put it all together and use them to create a fully integrated multimedia campaign. As an example, let's look at some work done for the American Legacy Foundation's truth® youth smoking prevention campaign. (Strategically, the campaign was brilliant, and though I won't go into it here, you should study the strategy behind this work. For our purposes today, we're talkin' tactics.)

truth® wanted to point out to teenagers that cigarettes contain ammonia. Their first idea, the basic platform, was this simple parallelism: "Cigarettes contain ammonia. So does dog poop."

Perfect. It's an unpleasant idea and a grotesque image. Next, after thinking for a while, they found their first execution (and it wasn't a TV spot or a print ad).

"Hey, what if we stuck small signs directly into actual dog poop in city parks? Signs with the message: 'Cigarettes contain ammonia. So does dog poop.'"

Boom. There's the outdoor. (Or what some call *guerrilla* advertising.)

Then they took the same small sign and turned it into a print ad. The ad featured three dog poop signs, die cut and ready for the reader to deploy. Boom. Print's done.

Then they filmed some truth volunteers at a park sticking these signs in dog poop as curious passersby looked on. Boom. TV's done.

An entire campaign from *one* idea, expressed seamlessly in several media—boom, boom, boom (Figure 8.3). Man, if advertising gets cooler than this, I haven't seen it. A warning here, though, from Saatchi's Tony Granger: "Simply checking the boxes across every possible new media channel is no longer enough to stand out. . . . Each piece of creative should stand on its own as a great expression of the big idea."[3]

This truth campaign did happen to employ some of our usual suspects (TV and print), so let's go back to our self-imposed rule and

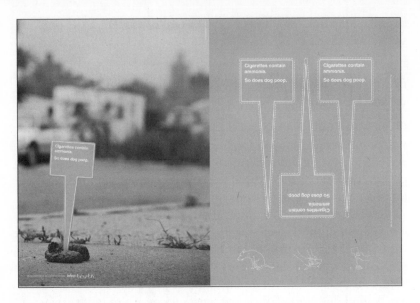

Figure 8.3   The sign in the dog poop reads: "Cigarettes contain ammonia. So does dog poop." An entire multimedia campaign from this one idea.

pretend TV and print don't exist. How could we promote, say, a retail client that needs some buzz for a new store—without TV or print?

IKEA decided to get buzz going for a store opening in Toronto by putting a living room full of their sleek furniture on the public sidewalk of the train station. But to make it an *event*, the creatives at CP+B* (Mike Lear and Dave Swartz) attached notes to the furniture that read: "Steal me." The copy went on to ask, "What better way to make a friend than to say, 'Excuse me, want to help me steal this sofa?' The two of you will then be able to look back at this day and say, 'Hey, remember that time we stole that sofa?' And you'll laugh. Of course, you and your new friend could always just go to IKEA and buy a Klippan sofa, seeing as they're only $250."

People didn't believe it at first, but after the first two strangers helped each other cart off a couch without the cops showin' up, the whole ensemble disappeared in an eight-minute scene of helpful, harmonious larceny.

---

*Yes, I know, yet another campaign created by Crispin Porter + Bogusky. If I seem to be favoring these guys a bit in this section, sue me. I use a lot of Volkswagen in this book for similar reasons: VW is a company that figured out how to do print and outdoor long before anyone else did. CP+B happens to be one of the leading agencies in executing integrated campaigns and in the innovative use of media.

Of course, the creative team was across the street filming the whole thing to post on the Web. IKEA repeated the exercise for a store opening in another city, and this time someone dropped a dime to the local news and the event was covered from a helicopter overhead. Roughly 10 grand to pull off, a quarter mil of free airtime, serious buzz, and no TV commercials.

With practice, you should be able to start thinking in big honkin' ideas like this more and more. Of course, not every job that slides cross your desk will require this type of thinking—just the really fun ones, the big ones, and of course, new business pitches. However, you may be able to create something big and cool out of a small print-and-radio assignment just by finding some nugget of a concept and blowing it up way beyond what's been asked for.

Try something naughty.

I do *not* mean do a pee-pee joke. (Oh lordy, please, please . . . no pee-pee jokes. No fart jokes. No scatology. *Please,* just stop it.)

What I *am* suggesting here is that you do something naughty. Maybe *naughty* isn't the right word. How about *controversial*? My thesaurus also suggests: *devilish, sneaky, disobedient, mischievous, willful, wayward, bad,* or *recalcitrant.* Do something you're not supposed to do. Break a rule of some kind. Come up with an idea that makes you say, "We can't do that, can we?" That's a sign it's a strong idea. The other question to ask is: "Will somebody talk about this idea if we do it?"

Sticking messages into dog poop at the park qualifies, I think, on both counts. It's a controversial sort of idea somebody might talk about.

Beaming an antigovernment message onto the side of city hall is naughty.

Airing a free video on a hotel's adult channel is naughty.

Running a small-space ad with a headline "Fur Coat Storage Services" is naughty. Well, it is when you know the rich ladies who called the number got a recorded message from People for the Ethical Treatment of Animals about the cruelty of the fur business and how they should "donate" their fur for proper burial.

In Warren Berger's book *Hoopla*, CP+B's Alex Bogusky observes, "If you're about to spend advertising dollars on a campaign and you can't imagine that anybody is going to write about it or talk about it, you might want to rethink it. It means you probably missed injecting a truth or social tension into it."[4]

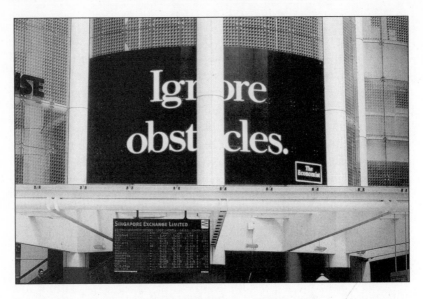

Figure 8.4   The Economist's *signature red tells the reader whose poster this is from 100 yards. And the pillars don't get in the way. They hold the concept up.*

A truth. A social tension. Now we're getting to the nut of it. Think of truth, or social tension, or naughtiness as the bad guy in a movie. Ever notice how the bad guy is usually a movie's most interesting character? Kids wanna be Darth Vader, not Luke. On Halloween, I've never seen anybody wearing a Jamie Lee Curtis mask; it's always Michael Myers. Bad is good. The bad guy disrupts. He changes things, makes them interesting. Bad means gettin' some "Bom Chicka Wah Wah" from the Axe Effect or doing things in Vegas that have to stay there. Bad is why the Subservient Chicken is wearing a garter belt.*

Do something devilish, disobedient, sneaky, mischievous, willful, wayward, bad, or recalcitrant. At every turn of the way, question authority.

Try doing something counterintuitive with a medium.

This is another form of naughtiness. Use a medium "incorrectly."

Write a 25-word outdoor board. Put your poster in exactly the wrong place, like they did with this one for the *Economist* (Figure 8.4).

---

*The Subservient Chicken's a long story, well reported in many other places. Google it.

Why not use radio for something besides retail? What if you mailed your posters and posted your direct mail? What if you embedded a radio spot in your transit poster? What if you used the newspaper's classifieds to sell a thought instead of a car? What if you used a huge outdoor board to do the work of a classified ad?

If you do an ad, does it have to be a flat page?

Try a pop-up, a gatefold, a scratch and sniff, a computer chip, something, *any*thing.

Typically, liquor companies trot out these print extravaganzas during the holiday season, spicing their inserts with talking microchips and pop-up devices. But why wait for the holidays when other advertisers might be doing it? Also, there are less expensive tricks you can try. Sequential ads. Scratch-off concepts. Die cuts. Different paper stocks, acetate film. There's even a magnetized paper now. What can you do with the ad itself to make it more than just an ad?

Crispin Porter + Bogusky's entire print buy for the MINI featured stunts like the one pictured here (Figure 8.5). They had to;

Figure 8.5 It's hard to see in this reprinting, but CP+B bought the center spread of Rolling Stone *magazine and had the MINI slaloming around orange-colored staples. The copy: "Find out why a MINI handles the way it does at MINIUSA.com."*

© 2007 MINI, a division of BMW of North America, LLC. All rights reserved. The MINI and BMW trademark, model names, and logo are registered trademarks.

Detroit was outspending them in magazines a hundred to one. So their stunts weren't just a couple of one-off's for the holidays; almost every single MINI ad was a stunt, each one basically an event held into a magazine with staples. One ad had peel-off decals to put on your MINI. Another featured a car-deodorizing pine tree. My favorite was a flattened cardboard milk carton inserted into the magazine. The copy invited you to reassemble it to look like an empty milk carton, which was just the excuse you needed to get in your MINI and motor.

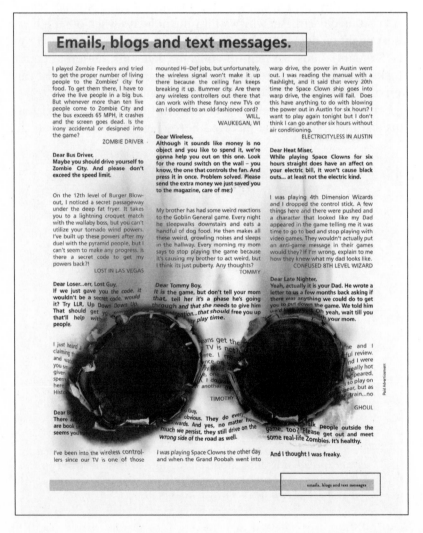

Figure 8.6   The F-15 on the other page is torching the editorial on this page.

One of the best events-in-a-magazine I've ever seen was a little two- by four-inch flip-picture book, pasted to the middle of a white page, with the words "The Golf TDi Diesel" printed on the cover. When you flipped the pages, you expected to see a little movie, a changing image of some kind. Instead, you saw a dashboard gas gauge with the needle staying, and staying, at "Full." The needle never moved. This little gem from BMP DDB Needham in London was a thing of beauty.

Your stunt doesn't always have to involve inserts. Check out this cool ad for the U.S. Air Force from GSD&M (Figure 8.6). Dummy

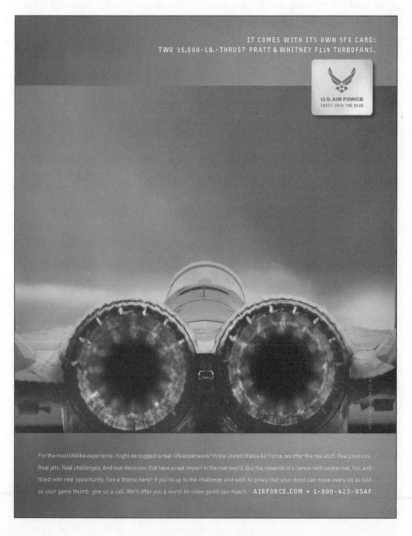

Figure 8.6   (Continued)

editorial copy on the left side is burnt to a crisp by the afterburners on the F-15.

Remember: Do something devilish, disobedient, sneaky, mischievous, willful, wayward, bad, or recalcitrant. At every turn of the way, question authority.

Instead of doing an ad, change the product.

You're never going to be at the agency one day and get a job request saying, "Change the product." But smart agencies are doing this more and more and are making a bunch of money for their clients in the process. Sometimes you'll just stub your toe on an idea. And sometimes it can come out of an agency brainstorming session, as it did at GSD&M with the "DING!" product for Southwest Airlines.

Inspired by the familiar flight-cabin "ding" that Southwest uses in its TV tagline (*"You're now free to move about the country"*), DING! is a downloadable program that immediately lets a customer know (with a small ding!) when a low fare is available to a favorite destination. Clicking on the message takes a customer to Southwest's online booking. So in addition to selling seats, it encourages customers to book online, which saves the customers and Southwest money.

As you can see, DING! wasn't an ad, but it made the client some serious money. Same thing happened at Burger King. It started with a video game developer asking Burger King if they wanted to buy some "signage" within a game. CP+B and Burger King renegotiated the deal and ended up with much more than just a BK logo way in the background of some fight scene: The King actually became a player in the game. Creative Director Bill Wright told me the success of this experiment led to bigger things: "After a year of development, three Xbox 360 games went on sale inside Burger King restaurants. So far [summer 2007], 3.2 million have been sold. And instead of just watching the King, people are playing him. Burger King has been turned into a legitimate game developer."

These are moneymaking ideas, not ads. Changing the product can even serve as an image campaign. Consider Molson Canadian's problem. "A beer has to signal something about who you are," said Wright in another conversation. "And when we found out our target audience thought Molson is the beer 'my uncle drinks in the basement when he watches hockey,' . . . we knew we had a problem."

To reach their younger target, creatives came up with "Molson Twin Label technology." Molson printed an additional label on the *back* of their bottles with one of 200 different horn-dog, testosterone-poisoned barroom "conversation starters," all of them certain to thrill any 20-year-old boy:

Let's get out of these wet clothes.

I'm not wearing any underwear.

Guess where my tattoo is.

Like we said back in Chapter 3, "Saying isn't the same as being." Molson didn't run an ad saying, "We're not the beer your uncle drinks in the basement." By changing the product, they *proved* they weren't.

Do anything but an ad.

In a recent interview on adcritic.com, Lee Clow said, "Everything is media." As an example, he said the Apple stores now in malls across America are "the best ads Apple's ever done." Similarly, Alex Bogusky said a drink cup at Burger King can have as much reach as a commercial on the Super Bowl.

Stores, cups—it's all media, and it's all canvas an ad person can use to paint a brand's story. Clow might agree with my painting metaphor, given that he sees TBWA/Chiat becoming what he calls a "media arts company." Media arts—that's actually a pretty cool way to think about what we do. But the key word here, folks, is *art*. Just because some building has a flat side doesn't mean we should put an ad there. If we do, we need to remember what Howard Gossage reminded us of back when we were discussing outdoor in Chapter 3: Our work, particularly in outdoor, must delight the people who see it. Delight them.

This is the attitude I encourage you to adopt if you ever have to create any guerrilla advertising, a term Wikipedia defines as "an unconventional way of performing promotional activities on a very low budget." It's a form increasingly popular with both clients and creatives, the former liking its ability to pinpoint a target segment, the latter its possibilities. When done well, like this piece for Norwegian Cruise Line, guerrilla ads delight audiences (Figure 8.7). The very environment where the ad appears affects the way people interpret it, and because their ad guard is down, it has an additional element of surprise. But if it's missing that element of art, it could

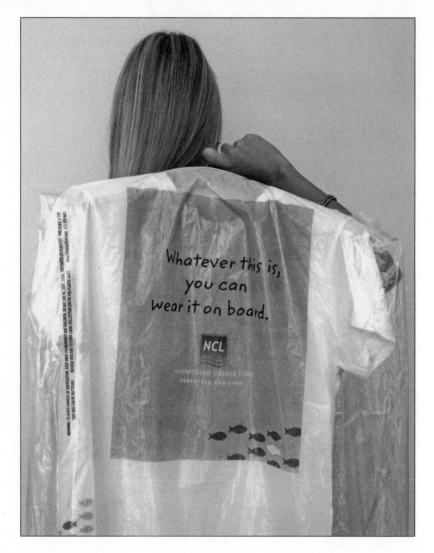

*Figure 8.7   What better place to tell potential cruisers about the easy
dress code aboard NCL than on their dry cleaning bags?*

feel more like corporate hijacking of the environment. In her book
Advertising by Design, Robin Landa gets to this very point.

> Guerilla advertising is effective when it is entertaining. It is offensive
> when it accosts or seriously intrudes. As advertising creeps more and
> more into our environment, we must be judicious about its placement
> and its effect on popular culture and on people. Respecting people is
> critical.[5]

Don't suck, people, is basically where I'm goin' with this. And don't let people make you suck, particularly in regard to outdoor and guerrilla advertising. This isn't a medium people can switch off.

One last thing: Unless you have something really important to tell me, please stay out of my bathroom stalls and off of my urinal pucks. Stuff like that—really *any* media being marketed by a vendor—has probably already lost its element of surprise anyway. The whole bathroom advertising gig reminds me of when my boys were little; they'd bring their fight to the outside of my bathroom door demanding that I immediately render judgment. Through the door I'd say, "Boys, can't this wait?"

Through the door I ask again today, can't the wheels of capitalism wait long enough for me to take care of business here? Lordy.

Don't even do an ad. Create an event instead.

Getting good PR for your client is one of the very best things you can do. Some of the most fantastic selling concepts I've ever seen weren't ads per se; they were events.

One was for Mothers Against Drunk Driving. To make their "ad," they parked the wreckage of an actual car on the back of a flatbed truck and put it on display on a busy downtown sidewalk. It was a police car, one in which a Minnesota sheriff died because of a drunken driver. Below the wreckage was a plaque with a description of the accident and the name of the law officer, a family man dead at the age of 36. No snappy headline. Just the ugly facts. And the car with its driver's side door punched in three feet. Nobody in that car could have lived. You could see it for yourself, and you walked away mad.

Another example that comes to mind is Diesel's insane idea for marketing its Intimate Collection. I would love to have been in the conference room when they presented this idea.

"Okay, basically, what we're suggesting is we're gonna have two pretty girls—both of whom we'll name 'Heidie'—and these two girls, they're gonna steal a bunch of this new underwear you got, kidnap one of your sales managers, and then lock themselves in a hotel for five days. Consumers will be able to talk to the Heidies by phone and online. And we'll broadcast the whole thing live on the Web."

Man ... I've been in meetings where suggesting "Let's run *two* newspaper ads" would put the account into review. But in this case, Diesel said yes, and their servers nearly melted down as customers jammed the lines trying to interact with the Heidies.

"Can you say my name on the air, Heidie?"

"Heidie, will you please play my favorite song?"

Everybody was in on the joke, and the entire promotion garnered massive PR because of its intelligent parodying of reality TV, MySpace, and the global fever dream of being famous for a Warholian 15 minutes. It was incredible.*

Half of creating an event is the event itself; the other half is leveraging it for all the public relations mojo you can get. Most of the ideas you've read about in this section were followed with a strong PR effort by the agency or the client's PR firm. The thing is, when your ideas are this cool, they're just as interesting as news as they are as advertising. For instance, I personally never saw the Starbucks coffee-cup-on-a-car-roof promotion; I only read about it later in the newspapers. Starbucks paid drivers to drive around town with one of their cups attached to their roof, and when passersby tried to alert the driver, they were handed a coupon for a free drink. The idea was cool, the event was cool, and, finally, just hearing about it was cool.

Create something so cool you don't have to pay people to watch it.

The other day at a parent-teacher conference I overheard this nice lady describing a problem with her teen daughter.

"Well, I went into her room—without knocking—and I caught her and her friends on the Internet looking at a video where a nice man in a suit talked about Verizon's terrific variety of affordable calling plans and the nation's widest coverage."

Okay, I'm kiddin'. Didn't happen.

The point is, people don't go on the Internet looking for boring stuff. And if you think it's difficult to get people to look at your spot on TV, it's even tougher to get them to look at your viral spot on the Internet. Viral advertising is generally any Internet-driven promotion in the form of video clips, interactive Flash games, or SMS text messages. The really good ones get passed along from one person to another and spread like global infection. Which is why I find it kind of funny whenever I hear someone say, "Oh, when we're done makin'

---

*Just so you know the conclusion, the siege came to an end when the son of Diesel founder Renzo Rosso cut a deal with the Heidies and freed the salesperson. The deal—which pulled the idea into other media—was to use the Heidies in a Diesel print campaign.

this commercial, we're gonna have it go viral." You decide to go viral about as much as the Beatles decided to "go famous." Before anything viral happens, somebody has to do something *extremely* cool.

I first saw Honda's famous "Cog" commercial (Figure 5.5) through a link in an e-mail, as did millions of others. Same with Burger King's "Subservient Chicken."

Then there was Ogilvy Toronto's marvelous "Evolution" commercial for Dove, which rode a wave of mass Internet interest all the way to the top prize at Cannes (Figure 8.8). In this simple commercial, we see an ordinary-looking woman sit down in front of a camera. From the sides come the hands of makeup artists, which begin to touch her up, to groom her. The hairstylist's hands follow; the lighting is similarly fussed over. A minute or so into it, this ordinary-looking woman is approaching cover girl material, and that's when her image is transferred to computer. Here, even more radical makeovers morph her image into the totally fake "10" we see up on a billboard and then the video ends. Two supers come quietly onscreen with the message "No wonder our perception of beauty is distorted. Take part in the Dove Real Beauty Workshop for Girls. Visit campaignforrealbeauty.ca."

Figure 8.8   From 0 to a "10" in 90 seconds.

The whole thing was set to a great piano track and, except for the words at the end, could have passed for a cool MTV video.

Janet Kestin, Creative Director at Ogilvy Toronto, assured me they did not "decide" to go viral.

"We really had no idea it was going to do what it did," she said in an interview. "It started with the art director/writer, Tim Piper, posting it on YouTube and at the same time Dove sent out an e-mail blast. A couple of days was all it took before it was on everything from CNN.com to BBC, even talk shows in Korea. It was starting to get momentum, but the posting on YouTube and the PR push were the real catalysts."

It would seem we're back to what Bogusky said earlier: "If you're about to spend advertising dollars on a campaign and you can't imagine that anybody is going to write about it or talk about it, you might want to rethink it. It means you probably missed injecting a truth or social tension into it."

Dove's "Evolution" had both of those. Kestin's partner, Nancy Vonk, adds: "As a society, we're so celebrity-obsessed and appearance-obsessed. Dove's Campaign for Real Beauty came at the moment when people were asking themselves, 'Have we gone too far?' It didn't hurt that it was released right when it was Fashion Week in New York City and there were lots of news stories about too-skinny models and all of that. To use Gladwell's phrase, it really did seem like a tipping point."*

"Evolution" indeed had a truth and social tension built into it. It also had pretty much everything else we've been talking about through this entire book. A quick look back at all the things we've talked about so far convinces at least me that Dove's "Evolution" was a big honkin' idea that hit on every cylinder.

> Say something believable. Say something relevant. Be simple. Try not to look like an ad. Open strong. Have one theme. Show, don't tell. Make sure your idea works fast. Reduce your number of moving parts. Find a villain. Tell the truth and run. Be provocative. Use simple language. Entertain throughout the spot. Leave a picture in the listener's mind. End dramatically. Don't suck. And create something so cool you don't have to pay people to see it.

"Evolution" did all of those things and more. What's *not* in "Evolution" is also important: There's no spokesperson telling you

---

*Malcom Gladwell's best seller *The Tipping Point* is good reading.

Dove is soft on your skin. Quoted in *Life After the 30-Second Spot*, Chuck Porter seems to agree that viral has its own rules.

> [S]o far, the only two ways I can see to get people to even pay attention to you in the interactive world are to offer information or entertainment. And if you really have dreams of viral, entertainment will always win. Imagine two sites. One has really useful information on caring for delicate fabrics. The other has the funniest joke you've heard since high school. Which one are you going to send to all your friends? . . . People are very tuned into the fact that whatever you forward to your e-mail list says something about *you*. And hardly anyone would ever send a salesman over to a friend's house.[6]

Invite the customer to play.

Instead of just saying something to passive viewers, why not make them active participants in your communication? Have them *do* something—something fun.

Involving the customer in the life of the brand is more than just a fun tactic, it's the way more things will be done in the future. Advertising was once exclusively the client's game; they broadcast their message to the masses and then waited to count the money. What was once a client-push strategy is becoming consumer-pull; particularly with younger customers who are increasingly experiencing brands through channels that are two-way. *("Well, well, Mr. Madison Avenue Man, it appears the Alberto Guardiani Italian goatskin loafer is now on the other foot.")* The attachment of younger people to their mobile phones, to the Web, and to texting is just the beginning of a sea change in advertising, where the metrics for success will be less about the number of "consumer impressions" and more about consumer involvement. The Web is, of course, the ultimate interactive medium, and the possibilities it offers are beyond what this little volume can hope to cover. But interactivity is not limited to the online world. IKEA's "Steal me" event we talked about earlier? That's a great example of inviting the customer to play. Or when Mars (the candy people) asked viewers to help them come up with their next color for M&M's? Very cool. Audi asked America to help them find a missing vehicle. Doritos asked viewers to submit finished commercials to air on the Super Bowl. Dove posted a billboard asking passersby to vote on their idea of beauty by using their cell phones, and then posted the results of the poll in real time.

KFC ran a TV spot with a promotional code buried in a single frame. Meanwhile, in a separate print and Web campaign, they told viewers to play back the spot frame by frame on their digital video recorders to find the code and its accompanying coupon. (The fact that viewers actually *went through* all this trouble to save a few pennies on something called a "KFC Snacker" probably says less about the penury of today's youth than it does about the potency of modern hydroponically grown marijuana.)

PARTING THOUGHTS.

The days of solving business problems by doing an ad or shooting a spot are over. In an interview, Rob Schwartz of TBWA/Chiat agreed and encouraged ad students to start seeing assignments on a much larger scale: "It's not just 'I can do one good print ad.' It's 'I can do a holistic, fully integrated, major, big chunky thought that is media infinite.' It can run on TV, it can run in print, it can run in someone's dinner conversation, the public relations people can work with it."[7]

In closing, I give the advice Mark Fenske offers: "If you are near a big idea, get out of its way. Lay flat."

Figure 9.1   An author of a book on creativity wrote:
"An idea is nothing more or less than a new combination of
old elements." And then there's . . . this, an ad for
Sony's Playstation.

9

"Toto, I Have a Feeling We're Not in McCann-Erickson Anymore."
Working out past the edge

PICASSO PROBABLY LEARNED TO DRAW a realistic head before he began putting both eyes on the same side of the nose.

Getting the eyes in the right place has been the subject of the first chapters of this book. Once you learn how, it's time to go further out. So take everything I've said so far and just chuck it. Every rule, every guideline, just give 'em the old heave-ho.

Let's assume you know how to sell a vacuum cleaner in a small-space ad with a well-crafted headline. Let's assume you know how to put a great visual idea on paper and how to come up with the sort of idea that makes colleagues who see it go, "Hey, that is cool."

Doyle Dane art director, Helmut Krone, had this to say on the subject:

> If people tell you, "That's up to your usual great standard," then you know you haven't done it. "New" is when you've never seen before what you've just put on a piece of paper. You haven't seen it before and nobody else in the world has ever seen it. . . . It's not related to anything that you've seen before in your life. And it's very hard to judge the value of it. You distrust it, and everybody distrusts it. And

very often, it's somebody else who has to tell you that the thing has merit, because you have no frame of reference.[1]

There's going to come a point in your job when the compasses don't work. When you're so far out there that up ceases to be up, west isn't west, and "Hey, great ad" is replaced with "What the hell is this?" Perhaps this is how the lay of the land looked when my friends Jelly Helm and Jamie Barrett (then of Wieden + Kennedy) came up with this ad for Nike (Figure 9.2).

What rules, what advice in this book could possibly have led a creative team to come up with this? None that I can think of. There is no bridge across some chasms. Only leaps of imagination can make it across. We're not talking about small increments of experimental thinking anymore, or reformulations or permutations, but entire new languages. New ways of looking at things.

Once you've learned to draw a realistic head, this creative outland is where you're going to need to go. This point is important enough that I've devoted this whole, albeit short, chapter to it. The last rule is this: Once you've learned the rules, throw them out.

Any further advice I give at this point is counterproductive to the creative process. It's as if I'm looking over the artist Jackson Pollock's shoulder saying, "I think you need another splat of blue over there."

But even out in deep space, there is one rule you are obliged to obey. You must be relevant.

You're never going to get so far out there that you can dare not to be relevant to your audience. No matter how creative you think an idea is, if it has no meaning to your audience, you don't have an ad. You may have art. But you don't have an ad.

"LOVE, HONOR, AND OBEY YOUR HUNCHES."
—Leo Burnett

Bernbach said, "Execution becomes content in a work of genius."

It is never more true than out here, where concepts can sometimes be all execution without the traditional sales message. To have such an execution succeed, you're going to need to know your customers better than the competition. You're going to need to know what they like, how they think, and how they move through their world. If your idea reflects these inner realities, you'll succeed, because your viewer's going to think, "This company knows me."

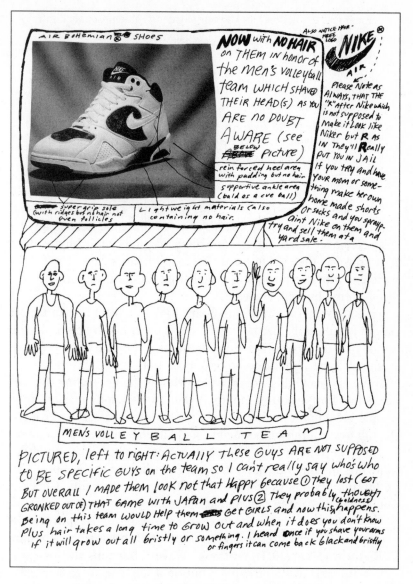

Figure 9.2   Nobody's broken more rules than Nike.

Here's a good example of how keen awareness of the customer, an intuition, and incredible production values colluded to make advertising history.

Consider the following TV script. There is no music.

BANKER: "There's a lot of paperwork here. There's always paperwork when you buy a house. First one says that you lose the house if you don't make your payments. You probably don't want to think about that but . . . you *do* have to sign it. Next says the property is insured for the amount of the note. And you sign that in the lower left corner. This pretty much says that nobody's got a gun to your head . . . that you're entering the agreement freely. Next is the house is free of termites. Last one says that the house will be your primary residence and that you won't be relying on rental income to make the payments. I hope you brought your checkbook. This is the fun part. I say that all the time, though most people don't think so. (Chuckle.)"

This was one of the TV spots for John Hancock Financial Services that swept every awards show at the time. Accompanying this voice-over were images of a young married couple buying their first house as they sat in front of a loan officer's desk. The scenes were cut with quick shots of type listing different investment services offered by John Hancock.

I'm sure that, on paper, the board looked a little flat. In fact, it probably still looks flat here. But this is precisely my point. In the hands of a director other than Pytka or a less seasoned creative team, this little vignette could have been flat.

But what made this storyboard work was the gut feeling the creatives had for the cotton-mouthed, shallow-breathing tension some people have upon buying a first home. They successfully brought the full force of this emotion alive and kicking onto the TV screen.

There were no special effects, no comic exaggerations, no visual puns, nor any other device I may have touched on in this book. Just an intuition two guys had, successfully captured on film. Check it out. It may be hard to find online, but it's worth a viewing.

While you're in the archives, look also for a spot called "Interview" for United Airlines, done by Bob Barrie and Stuart D'Rozario (Figure 9.3). Nothing "clever" happens in this spot, either. It just shows a guy shave, put on a suit, and fly to some far-away city for a job interview. There's no dialogue, and if there's any drama to the spot it's when he realizes he put on mismatching shoes. But the interview goes well, and he gets a call that makes him do a small jump for joy in the street. As we see him sleep in the plane on his way home, the voice-over says, "Where you go in life is up to you. There's one airline that can take you there. United. It's time to fly."

If none of this exactly blows your socks off, again, that's the point. What makes this spot so different and so good is the understated

Figure 9.3   Set to Gershwin's classic "Rhapsody in Blue," the United campaign was all in the execution. This frame's from a spot called "Rose."

illustration style used in place of film. Go online somewhere, find the spot, and watch it. Like Bernbach said, "Execution can become content." How you say something can become much more important than what you say.

Mark Fenske told me, "You cannot logic your way to an audience's heart." People are not rational. We like to think we are, but we're not. If you look unflinchingly at your own behavior, you may agree that few of the things you do, you do for purely rational reasons. Consumers, being people, are no different. Few purchases are made for purely logical reasons. Most people buy things for emotional reasons and then, after the fact, figure out a logical explanation for their purchase decision.

So that's the other piece of advice: Trust your intuitions. Trust your feelings. As you try to figure out what would sell your product to somebody else, consider what would make you buy it. Dig inside. If you have to, write the damn strategy after you do the ad. Forget about the stinkin' focus groups and explore the feelings you have about the product.

If an idea based on these feelings makes sense to you, it'll probably make sense to others. So sort out the feelings you have about the product and then articulate them in the most memorable way you can. Someone once told me that the things about myself that are the most personal are also the most universal. Trust your instincts. They are valid.

––––––

BUILD A SMALL, COZY FIRE WITH THE RULE BOOKS. START WITH THIS ONE.

It's been said there are no new ideas, only rearrangements. Picasso himself said, "All art is theft." Historian Will Durant wrote, "Nothing is new except arrangement."

I've used logic like this to defend ads I've written that were sound and good, but weren't *new* ideas. I think I was wrong. Instead, I think it's better to believe there really are whole new ways of communicating, ways that nobody has discovered yet. I urge you to look for them.

In 1759, Dr. Samuel Johnson wrote, "The trade of advertising is now so near to perfection that it is not easy to propose any improvement."[2] That was written in 1759, folks; probably with a quill pen. I don't want to make the same mistake with this book. So I repeat: Learn the rules in this book. Then break them. Break them all. Find something new. It's out there.

Figure 10.1   As it turns out, there are actually quite a few things "more powerful than an idea whose time has come." There's the marketing manager, the product manager, the research department, the CEO, the CFO, and that loud, opinionated guy who shows up at every focus group.

10

Only the Good
Die Young

The enemies of advertising

IN A PERFECT WORLD, IT WORKS LIKE THIS. You come up with a great ad. You take it over to the client, and they agree it solves the problem and approve it for production.

In all my years in the business, this has happened a total of three times. What usually happens is your ad dies. I don't know why it is this way, but it is. Get ready for it. It doesn't matter how good your ad is, it can die. I once watched a client kill a campaign between sips of coffee. Two months in the making, and he killed it all—every TV spot, every magazine ad, and every newspaper ad—with one chirpy line.

"Good first effort."

The thing to remember is, clients are perfectly within their rights to do this. We are in a service business. And our service isn't over when we present something we like. It's over when we present something *they* like. The trick is to do both, the first time.

There are good clients out there. Bless them. When you have one, serve them well. Work nights for them. Work weekends. You will produce the best work of your career on their behalf.

And then there's the other kind: the really tough clients. I'm not talking about the ones who hold your feet to the fire and push for greatness. This is about the ones who misbehave. Fortunately, good clients outnumber them. But the bad ones are out there, and you need to be able to spot them. Here are some of the kinds I've run into in my career. Let me rephrase. Here are some of the kinds that have run over me in my career.

There isn't a lot you can do about them. They're like mines buried in the field of advertising. Try not to step on any.

THE SISYPHUS ACCOUNT.

Those familiar with Greek mythology know Sisyphus, the king of Corinth. The gods sentenced him to an eternity in hell, pushing a large rock up a hill. He'd get it to the top, only to watch it roll to the bottom, where his job awaited him again.

So how do you spot an account like Sisyphus Corp.? By the smell of foamcore—that stiff board that agencies use to mount ads for presentations. You'll notice the smell the minute you get off the agency elevator. They won't tell you what it is during the interview, but you'll find out soon enough.

The creative director comes in and says, "I'm putting you on Sisy Corp. You're perfect for them." You'd be excited about it, were it not for the pallid look of the passing secretary who overhears your assignment.

Pretty soon you start to catch on. One day you're walking down the hall and you notice you've never seen an ad for Sisyphus displayed up on the wall. Not one. Then you see the delivery guys from the local art supplies company; they're in the lobby again with another cart full of foamcore. *(Weren't they just here yesterday?)*

Then one day you're looking for markers in the storeroom and you find 200 dead storyboards for Sisyphus, all of them great ideas, all dead as doornails and hidden in the corner like Henry VIII's closet of heads.

When they hired you, they told you Sisyphus Corp. was the next VW. The next Energizer Bunny. "We're turning it around." But now you're starting to understand: Corporations like Sisyphus don't want to actually *run* advertising. They want to look at it. They want to talk about it. They want to have meetings about it. But they won't run an ad. Not this year. anyway.

"If we were to run advertising—we're not, but if we *were* to run an ad—could you show us what it might look like?"

You've just been handed a shovel and told to feed the Foamcore Furnace. You will work as hard as somebody whose ads are actually being published. You'll spend the same late nights and long weekends and order in the same pizza. But when the year is over, you'll have nothing to show for it but some ads mounted on foamcore and a pizza gut.

This kind of account, while it can drive you crazy, isn't the worst. (More on them in a minute.) They're like blind giants, a Cyclops with something under his contact lens. They're big. They have money. And if they lumber about and head in the wrong direction, it hardly matters. As long as they make their numbers, they don't care. They've lost the entrepreneurial spirit. Winning isn't important. Not losing is.

There isn't much you can do about this kind of account. There's an old saying: "The only way out is through." Sometimes it's best simply to feed the beast its daily minimum requirement of concepts and then sneak out to a movie when the Foamcore Gods aren't hungry. Call it "paying your dues." After you've put in a few months papering the walls of your client's meeting rooms, appeal to your creative director. Show him your battle scars. If he's any good, he'll occasionally put a fresh team in front of Sisyphus's rock.

Sisyphus isn't the worst kind of account. Not by a long shot. There's another enemy of good advertising. Fear.

THE MEAT PUPPET.

A very talented woman named Lois Korey, an ad star from the 1960s, described this kind of account:

> Clients seem to get the advertising they deserve. The good ones, they're risk takers. They're willing to risk failures for extraordinary success. . . . The bad clients? Fear dribbles down from the top. No one says so, in so many words, but you know no risks will be tolerated, no rules will be broken, that mediocrity is the measure by which your work will be weighed.[1]

Fear dribbles down from the top, says Ms. Korey. The Chinese have a more colorful phrase: "A fish stinks from the head."

You can actually smell it on the vice presidents, the fear. No amount of roll-on is gonna cover up their terror of the boss. It may be their boss, or their boss's boss—it doesn't matter.

But the boss has done a terrible thing to these vice presidents. He has put them in charge of something they're not in charge of. The nameplate outside their cubicle may sport words like "Assistant Director of Marketing." But they are not directing marketing or anything else, for that matter. They are, in effect, meat puppets.

Invisible strings, thin but powerful, dangle down from management and are attached to every part of their bodies. Everything these guys do, everything they think, every memo they write, every decision they don't put off, will be second-guessed.

When you're a meat puppet, what you do is say "No." An ad lands on your desk, and that invisible string connected to your hand makes you reach for the big NO stamp, pulls it back over the ad, and wham!

"NO!"

I have seen fear completely unravel a meat puppet.

She was the director of marketing for a large corporation whose name you'd recognize. She needed a TV spot, just one 30-second spot, for a new product being introduced the following spring. It was a great product. It deserved a big, wonderful introductory spot. We worked hard and presented an idea we believed was very good.

We flew in. Shook hands. Found a room with an easel, did our setup, and unveiled. She looked at the storyboard, looked at her notebook, then wrote something down. (When clients do this, I always assume it's: "Begin new agency search immediately.") She looked up and said, "I just don't like it."

The strategy wasn't the problem. How we were saying it wasn't the problem.

"I just don't like it."

Good clients are allowed this. If they're buying good work most of the time, well, they deserve to have those simple human reservations we all feel now and then. We decide to let her play the "Just don't like it" card. Fine. We go back. Time is running out, so we bring three storyboards to the next meeting. Luckily we're on a streak and all three are good. We'd have been happy to go with any one.

"I just don't like it."

"All three?"

"I just don't like it."

"What is it you don't like?"

"I can't say." And then she said the one thing all the really bad clients say sooner or later. "I'll know it when I see it."

Copywriter and author Dick Wasserman said this phrase is tantamount to a general telling his armies, "March off in all directions, and when I see where one of you is headed, I'll have a better fix on where I'd like the rest of you to go."

And so we marched off in all directions. Meeting after meeting was adjourned with, "I just don't like it." The boards piled up. After a while, we didn't bother to fly in for meetings and started e-mailing scripts, always getting the same answer.

Some 25 boards passed before her. And 25 died. I assure you, we didn't give up. It was a good product. A fallow field lay before us. We presented good work right up to the end.

"I just don't like it."

Time began to run out. Directors' January schedules were filling up. The media was bought and the client was panicking. Client panic sometimes works in the agency's favor. Not this time. She asked for more. In the final phone meeting, the agency simply refused to provide any more boards.

And the client unraveled. I mean, she completely fell apart.

I remember listening to her voice on the speakerphone, hearing it begin to waver. She began to cry and then, God help me, beg like a junkie for more work.

She had become addicted to indecision.

"Come on! It doesn't even have to be a 30. Gimme a stinkin' 15. I'll take a 15! You got to have some 15s! Oh baby, baby, come to momma with another board." (Okay, she didn't say exactly that, but . . . she said exactly that.) I'd never seen anything like it. It got worse, too.

Somehow, around board number 29, she bought something. The agency wasn't proud of the piece. We were just holding our noses, hoping to simply produce the thing and pray we would prevail on the next assignment. A second-tier director was chosen. A location in Miami was scouted and approved. There was a listless prepro meeting. Sets built. The team assembled in Florida the night before the cameras rolled. And the phone rang.

In the 11th hour, in the 59th minute, and at the tail end of the 59th second, the client's antiperspirant failed again. "I just don't like it."

The agency was forced to come up with a new concept and do it under the constraints of an existing set and a locked-off budget.

Which is a lot like being told to build a plane, and here's a coffee can, a crayon, and an old copy of *Sports Illustrated*. It was insane. It was like that famous line from journalist Bill Mellor: "We are sorry. But the editor's indecision is final."

These incredible dervish-like turnarounds are known as "doing a 360°." It's like doing a 180°, but twice. It could be argued that this client did a 540° or even a 720°. (A 900° was once observed in Brussels, but no verification was available as this book went to press.)

The agency had to go back to the drawing board yet again. This time, getting the idea took just 10 minutes. The tired writer and the dispirited art director walked to the end of a nearby pier and just sat there looking out at the ocean.

Idea number 30 limped into the writer's mind like a sick dog with its ribs showing, and the writer said, "Okay, what if we did this?"

The art director looked at the dog. The dog looked up at the art director.

"Fine."

They took their sick little animal of an idea and walked it back down the dock toward the nearest phone.

The client loved it.

It should come as no surprise that the final spot sucked. It was so bad we were trying to change channels on it during the final editing session. "See what else is on," someone would say. What is surprising is how the client later decided they didn't like it and blamed the agency. "Why aren't our commercials as good as the work you do for your other clients?"

The spot never aired. I swear this happened.

There is a list I've seen posted on bulletin boards in many agencies. One of those jokes that get photocopied and passed around until the type decays. This was the list:

THE SIX PHASES OF AN ADVERTISING PROJECT

1. Enthusiasm
2. Disillusionment
3. Panic
4. Search for the guilty
5. Punishment of the innocent
6. Praise and honors for the nonparticipants

What was once a joke tacked to a bulletin board had become grim reality. What began with enthusiasm ended as a new agency search.

Funny thing, though. While the account did leave the agency, a month later we heard the woman was fired.

And, wouldn't you know it, in her absence the client's advertising improved. Which is always a little hard to take. I mean, the mature thing to do is wash the blood off your hands, wave good-bye to an account, and wish them the best. But you secretly wish your old girlfriend, after she dumps you, ends up dealing crack from a culvert or pushing a mop at the Bun 'N' Burger. Currently, the on-the-job life expectancy of the average chief marketing officer is a scant 23 months[2] before they're fired and replaced by the next one (who always has his own ideas, if not his own agency). This often means the only steady hand on the rudder of a brand is the ad agency's junior account person.

I had another client who was a meat puppet, working in a company run by fear. He was about as far down the corporate food chain as you could get—cubicle plankton. He even looked the part: that pale-white kind of guy who always gets killed in the first five minutes of a movie. Yet, to get an ad approved, you had to run it by this guy. And a bullet from his ratty little Saturday night special was as deadly as any other.

He was perhaps the tensest person I ever met. One morning, he was seen standing in front of the company coffee machine holding an empty cup, growling through clenched teeth, "Brew, goddammit." He had such high blood pressure, we worried that if he sustained even a paper cut, arterial spray would redden the ceiling.

But as scared as he was, he had a little power game he ran. It was brilliant. Whenever you presented ads to him for his approval, he wouldn't look at you. Or the ads. Wouldn't look at all. He'd just stare down at his legal pad in front of him.

There you were, having taken a two-hour plane ride, lugging your portfolio in and out of cabs to arrive in his conference room. You did your setup and then presented the ads, ta-da! . . . to the top of his head. And if it was a visual concept, it drove you crazy. Because you found yourself having to use words to explain an image that you came up with to avoid using words in the first place.

He, too, was a meat puppet. Unable to make any decision without imagined repercussions from above, he chose to make none and, instead, passed his decision on to the next guy up the food chain.

There is nothing you can do about a meat puppet. Your boss is going to have to go above him, to whoever's yanking his strings. Such a decision is not yours to make, and you'll need one of your higher-ups to talk with one of theirs. Sometimes it works. You may discover the client culture isn't, in fact, fear-based and that your contact person is living in a backwater of fear he created on his own.

PABLUM PARK.

It's a 10 o'clock meeting on Monday morning at Martini, Yesman & Longlunch. Coats come off and hands are shaken. Coffee poured and ties flattened. Everybody's excited because the client, the big regional power company, wants a new campaign.

"Okay," asks the agency, "about what?"

"Well, just about us. You know. *Us*."

"Okay, but what about . . . *us*?"

"We care."

"You care?"

"We care."

"You care about what?"

"We just . . . care."

"Okay, I get the caring. I get it. But what is it you care about?"

"Why do we have to care about anything in particular? Just a general sort of caring, I think, would be fine. In fact, Dick here was just saying on the way to the agency how that would be a workable theme-slogan sort of thing—'We Care.'"

Dick nods, sagely.

Uh-oh. It's a client with absolutely nothing to say. You are now entering Pablum Park. Abandon all relevance, ye who enter here.

A power company is a good example of this kind of client. There's nothing they can say without ticking customers off. Why they advertise at all is beyond me. Where else are you going to "shop" for electricity? ("Oh, I think I'll use that plug over there.") Many hospitals and health care plans have the same problem. They can't say, "Our doctors are better than their doctors." They can't say. "We cost less." They can, however, say, "We *care*."

So the Pablum Machine is turned on, and everything begins to run together in a saccharine slurry of Caring and Sharing and People Helping People. In fact, Pablum Park is populated entirely by "People People®."

"We're not just a giant corporation. We're People People® Helping People."

In Pablum Park, the police are "People Protecting People from People." Morticians are "Living People Helping Dead People." And lawyers are "People, Trying to *Be* People, Trying People."

If you watch even an hour of television, you'll see many commercials spouting drivel. Peel away the bluster and bombast, the jingles and clichés, and you'll find drivel. Nothing of substance. Words that sort of *sound* like you should be paying attention to them, but are ultimately empty.

The best drivel I've ever read was in a wonderful parody called *Patriotic Spot—60 Seconds*, by Ellis Weiner. I reprint it here in abbreviated form.

> You're waking up, America. It's morning—and you're waking up to live life like you've never lived it before. Say hello to a whole new way of being awake, America. Say hello to us. . . .
>
> We're watching you, America. We're watching you when you work—because, America, you work hard. And we know that afterward you've got a mighty big thirst. Not just a thirst for the best beer you can find. But a thirst for living. A thirst for years of experience. America, you're thirsty. . . .
>
> America, say hello to something new. Say hello to quality. Quality you can see. Quality you can feel. Quality you can say hello to. (How do you spell "quality," America? Real quality—quality you can trust? The same way we've been spelling it for over a hundred and fifty years.) . . .
>
> We're Number One. You're Number One. You're a winner, America. And we know what you're thinking. We know how you feel. How do we know? Because we take the time to tell you. We take the time to care.
>
> And it pays off. We're here, America. And the next time you're here—the next time we can tell you who we are and what we do—we'll be doing what we do best.[3]

You're not completely without hope with this kind of client. But it'll take some work on your part. Every client has a story. Even the big, ugly ones with names like "Syntheti-Corp" have a story that can be made relevant and meaningful to the average reader.

International Paper's trade campaign by Ogilvy & Mather back in the 1980s is a good example. International was a faceless corporation that made a product not famous for brand loyalty—paper.

How to write with style

By Kurt Vonnegut

International Paper asked Kurt Vonnegut, author of such novels as "Slaughterhouse-Five," "Jailbird" and "Cat's Cradle," to tell you how to put your style and personality into everything you write.

Newspaper reporters and technical writers are trained to reveal almost nothing about themselves in their writings. This makes them freaks in the world of writers, since almost all of the other ink-stained wretches in that world reveal a lot about themselves to readers. We call these revelations, accidental and intentional, elements of style.

These revelations tell us as readers what sort of person it is with whom we are spending time. Does the writer sound ignorant or informed, stupid or bright, crooked or honest, humorless or playful – ? And on and on.

Why should you examine your writing style with the idea of improving it? Do so as a mark of respect for your readers, whatever you're writing. If you scribble your thoughts any which way, your readers will surely feel that you care nothing about them. They will mark you down as an egomaniac or a chowderhead – or, worse, they will stop reading you.

The most damning revelation you can make about yourself is that you do not know what is interesting and what is not. Don't you yourself like or dislike writers mainly for what they choose to show you or make you think about? Did you ever admire an empty-headed writer for his or her mastery of the language? No.

So your own winning style must begin with ideas in your head.

1. Find a subject you care about

Find a subject you care about and which you in your heart feel others should care about. It is this genuine caring, and not your games with language, which will be the most compelling and seductive element in your style.

I am not urging you to write a novel, by the way – although I would not be sorry if you wrote one, provided you genuinely cared about something. A petition to the mayor about a pothole in front of your house or a love letter to the girl next door will do.

2. Do not ramble, though

I won't ramble on about that.

3. Keep it simple

As for your use of language: Remember that two great masters of language, William Shakespeare and James Joyce, wrote sentences which were almost childlike when their subjects were most profound. "To be or not to be?" asks Shakespeare's Hamlet. The longest word is three letters long. Joyce, when he was frisky, could put together a sentence as intricate and as glittering as a necklace for Cleopatra, but my favorite sentence in his short story "Eveline" is this one: "She was tired." At that point in the story, no other words could break the heart of a reader as those three words do.

Simplicity of language is not only reputable, but perhaps even sacred. The *Bible* opens with a sentence well within the writing skills of a lively fourteen-year-old: "In the beginning God created the heaven and the earth."

4. Have the guts to cut

It may be that you, too, are capable of making necklaces for Cleopatra, so to speak. But your eloquence should be the servant of the ideas in your head. Your rule might be this: If a sentence, no matter how excellent, does not illuminate your subject in some new and useful way, scratch it out.

5. Sound like yourself

The writing style which is most natural for you is bound to echo the speech you heard when a child. English was the novelist Joseph Conrad's third language, and much that seems piquant in his use of English was no doubt colored by his first language, which was Polish. And lucky indeed is the writer who has grown up in Ireland, for the English spoken there is so amusing and musical. I myself grew up in Indianapolis, where common speech sounds like a band saw cutting galvanized tin,

> Should I act upon the urgings that I feel, or remain passive and thus cease to exist?

> To be or not to be?

"Keep it simple. Shakespeare did, with Hamlet's famous soliloquy."

Figure 10.2   Long-copy ads can be great. Even if a customer doesn't read every word, they make it look like the company has a lot to offer.

Yet their campaign of award-winning ads was exquisitely readable (Figure 10.2). Above a spread filled with long, well-written copy were headlines like: "How to improve your vocabulary." Or "How to enjoy poetry." Each ad was authored by a marquee name like James Dickey or Kurt Vonnegut. And at the end of the ads, the copy seamlessly brought you around to International's take on the deal: "We believe in the power of the printed word."

"Be merciless on yourself. If a sentence does not illuminate your subject in some new and useful way, scratch it out."

and employs a vocabulary as unornamental as a monkey wrench.

In some of the more remote hollows of Appalachia, children still grow up hearing songs and locutions of Elizabethan times. Yes, and many Americans grow up hearing a language other than English, or an English dialect a majority of Americans cannot understand.

All these varieties of speech are beautiful, just as the varieties of butterflies are beautiful. No matter what your first language, you should treasure it all your life. If it happens not to be standard English, and if it shows itself when you write standard English, the result is usually delightful, like a very pretty girl with one eye that is green and one that is blue.

I myself find that I trust my own writing most, and others seem to trust it most, too, when I sound most like a person from Indianapolis, which is what I am. What alternatives do I have? The one most vehemently recommended by teachers has no doubt been pressed on you, as well: to write like cultivated Englishmen of a century or more ago.

6. Say what you mean to say

I used to be exasperated by such teachers, but am no more. I understand now that all those antique essays and stories with which I was to compare my own work were not magnificent for their datedness or foreignness, but for saying precisely what their authors

meant them to say. My teachers wished me to write accurately, always selecting the most effective words, and relating the words to one another unambiguously, rigidly, like parts of a machine. The teachers did not want to turn me into an Englishman after all. They hoped that I would become understandable – and therefore understood. And there went my dream of doing with words what Pablo Picasso did with paint or what any number of jazz idols did with music. If I broke all the rules of punctuation, had words mean whatever I wanted them to mean, and strung them together higgledy-piggledy, I would simply not be understood. So you, too, had better avoid Picasso-style or jazz-style writing, if you have something worth saying and wish to be understood.

Readers want our pages to look very much like pages they have seen before. Why? This is because they themselves have a tough job to do, and they need all the help they can get from us.

7. Pity the readers

They have to identify thousands of little marks on paper, and make sense of them immediately. They have to *read*, an art so difficult that most people don't really master it even after having studied it all through grade school and high school – twelve long years.

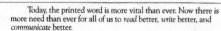

"Pick a subject you care so deeply about that you'd speak on a soapbox about it."

So this discussion must finally acknowledge that our stylistic options as writers are neither numerous nor glamorous, since our readers are bound to be such imperfect artists. Our audience requires us to be sympathetic and patient teachers, ever willing to simplify and clarify – whereas we would rather soar high above the crowd, singing like nightingales.

That is the bad news. The good news is that we Americans are governed under a unique Constitution, which allows us to write whatever we please without fear of punishment. So the most meaningful aspect of our styles, which is what we choose to write about, is utterly unlimited.

8. For really detailed advice

For a discussion of literary style in a narrower sense, in a more technical sense, I commend to your attention *The Elements of Style,* by William Strunk, Jr., and E.B. White (Macmillan, 1979). E.B. White is, of course, one of the most admirable literary stylists this country has so far produced.

You should realize, too, that no one would care how well or badly Mr. White expressed himself, if he did not have perfectly enchanting things to say.

Today, the printed word is more vital than ever. Now there is more need than ever for all of us to *read* better, *write* better, and *communicate* better.

International Paper offers this series in the hope that, even in a small way, we can help.

If you'd like to share this article with others–students, friends, employees, family–we'll gladly send you reprints. So far we've sent out over 15,000,000 in response to requests from people everywhere.

Please write: "Power of the Printed Word," International Paper Company, Dept. 5X, P.O. Box 954, Madison Square Station, New York, NY 10010.

INTERNATIONAL PAPER COMPANY
We believe in the power of the printed word.

Figure 10.2   (Continued)

THE KONCEPT KRUSHER 2000®.

This actually happened.

After several weeks of work, we finished a campaign for a large account and presented it to the client. They approved it, "pending research."

The account guys sent the boards to an advertising research firm retained by the client. A week later, the results came back. We'd scored okay with the traditional focus group tests. But we'd failed the "Andrea" test and had to start all over.

"What is the 'Andrea' test?" I asked the client.

With a straight face, she said, "Well, the thing is, we give your storyboards to a guy there at the research place. And he and another guy, they take it into a room and they close the door and then come out about, oh, three hours later with the results. And we know if your spot works. Yours didn't. I'm sorry."

"But what did they *do* in there?"

"The research firm tells us that's proprietary."

"Pro . . . can I *talk* to this 'Andrea'?"

"'Andrea' is just the name for the test. There is no Andrea and the methodology is proprietary, as I've said. They don't have to tell us what they do in there. The results they come out with always seem to be right on the money."

I stood there, blinking. The client, I'm sure, thought I was trying to think of some counterargument. But what I was thinking about was social work. *("I like people. I could help someone, maybe a little kid. It would be nice to get away. Peru or something. Maybe a little shack. Wouldn't be so bad.")*

I came to in the cab on the way to the airport, holding a fat spiral notebook full of all the things wrong with my ads, courtesy of "Andrea."

Clients who rely on test results to approve work will always be with us. There's no escaping it. That's the good news. The bad news is, with some clients, research will kill all of your work all the time.

A few large corporations have whole floors devoted to advertising-slash-research, and they have it down to a system. They feed your storyboards into one end of a process that's very much like a machine, with a name like, I don't know, "Koncept Krusher 2000." As your campaign goes through the device, you hear all kinds of nasty things happening . . . *("It's negative!" Muffled sounds. "We can't say that." Unidentified thwacking noise. "Why can't they all be happy?")* . . . and what comes out the other end you wouldn't want to air on a clothesline, much less network television.

The *really* bad news is that there isn't a thing you can do about it. Once these huge research machines are in place, they're usually there to stay. Somebody somewhere is making a *lot* of money off this research (and it isn't the client). No good idea will ever get out alive. Generally, it's the older, larger clients who've been advertising for years that have an overheated K/K 2000 down in the basement, running day and night.

I worked for several clients like this, where I think I did some of the best work of my career. But you've never seen it. On one particularly baneful project I remember, the Krusher must've been set on "high" because it went through hundreds, literally hundreds, of storyboards.

After I burned out on the project, the agency threw other people at the snapping jaws of the research machine. And then another team. And another. A full year later, the Krusher spit out this tepid little storyboard that both research and the client had approved.

There on the conveyer belt lay the TV spot—a trembling, pathetic thing that did not like being looked at directly. A sort of marketing Frankenstein—chunks of different departmental agendas and mandates, all sewn together by focus groups and researchers into something that looked like a TV spot but was, in fact, an abomination. We should have hammered a spike through its heart right there.

Koncept Krushers can be bigger machines than just a client's research department. The whole company may, in fact, be structured to blowtorch new ideas. This sounds cynical, I know, but I've seen it. I've stood right next to these furnaces myself and felt the licking of the flames.

Try this on.

The client in question was one of those Sisyphus accounts I described earlier. A big Fortune 500 company. Huge. The kind that asks for tons of stuff that's always due the next morning and you find out later it's for a product they're thinking about introducing 10 years from now.

So, anyway, this poor art director is stuck on a Sisy Corp type of account. She doesn't know this, so the day she gets a job for a big TV commercial, she's excited, right?

Well, she and her partner begin working on it. After a vast amount of work, they have a couple cool ideas. I mean some really smart things that also happen to be potential award winners (or "podium wobblers," as they're called in Britain).

Cut to next scene, meeting number 1 with the client—all of their ideas are dead. The reason? Doesn't matter. (You'll see.)

So they get to work on another series of ideas to present in meeting number 2. Days later, there's excitement in the creative department, rejuvenation. "We've done it again!"

Time wipe: It's meeting number 3. The client opens the meeting by announcing they've changed the strategy.

Okay, here's where we cut to that movie cliché—the clock hands spinning 'round and 'round, the calendar pages flying off the wall. The changes keep coming in. The client doesn't like the idea. Or they cut the budget. Or they change the product, or they change the strategy. One time it's the client *himself* who's changed—fired, actually—and now there's a new client who wants something totally different. Whatever it is, it's always something.

It gets worse.

During meeting number 4 through number 63, the campaign is watered down, softened, and diluted so much that the final commercial is precisely as interesting as a bag of hair. The last interesting thing in the commercial is successfully removed in meeting number 63. An optimist might say that things should have gone smoothly from here on out. *("For cryin' out loud. It's a bag of hair! What's to complain about?")* But there are no optimists in advertising.

It's Friday. The scheduled day of meeting number 64.

Meeting number 64 isn't even a very important meeting, given that the CEO signed off back around meeting number 50 or so. But there needed to be a few dozen more "For Your Information" sort of presentations, and if any of them went badly the agency would have to start over.

The meeting begins. The art director goes through the old moves, trying to remember the fun of presenting it the first time. But there's no spark left. She just . . . presents it.

The client sits there. Says nothing at first.

The client then reaches down into her purse and pulls out a small Kermit the Frog doll. (This really happened.) It's one of those flexible dolls, and she begins bending the frog's arms around so that its hands are covering its ears. Then the client says: "Mr. Froggy doesn't like some of the things he's hearing."

This really happened.

The client actually said, "Mr. Froggy doesn't like some of the things he's hearing" (Figure 10.3).

Let me put it this way. There are two kinds of hell. There's "Original" and then there's "Extra Crispy." This was Extra Crispy.

Well, Ms. Froggy-Lady, as she came to be known, wasn't able to kill the commercial, only make it a little worse—a feat in itself. And so, finally, in meeting number 68, the whole company had signed off on this one storyboard.

All in all, it took 68 presentations to hundreds of MBAs in dozens of sweaty presentation rooms. In fact, there were some sarcastic agency memos to the media department suggesting that since

tomlichtenheld.com

Figure 10.3   I'm not kidding. This really happened.

the commercial had been shown to thousands of people *already,* there may not be a need to air it at all.

The creative team went back to the agency, opened two beers, and sat looking at the sunset through the windows of their offices on the 30th floor. There, over the body of the original storyboard that lay on the floor, they performed an advertising postmortem, discussing the more shocking moments of its horrifying death.

Eavesdropping, a casual listener might have thought the two had just come out of the theater and were talking about a horror movie. *("Yeah! And remember that really scary part where they put that awful . . . 'thing' on the overhead projector? Man, I did* not *see that coming at all.")*

That's when they noticed something out their window—something disturbing.

Outside their window was a 40-story building.

The thing is, the 40-story building wasn't *there* the day they began working on the commercial.

With horror, the creative team realized that a building had been raised, built from a 30-foot-deep hole in the ground and 40 stories into the sky, faster than their little 12-frame storyboard had been destroyed and approved.

Why do I tell you this? To chase you away from the business?

No, to steel you for it.

This stuff happens all the time. And keep in mind, none of these clients were stupid people. (Well, we can discuss Froggy-Lady later.) They were all pretty sharp businesspeople, trying as hard as they could to solve a problem for their brand. But as smart and nice as they all were individually, a calcified approval process had crept into the company's structure, and it became completely impossible to get a decent idea out the door.

This happens all the time. Be ready.

———

THE LIZ ACCOUNT.

Then there's Liz. Liz is a glamorous and famous brand. *Everyone* knows Liz.

Over the years, the Liz account moves its tired old derriere from agency to agency to agency to agency. Every shop along the way thinks, wow, what a catch, and a year later every one of them has that hangdog look of desperation.

The thing is, many Liz companies make products that are incredibly great. But you couldn't tell it by their ads, which are always terrible no matter which agency they're currently shacking with. Good products, though, and that's the shame of it.

About once every two years, you'll see this client's name pop up in the trades: The honeymoon's over, old agency is out, new agency in. Photos are taken of big smiles shaking hands in front of banners with corny lines like "Partners in Progress" or "Thanks for the Biz, Liz."

"Compton & Curry Walk Away with $65M Liz-Co," reads *Adweek*. Six months later, Compton is in chemical-dependency treatment and Curry's on the phone to *Adweek* with something about "creative differences." Liz is back at the altar and agencies are lining up, lured by the siren song of that blue-chip logo still looking "okay" after all these years.

I have a friend who just started working for a Liz client.

One day the client phones my friend, says, "Okay, I want you guys to start thinking about our next TV campaign. And don't worry. I already have the elephant."

She was serious. She actually said, "Don't worry. I already have the elephant."

She had, in fact, already booked an elephant through an animal trainer. She didn't have the idea all worked out but felt certain that the marketing answer was somewhere in the whole pachyderm thing. All that was left for the agency to do was coax the idea out of its pen at the zoo and onto prime-time TV.

See, Liz's problem is that she thinks she knows advertising; she already has her own executions in mind. She knows enough to recognize somebody else's good work when she sees it, which is why she's always flirting with the good agencies. But she doesn't know enough to let them solve the problem. She thinks she knows better.

Once they're in bed with her, the mask comes off and Liz says, "All right, scribblers, here's the idea I want executed," and she proceeds to bend them around like red licorice.

One morning, long after the excitement of that famous logo is gone, you'll roll over in bed and see Liz without makeup. Not a pretty sight.

But Liz, as certain as she is of her own ideas, is nice about it. Worse than a Liz client is one who bullies you. Mistreats you. There aren't many, but they're out there.

THE BULLY.

There is another kind of bad account. The account run by the Bully client. Bullies anywhere are bad. But Bullies with real power are enough, as Anne Lamott says, to make Jesus drink himself to sleep.

Bullies aren't born that way. They develop over many years, like wine gone sour in a forgotten cellar. They come out of the cellar with a vast amount of knowledge, all of it wrong, down to the syllable. The one I'm thinking of had been in the business some 20 years when I was put on his account.

He had spent most of his career on a second-rate brand of beer and was personally responsible for one of the worst campaigns ever to foul a TV set. And he was so proud of that beer campaign. Women with big breasts. Wild beach parties with lots of what he'd call "jiggle." And always ending with that tired old shot, a bartender holding two frosty bottles in each hand, offering them to the camera. "Product ID!" he'd say.

He would brag about this awful campaign, measuring our work by it one day, smacking our hands with it the next. When it was just us guys in the room, he'd say, "You wanna know why that campaign worked? I tellya why that campaign worked. We had girls with them big ol' titties and trucks and everything."

I'm not kidding. He said that. It was like every nightmare Gloria Steinem ever had about the way some men behave behind closed corporate doors. He was a pig.

Even his boss knew his beer campaign stank and would occasionally interrupt him in midbrag to tell him so. The Bully would good-naturedly chuck his boss's shoulder and remind him of the slight upward drift of his beer's sales curve.

He projected his own inadequacies onto the market and made the mistake of thinking that the customer is none too bright. And it was reflected in the advertising he forced all of his agencies to do. Pile-driving, "no-nonsense" nonsense.

During your career in advertising, you will meet this man. He will know nothing about advertising but will wield great power. "All hat and no cattle," I've heard him described. No argument will be eloquent enough to sway him from his sledgehammer approach to advertising. There is no poetry in the man. No subtlety. He is a paper tiger. A tin-pot despot lording over his little product fiefdom, spouting rules from advertising's Bronze Age, and pointing to modest sales increases whenever his excesses and crudities are exposed.

And the day all intelligence in American advertising dies, he should be brought in for questioning.

HALLWAY BEAST #1: THE HACK.

Yes, clients can misbehave. Thank God, most of them don't. And to account for all that awful work you see on TV every night, those bad clients must have a few friends on the agency side of the business. They do.

Like everything else in life, America's list of agencies makes up a big bell curve. There are a few truly great agencies, then a whole bunch of agencies that are just okay, and then a few bad ones.

To get off to the right start in this business, you're going to need to know how to spot those bad agencies. And it's not as easy as you think. Just because an agency has a commercial in the latest awards annual doesn't mean you want to work there.

What you've got to do is, during your interviews, look for The Hack. (Let's call him Hallway Beast #1. There are others in the menagerie.)

The first warning sign that you're in the presence of a Hack is that he'll somehow bring up his One Good Ad from Way Back. He won't call it that. In fact, he'll show it to you and say something like, "This is the kind of work we do here." That's when you notice the ad is on brittle, yellowing paper from a magazine like *Collier's*.

All Hacks have one of these ads. They made their name on it. They've been riding its tired old back for decades and look about as silly doing it as Adam West now looks in his old Batman suit.

It can be a great ad. Doesn't matter. Ask yourself, what else have they done? Talented people with a gift for advertising keep doing great work, time and again, for a variety of clients.

Another warning sign that should send your Hack-O-Meter into the red is how they talk. And how they do talk. In fact, talk is all a Hack can do, being incapable as he is of producing an ad that a fly won't lay eggs on. He'll know the buzzwords. And worse, he'll have a few of his own. "At this agency, we believe in advertising with Clutter-Busting® Power." If you hear something like this, just drop your portfolio and run. You can put together another book. Just run. Don't risk the elevator. Go for the stairs.

Agencies are the way they are for a reason. It's no accident they're doing awful work. They have clients on one side asking for awful work, Hacks on the other side giving it to them, and a guy in the middle counting all the money. Talk is cheap. Especially talk about how "we're going to turn this place around." If you hear this phrase, you should turn around. Again, go for the stairs.

The quintessential giveaway, however, is the creative director who denigrates creativity in general and awards shows in particular. This was the kid in the playground who didn't have a big red ball, so he told the other kids, "Big red balls are stupid." He can't do it. So, of course, he's going to denigrate it.

Some of these guys kill ideas simply because they're unable to generate ideas of their own. In fact, to kill what you've come up with actually seems like an idea to them. They'll go: "Hey wait! Shhhhh! . . . I have an idea! Let's *not* do your idea!" Their ideas are like antimatter. They don't really exist until yours does and when they meet, they're both gone in an instant.

In an interview, this guy will look you straight in the eye and say,

"Creativity is overrated. Client sales is what we're all about." He'll get out a case history. Show you some commercials he'll call "hard-working" and then tap his finger on a number at the bottom of the results page. "This, my little friend, is what we do."

Someday I'd like to try an experiment. It will cost $40 million. I'll give a fifth-grader a brand name and tell him to shoot a commercial. Whatever he comes up with, I'll spend the rest of the $39-some million airing on prime time. In a couple of months, I'll bet Little Jimmy can take off his baseball glove and tap his finger on a similar sales increase. The point is, with a two-ton sledgehammer even a fifth-grader can ring the bell at the top. (I suspect Mr. Whipple's war chest of several trillion had something to do with his high recall scores.)

On the other hand, you have what's called *creative leverage*—beating out the competition's advertising by doing something that is more interesting. Years ago, writer Ed McCabe said, "Disciplined creativity is often the last remaining legal means you have to gain an unfair advantage over the competition."

Compare that quotation from McCabe with this next one. I can't print this man's name, but to a national trade magazine he said blithely and without shame, "Sheer repetition can build awareness and equity for a client even if an ad is not considered creatively brilliant. A dumb dollar beats a smart dime any day."

Sheer repetition? If I were this guy's client, I'd take my dumb dollar over to an agency that can give me 10 times the wallop with a dime's worth of sheer brilliance.

Hacks get easier to spot as they feed and prosper. In their mature years, they sprout long titles, some growing up to 10 inches in length. Recently, I saw a picture of a Hack in *Adweek*, and below it, this title: "Executive Vice President/Vice Chairman/Chief Creative Director North America/General Manager/Worldwide Coordinator." I'm not kidding—word for word.

Agencies may keep them on, sort of as expensive hood ornaments. They'll trot them out at big pitches, but during the rest of the year they'll give them what I call a "Nerf account"—something they can bat around without hurting themselves or anybody else. They are well known, as one wag put it, chiefly for being well known.

A closing thought on Hacks. One of the great things about this business is that you'll be surrounded by vibrant, interesting, and genuinely nice people. I don't know why the industry attracts them, it just does.

And Hacks are no exception. Most of the ones I've known are people just as nice as you could want to meet. After office hours, they're great fishing buddies, loving mothers, and intelligent bridge partners.

But I warn you against joining their team during working hours. As a junior, you'll learn bad habits from them, habits that will be hard to break, even when you come under the tutelage of more talented teachers. We improve by surrounding ourselves with people whose work we admire.

THE GOLDEN HANDCUFFS.

If you take a job at a big, dull agency, you might, without your seeing it happen, slip into a pair of "golden handcuffs." That big agency may be willing to pay you a lot of money to crank out the dull ads. You get used to the money. A couple of years go by, and as your bank account fills with money, your book fills with bad ads—ads you can't show without embarrassment or explanation.

Agencies will do all kinds of silly things to keep you happy at your desk cranking out bad stuff. I remember at one agency they started handing out "vice presidencies" like candy from a Pez dispenser. Anybody who complained or was seen putting his portfolio together was suddenly a vice president.

After a while, though, it seemed almost everybody in the creative department was a VP, and the distinction began to lose its luster. That didn't stop them. They just started handing out secret vice presidencies.

The boss would motion you into his office. He'd say, "We love your work. You're gonna be a superstar. So we're making you a vice president, but . . . uh, we don't want you to tell anyone. Some people, well, they aren't as good as you and aren't being promoted." By the time I left, the entire creative department was full of "superstars" who were vice presidents, half on the up-and-up, and half "secret" vice presidents.

Most of the time, these "assistant-vice presidencies" and other titles don't add up to much anyway. I had a friend who worked for a large, stuffy old agency. The morning after he was promoted, he was standing outside his cubicle chatting with a coworker. The kid from the mail room shows up with a hammer and says, "Your name Buchner?" My friend nods yes. The kid proceeds to wedge one corner of the cubicle open, hammers in a modular two-foot extension piece, says "Congratulations," and walks away.

HALLWAY BEAST #2: THE PRIMA DONNA.

Hallway Beast #2: the Prima Donna. This is the writer or art director who thinks he is God's gift to advertising. And they are all *over* this business.

The one I'm thinking of right now had that one dead giveaway, something all PDs share—the Swagger. That walk people get when they think their DNA is better than everybody else's. There he goes now, down the hallway. And in his hand, a paper bearing his latest brilliant headline. *(Oh, how I wish he'd let me see what it is now and not make me wait till next year's awards annuals come out.)*

Why they develop the Swagger, I don't know. I mean, if that paper was a blueprint for world peace instead of a coupon ad for Jell-O, okay, sashay a little bit. But the PD seems to have forgotten what he does for a living. He's a word-slinging schmuck like the rest of us. But you'll never convince a Prima Donna he's the same species as we.

Wherever the Prima Donna is swaggering, when he gets there you can bet he'll have something nasty to say about either how excruciatingly dumb account executives are or what blind bastards every single one of his clients is.

But you, you're okay—that is, if the Prima Donna is standing within 10 feet of you. PDs obey what I call the 10-Foot Pinhead Rule. Anyone farther than 10 feet from the Prima Donna is a pinhead. He'll walk into your office and say, "Oh, you wouldn't believe the pinhead I was just talking to." Of course, the rule applies when he leaves your office. Eleven feet down the hallway, he'll be telling whomever he's with, "God, I'm glad we left that pinhead's office."

Prima Donnas would have made great Nazis, because they cultivate an air of entitlement and genetic superiority. Each one believes he is the center gear in capitalism's great machine. What the pen of Herr Donna writes today will tomorrow be on the lips of all the haggard supermarket moms he makes fun of in his off-hours.

You see, Prima Donnas have so much to teach us. If we would only listen. But as the years go by and he casts more of his pearls before swine, his poison ferments and his talons curl. Prima Donnas just get mean.

It's like this: When I look out my tall office building, I think all the people look like ants. He thinks that when he's on the street.

There was this one Prima Donna I remember. His first day at work he called the office manager in and calmly directed that his desk be raised three inches. Three inches—I'm not kidding. Apparently, his keyboard had to be a certain distance from his chin to invoke the visions. When he could bully the producers into it, he'd fly only first class. And any suggestions from coworkers on how to improve an idea were laughed off or explained away. It got so bad finally that no art director would work with him. He was about to be fired when he quit and took a job somewhere else.

The hurt and anger he left behind in the agency lingered for some time. Secretaries came out of hiding and admitted to farting in his office when he was gone. After a while, we tried to be philosophical about his character. The best we could say about him was: "If you cut him open, you'd find a heart of gold. And if you didn't, hey, you've cut him open."

HALLWAY BEAST #3: THE WHINER.

Lord knows, I've been one of these. And in my early years, I wasted a lot of time doing it. (Does this chapter count as whining? Don't answer.)

It has been said that whining is simply anger coming through a very small hole. If so, then the Whiner is a very angry little man.

What he whines about most is his job. And he whines all the time. All of his clients suck. All account executives suck. The sad part is, if he could just convert half the energy he spends whining in the hallways to working in his office, he'd be doing better work. Yes, that work might die because sometimes a client may, in fact, suck. But those are the breaks of the business. Get over it.

The Whiner can have a job at the best agency in the world and he'll find something to bitch about. And it's such a *disconnect* to listen to a Whiner strum his blues as he reclines amid the opulence of a large ad agency.

You'll find him whining in the employee kitchen while guzzling his 80th free Coke and eating a free lunch. (*"My book is* so *at the headhunter's."*)

You'll find him in a first-class seat of a jet on the way to a commercial shoot in sunny California, bitching about how they made him mention the client's product in a commercial about the client's product. *("That is, like, so expected.")*

You'll find him working in a comfortable conference room, grousing about having to work on smaller jobs like a brochure or direct mail. *("My old partner is on a TV shoot right now and I'm here doing this crap.")*

Whiners can be poison to other people in the agency. It's hard enough to keep your spirits high in this business, and it doesn't help to have a Whiner draped over the chair in your office, going through the agency phone list rating employees. *("Loser, Hack, Mule, Mule, Hack, Loser...")*

When the Whiner moves on to that agency he thinks is so much better, it's the old truism: "Wherever you go in life, there you are." To his horror, he discovers ad agencies are pretty much the same everywhere. There are hard clients, misguided research, and unreasonable deadlines everywhere, and because that's all he focuses on, these Harpies will follow him throughout all of his sad days.

I'm not saying you can't whine. It's good to let off some steam now and then. True Whining, however, has a vituperative edge to it. It's toxic. Pestilential. There's no hope in it. After a while, you wonder why Whiners don't just leave the business altogether.

Cut to the next scene, the Whiner's new job at the shoe store: "I should get a job over at Foot Locker. Those guys are so good. This place sucks."

HALLWAY BEASTS #4 AND #5: WACK JOBS AND SLASH WEASELS.

If this book were politically correct, our next Hallway Beast might be described as a person who "does things differently." But this is not that kind of book.

I'm talking about people who are *total* Wack Jobs. Crazy as six-toed cats on crack in a Chinese whorehouse.

What makes Wack Jobs such interesting specimens is that they look crazy even in the loosey-goosey atmosphere of an ad agency. I'm remembering this one guy who could write only if he was wearing a full-face knit ski mask. Or this other one who could write only on days that were approved by his astrologist.

Also legendary was the Wack Job who had so little life outside the agency that he slept there. When you worked late at the agency, you grew used to the sight of him in his underwear walking through the hallways to the bathroom for a midnight pee. Which reminds me of this other guy who stood at the urinal in the company men's room with his pants and underwear dropped all the way down around his ankles. When you came into the bathroom he would give you a look that just *dared* you to say anything.

Wack Jobs usually have very screwed-up personal lives that they vaguely allude to in the few meetings they turn up for.

"Sorry, I'm late. I was in court."

"Oh, jury duty?" someone asks.

"No."

"Ooooooookay, well, let's start our meeting, shall we?"

WJs move from giving you no information about themselves *("I'm from . . . out West.")* to giving way too much. In the middle of a meeting, they'll lean over and whisper something like, "Years ago my mother was killed by clowns, and I feel sad today."

Sometimes that excess information is medical. We had this one Wack Job call in sick and leave a long voice mail with grisly details about the viscosity of his mucus and the water content of his phlegm. The voice mail was played publicly at maximum volume the entire week.

The most damaging kind of Wack Job is the crazy creative director. One of the early warning signs of possible wackage in a CD is a proliferation of props in his office—like those giant six-foot pencils. A giant wristwatch on the wall. A giant anything, really. Or a dentist's chair. *("See, it's an actual dentist's chair!")* Jukeboxes and pinball machines are popular; mannequins, too.

Wack Job CDs think their office props say, "I'm creative! Who knows *what* I'll say or do next?" What they say or do next, however, is driving everyone insane because they change their minds about the work right up to the last minute.

I have a friend who worked for a Wack Job. Crazy-ass boss comes into my friend's office one hour before a client meeting with huge changes to the campaign. When my friend groans, the WJ whips out a small vial of pills and says, "Sure you don't want to split a Xanax?"

CDs can stay crazy even on vacation. I remember getting a phone call from a CD's assistant: "Jim called from Barbados to kill that campaign he approved. Fax new ideas to his boat tonight, okay?"

Wack Jobs are, of course, relatively easy to spot in the agency hallways. More insidious is the Slash Weasel.

First thing you need to understand is the word *slash.* In ad parlance, it means "shared credit." When an ad is accepted into a national awards show, the credits are listed below the ad. And when two people contribute to an ad's art direction or its writing, their names are listed together, separated by a slash (/).

But those names in the award books? That's credit. And credit is what the Slash Weasel craves. So he'll creep around the creative department trying to get "slashed" into the credit lines of other people's work. They're basically the goal hangers of advertising. To ride your coattails, a Weez thinks all he has to do is make a suggestion about your ad. Upon seeing your work, he'll rattle off a couple of "Did you try . . ." statements and walk away. Later, he'll insist he "helped" with your work and will include your ad in his portfolio. This really happens.

Remember that saying, "There is no 'I' in team"?

Well, there's a "we" in weasel, which is why they throw the word around a lot regardless of whether they're part of your team or any other. They'll just stand in your office when the boss comes by and go, "Man, we really like these ads a lot." Another stunt is to pop into the creative director's office right before you present and say something like, "You're really gonna like what you're about to see."

There's not much you can do about a Weez except steer clear. What's sad about them is that Slash Weasels sometimes actually have talent. The problem is, they're in the business for the wrong reason—they don't care as much about their clients' brands as they do their own.

HALLWAY BEAST #6: THE HOUR GOBBLER.

Hallway Beast #6 isn't a person. It's a thing. The Meeting. If you see one, run.

Run, little pony, run, and *never* look back.

If the wheels of capitalism ever grind to a halt, the agenda of a meeting will be found caught in the gears. And in the advertising business, meetings thrive like mutant weeds, making actual work impossible.

There are meetings with doughnuts and meetings without doughnuts. Meetings to talk about ads you're going to do and meetings to talk about the ads you just did. All these meetings will be held in small, windowless rooms heated to forehead-dampening temperatures by overhead-projector bulbs and all held during that torpid postlunch lull around 2:30.

As a junior, you probably should just shrug and show up for any meeting you get memo'd on. But as your radar develops, you'll start to be able to detect which meetings are important—where big plans are made and things get done—and which aren't.

The ones I'm talking about are those meetings that are called because somebody needed something to do. "Background" meetings. Or "touching base" meetings. These aren't called because decisions need to be made. They're just called. And oh, how they go on. I was in one of these Hour Gobblers once, and I swear time actually stopped. I'm not kidding. Swear to God, as plain as day, the second hand on the wall clock just *stopped*. No more tick-tock. Just . . . tick. . . . and that was it.

It was a particularly useless meeting and three hours long. Just when we thought we were going to get out, someone raised his hand and asked a question—the kind of tired, lifeless query I call a "meeting extender." A meeting extender is a question like: "Well, Bill, how do those figures compare with the results from *Chicago*?" That's when the clock stopped and began to sag like a Dali painting.

Speakerphone meetings are the worst. And the worst of the worst is the three-way speakerphone, client-on-a-car-phone conference call meeting. There you are, eight nervous people all huddled around a little black box, listening to an art director in L.A. describe a picture nobody can see, to a client nobody can hear.

Ending a meeting is an art it pays to develop. When the business at hand seems at an end even though the meeting is not, start stacking your papers together, evening up the edges, the way news anchors do at the end of their broadcast. It's body language that says, "Well, nothing interesting is going to happen anymore in this room."

I hate it when I get sucked into an Hour Gobbler and have no work I can sneak into the meeting. I usually start writing jokes to myself to pass the time. In one meeting, I remember trying to make my buddy Bob Barrie laugh and instead blew my own cover. I started writing a joke: "Bob's List of Things to Do." I thought I'd just slip it under his nose. Try to crack him up. So I started scribbling:

BOB'S LIST OF THINGS TO DO:

1. Ointment on rash??
2. Rotate bricks under car in front yard.
3. Apologize to that kid's parents.
4. Wash blood out of clown suit.
5. Peek under scab.

When I wrote "Peek under scab," I did one of those bursting laugh-out-loud kind of explosions, and the whole room stopped thinking about Chicago and glared at me for an explanation. I simply had to fess up: "Hey, I'm sorry, I just thought of something funny, completely unrelated to these proceedings. I'm very sorry. Please continue."

But the image of Bob Barrie peeking under a knee scab finally did me in. I just collapsed, boneless, and had to excuse myself from the room.

But it got me out of the meeting.

Yet as much as I try to avoid meetings, all the really important stuff in this business ultimately happens in one meeting—the client presentation.

This is where all the hard work you've done lives or dies. And where the future audience of a storyboard is decided. Will it be millions of people seeing your TV commercial on the Super Bowl? Or a janitor who glances at the big board with funny drawings before cramming it into the rolling garbage can?

It's an important meeting. Be prepared.

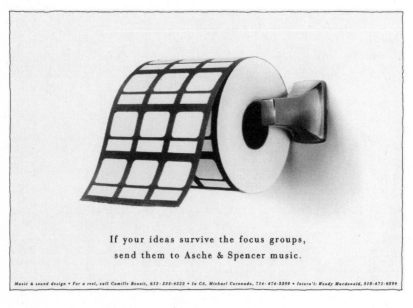

If your ideas survive the focus groups,
send them to Asche & Spencer music.

Music & sound design • For a reel, call Camille Benoit, 612-555-4322 • In CA, Michael Coronado, 714-474-5290 • Intern'l: Wendy Macdonald, 310-471-0599

*Figure 11.1   In focus groups, bad things happen to your storyboards.
Very bad things.*

▌▌

Pecked to Death by Ducks
Presenting and protecting your work

▬

ABOUT 20 PERCENT OF YOUR TIME in the advertising business will be spent thinking up ads. 80 percent will be spent protecting them. And 30 percent doing them over.

A screenwriter was looking out on the parking lot at Universal Studios one day. It occurred to him, said this article, that every one of those cars was parked there by somebody who came to stop him from doing his movie.

The similarity to advertising is chilling. The elevator cables in your client's building will fairly groan hauling up all the people intent on killing your best stuff.

When word gets around the client offices that the agency is here to present, vice presidents and assistant vice presidents will appear out of the walls and storm the conference room like zombies in *Night of the Living Dead*, pounding on the door, hungry arms reaching in for the layouts, pleading, "Must kill. Must kill."

I have been in meetings where, after the last ad was presented, an eager young hatchet man raised his hand and asked his boss, "Can I be the first to say why I don't like it?"

I have been in meetings surrounded by so many vice presidents, I actually heard Custer whisper to me from the grave, "Man, I thought I had it bad. You guys are, like, so dead."

You will see ads killed in ways you didn't know things could be killed. You will see them eviscerated by blowhards bearing charts. You will see them garotted by quiet little men bearing political agendas. A comment from a passing janitor will pick off ads like cans from a fencepost and casual remarks by the chairman's wife will mow down whole campaigns like the first charge at Gallipoli.

Then there's the "friendly fire" to worry about. A stray memo from your agency's research department can send your campaign up in flaming foamcore. Your campaign can also be fragged by the ill-timed hallway remark of an angry coworker.

War widows received their telegrams from ashen-faced military chaplains. You, however, will look up from your desk to see an account executive, smiling.

"The client has some issues and concerns about your ads."

This is how account executives announce the death of your labors: "Issues and concerns."

To understand the portent of this phrase, picture the men lying on the floor of that Chicago garage on St. Valentine's Day. Al Capone had issues and concerns with these men.

I've had account executives beat around the bush for 15 minutes before they could tell me the bad news. "Well, we had a good meeting."

"Yes," you say, "but are the ads dead?"

"We learned a lot."

"But are they dead?"

"Wellll, . . . your ads are, they're with Jesus now."

When you next see your ads, they will be lying in state in the account executive's office. Maybe on the desk. Maybe down in between the desk and the wall. (So thoughtless.) Maybe they'll bear crease wounds where they were crudely folded during the pitch team's hasty medevac under fire.

But you'll remember them the way they were. *("They look so . . . so natural.")* Say your good-byes. Try to think about the good times. Then walk away and start preparing for the next attack. I hear the drums.

What follows are some quixotic arguments that may help protect your loved ones in future battles. If you find any of them useful, I recommend you commit them to memory. Go into meetings armed and with the safety off. It's my experience that what a client decides in a meeting stays decided.

———

PRESENTING THE WORK.

Learn the client's corporate culture.

Spend as much time with the client as you can. Talk to the quiet guy from R&D. Tell jokes with the product managers. The more they know you, the more they're going to trust you. The more they trust you, the more likely they are to buy these strange and disgusting things you call ideas.

But you're going to learn something about them, too. You're going to get a feel for the tone of this company. How far they will go. What they think is funny. You'll save yourself a lot of grief once you understand this. Remember, they see you as their brand ambassador. They're trusting you to accurately translate their corporate culture to the customer.

This doesn't mean doing the safe thing. It means if your client is a church, you probably shouldn't open your TV spot with that scene from *The Exorcist* where Linda Blair blow-chucks split pea soup on the priest.

Present your own work.

Nobody knows it better than you. Nobody has more invested in it than you. And if you screw up, you have nobody to blame but you.

Two addenda: (1) If you are a truly awful presenter, don't. At least not the big campaigns. Better to have a skilled account person or creative director sell them. (2) Learn to present. It's a skill, and like any other skill, the more you do it the better you'll get. Start small. Sell a small-space newspaper campaign. Present to the account folks. Just do it. Creatives who can brilliantly present work go a lot further and make more money in this business than those who cannot. Not being able to present your own work (or the work of other people) will handicap you throughout your entire career. Pilots can't be afraid of heights. It just doesn't work.

Practice selling your campaign before you go in to present.

Don't just wing it. I used to think winging it was cool. But that was just bravado. As if my ideas were so good they didn't need no stinking presentation. Wrong. Practice it.

Don't memorize a speech for your presentation.

Trying to memorize written material will make you nervous. You'll worry you're going to forget something. Write out a speech if it helps you organize your thoughts, but toss it when you're done. All you need to do is establish what marks you have to hit along the way and then make sure you hit them. "I need to make Points A, B, and C." Once you see the light go on in a client's eyes regarding A, move on to B.

Don't be slick. Clients hate slick.

You know all those unfair stereotyped images we sometimes have about clients? Uptight, overly rational, number-crunching politicians. They've got a similar set of incorrect images about us. Slick, unctuous, glad-handing, promise-them-anything sycophants. Is it fair? No. But that's the thing about stereotypes. You're a little behind before you even start. So don't be slick.

But if you're not slick, what should you be?

Be yourself. Be smart. Be crisp, be to the point, be agreeable. Don't be something you aren't. It never works. You will appear disingenuous, and so will your ideas.

Keep your "pre-ramble" to an absolute minimum. Start fast.

That doesn't mean start cold. It's likely you'll have to do some amount of setup. But make it crisp, to the point, and fast.

There is a good book on the art of good presentations called *I Can See You Naked*, by Ron Hoff. I recommend it. One of his points is this: The first 90 seconds of any presentation are crucial. "*Plunge* into your subject," writes Hoff. "Let there be no doubt that the subject has been engaged."[1]

In those first 90 seconds, the client is unconsciously sizing you up, making initial impressions, and probably deciding prematurely whether or not they're going to like what you have to say. So don't wade into the water. Dive.

Don't hand out materials before you present.

Stay in command of the room. The minute you hand a script to a client, you're competing with the script. Clients are human and naturally want to get to the good stuff. They'll start taking peeks.

In fact, when I present a TV storyboard, I'll sometimes cover up a number of frames to keep the client from getting ahead of me. Perhaps the best method is not to use a storyboard at all. A client usually looks at a storyboard and sees nine frames of "kooky, wacky stuff" and one frame of his logo. The math that goes through his head isn't pretty. It's usually better to work from a script and one key frame. Talk them through the broad strokes. Play a movie in their heads. And bring out a board later on only to discuss details.

Whatever you do, stay in control of the room's attention.

Don't present your campaign as "risk-taking work." Clients hate that.

In the agency hallways, it's fine to talk about work being "risk taking." But it's just about the worst thing you can say to product managers. They don't want risk. They want certainty. Whether certainty is possible in this business remains in doubt, but clients definitely do not need to hear the R word.

Find other ways to describe your campaign. For instance, "It goes against the grain." Anything is more palatable to a client with his job on the line, a mortgage to pay, and two kids to put through reform school.

Okay, before we go on to the next paragraph, I just want to say that is really good. I worked on it a long time and it may in fact be the best paragraph of this whole book. I think you're going to love it.

Before you unveil your stuff, don't assure the client that they're "going to love this."

This is known as "leading with your chin." Somebody's gonna take a swipe at it just to keep you humble.

As they say in law school, don't ask a question you don't know the answer to.

Same thing in presentations. Anticipate every objection you can and have a persuasive answer in the chamber, locked and loaded.

If you're presenting print work, why not paste the ads into one of the magazines in which they'll be appearing?

If you've done it right and the ads avoid the visual clichés of your category, they should be head and shoulders above the clutter. You don't have to say, "Trust us." You can hand the magazine over to the client and say, "See for yourself."

Never show a client work you don't want them to buy.

I guarantee you, second-rate work is what clients will gravitate to.

The reasoning I have used to allow myself to present so-so ads goes like this: "Well, we gotta sell something to get this campaign going, and time is running out. So we'll present five ads, but we'll make sure they buy only these three great ones. The two so-so ones we'll include just to, you know, help us put on a good presentation. They'll be filler."

But what happens is, the client will approve the work they feel safer with, less scared by, and that is almost always the second-rate work.

Conversely, don't leave your best work on the floor at the agency.

"Oh, the client will never buy this." How do you know? They may surprise you. They may not. But don't do their work for them. McElligott once told me, "Go as far as you can. The client will always bring you back."

At the presentation, don't just sit there.

No matter how right your campaign may feel to you, it's not going to magically fly through the client approval process. Even if the client appears to buy it outright, sooner or later they'll start taking potshots. "Little changes" here and there, here and there.

You need to learn to be an articulate defender of your own work. Don't count on your account executive to do it. Don't leave it to your partner. Pay attention in the meeting. Try to understand exactly what might be bothering your client. And then take the initiative to either fix the problem to your satisfaction or come back with the most articulate defense you can.

As you form a defense, your first instincts may be to build a bridge from where you are to where your client is. *("If only I could get them to see how great these ads are.")* Instead, get over to where your client is and build a bridge *back* to your position. With such an attitude, your argument will be more empathetic and more persuasive. Because you are seeing the problem from your client's perspective.

Base your defense on strategy.

Your client is not sitting at his office right now twiddling his thumbs, waiting for you to bring in your campaign. A director of marketing for a consumer products company may spend as little as 5 percent of his time on advertising issues—the balance on manufacturing, distribution, financing, and product development. In fact, the managerial strengths that got him to his position in the first place likely had nothing to do with his ability to judge advertising.

Keep this in mind when you go in to present: It isn't a client's job to know great work when they see it. They're generally numbers people.

Copywriter Dick Wasserman put it this way: "Corporate managers are inclined towards understatement. They value calm and quiet, abhor emotional displays, and do everything possible to make decisions in a dispassionate and objective manner. Advertising rubs them the wrong way. It is simply too much like show business for their taste."[2]

To prevail with an audience like this, Alastair Crompton says, "[T]hink like a creative person, but talk like an accountant."[3] Don't defend the work on emotional grounds or on the creativity of the execution. *("This visual is, I'm tellin' you, it's monstrous. It kills.")* Instead say, "This visual, as the focus groups bear out, communicates durability." Base your defense on strategy.

You must be able to strategically track, step-by-step, how you arrived at your campaign. That means having all the relevant product/market/consumer facts at your fingertips. There's no such thing as bulletproof, but your ads might be able to dodge a few rounds if you can keep the conversation on strategy alone. After all, that's something the client had a hand in authoring. It's a scary thing to do, but let the work's creativity speak for itself.

Buying creative work is hard. Cut your client some slack.

Before you get angry at a client for not immediately signing off on your brilliant idea, put yourself in his shoes. It's hard buying creative work.

In a subjective business where there are 30 "right" answers for every problem, deciding which ad to go with is, at best, a mix of business acumen, gut instinct, second-guessing, and a scarecrow in a cornfield pointing down two yellow-brick roads.

Buying creative work is hard. Remember this the next time your work is on the table. Help your client by offering rational reasons to support what is essentially an emotional decision.

"They might be right."

According to ad legend, Bill Bernbach always carried a little note in his jacket pocket. A note he referred to whenever he was having a disagreement with a client. In small words, one sentence read, "They might be right."

Here's my advice, and it starts a few rungs further down the humility ladder: Always enter into any discussion (with clients, account executives, anybody) with the belief that there is a 50 percent chance that you are wrong. I mean, really *believe* in your heart that you could be wrong.

I think that such a belief adds a strong underpinning of persuasiveness to your argument. To listeners, it doesn't feel like you're forcing your opinion on them.

I often think of the analogy of the two kinds of ministers I have seen. A quiet and anonymous minister at a small church who invites me to explore his faith. And the noisy kind I see on TV, sweaty and red-faced, telling me the skin's going to bubble off my soul in hell if I don't repent now.

Which one is more persuasive to you?

Listening doesn't mean saying "yes."

Listen, even when you don't want to. It doesn't cost you anything to listen. It's polite. And even if you think you disagree, by listening you may gather information you can later use to put together a more persuasive argument. (As they say: "Diplomacy is the art of saying 'nice doggie" long enough to find a big rock.")

I think our culture portrays passive postures (such as listening) as losing postures. But I think listening can help you kick butt. Relax. Breathe from your stomach. Listen.

You do not have to solve the problem in the meeting.

Be like that repair guy you see in the movies. Blow your nose, scratch yourself, and say, "Well, looks like I gotta take 'er back to the shop."

Seriously. It's tempting to want to alleviate client concerns by fixing something on the fly right there in the presentation. If it's an easy and obvious one, well, go ahead. But resist the temptation to do any major work there in the room.

Listen. Note their concerns. Play the concerns back to them so they know you heard them. And then say, "Let us come back tomorrow and show you how this can work."

In *The Creative Companion*, David Fowler put it this way:

> [For] now, listen to the input you've received and solve the problem on the terms you've been given. Your anger is beside the point right now. Once you've proven you're a trooper by returning with thinking that follows the input, you can bring up your original idea again. It may get a better hearing the second time. Then again, it may have been a monkey [of an idea] all along. Or, most likely, you'll have forgotten all about it, because you're onto something better.[4]

Choose your battles carefully.

No matter how carefully you prepare your work, no matter how impeccable you are about covering every base, crossing every "t," dotting every "i," the red pencil's gonna come out. Clients are going to mess with your visual and change your copy.

H.G. Wells wrote, "No passion in the world is equal to the passion to alter someone's draft."

We need to pause here for a minute so I can make this point as clear to you as I am able. It's an important one.

Millions of years of evolution have wired a network of biological certainties into the human organism. There is the need to eat. There is the need to sleep. And then, right before the need to procreate, is the client need to *change* every ad his agency shows him. This need is spinal. Nothing you can do or say, no facts you lay down, no prayers you send up, will stop a client from diddling with your concept. It's something you need to accept as reality as early in your career as you can.

It didn't start with you, and it'll still be going on when some Detroit agency takes in the campaign for the new antigravity cars. The fact is, we're in a subjective industry—partly business and partly art. Everybody is going to have an opinion. It's just that the clients have paid for the right to have their opinion. Advertising, ultimately, is a service industry.

Consider the drawing reprinted here (Figure 11.2): a client making

*Figure 11.2   Except for the clothes, this 1930 engraving of a client changing
a writer's copy looks like it could have happened yesterday.
(© Reprinted with permission of Dartnell Corporation.)*

changes to an ad as a frustrated copywriter looks on. I found it in a
book called *Confessions of a Copywriter*, published in 1930 by the
Dartnell Corporation. That date again—19*30*.

They were doing it then, and I suspect they've been doing it since
earliest recorded history. I have this image of a client in Egypt, 3,000
years before Christ, looking at some hieroglyphs on the walls of the
pyramids, saying, "I think instead of "⏃⏀⏚⏛⏁⏂," we should say,
"⏁⏀⏚⏛⏃⏂."

Get used to it. Even some of the writing on this page about rewriting was rewritten by my publisher's editor. Nothing is safe.

I say, if they want to mess around with your body copy, let them. If they want to change the colors from red to green, let them. Any hieroglyphs they want to change, let them. Protect the *pyramid*. If you get out of there with the big idea intact, consider yourself a genius.

Tom Monahan says, "[Squabbling over body copy and other details is] not where the advertising battles are won. Ideas—big, differentiating, selling ideas—are what win. And anything that takes away even an ounce of energy from the creating or selling of those ideas is misdirected effort."[5]

The moral: Don't win every battle and lose the war.

RESEARCH: BE AFRAID. BE VERY AFRAID.

Research isn't science.

Here's how advertising works: You toil for weeks to come up with a perfect solution to your client's problem. Then your campaign is taken to an anonymous building on the outskirts of town and shown to a focus group—people who've been stopped on the street the previous week, identified as target customers, and paid a small amount of money for their opinion.

After a long day working at their jobs, these tired pedestrians arrive at the research facility and are led into a small room without windows or hope. In this barren, forlorn little box, they are shown your work in its embryonic, half-formed state while you and the client watch through a one-way mirror.

Here's the amazing part. These people all turn out to be advertising experts with piercing insights on why every ad shown them should be force-fed into the nearest shredder fast enough to choke the chopping blades.

Yet, who can blame them? They've been watching TV since they were kids and have been bored by a hundred thousand hours of very, very bad commercials. Now it's payback time, Mr. Madison Avenue Goatee Man. And because they're seeing mere storyboards they think, wow, we get to kill the beast *and* crush its eggs.

Meanwhile, in the room behind the mirror, the client turns to you and says, "Looks like you're workin' the weekend, idea boy."

Welcome to advertising.

A committee, it has been said, is a cul-de-sac down which ideas are lured and quietly strangled. The same can be said for the committee's cousin, the focus group. But this research process, however wildly capricious and unscientific, is here to stay.

Clients are used to testing. They test their products. They test locations for their stores. They test the new flavor, the packaging, and the name on the top. And much of this testing pays off. So don't think they're going to spend a couple of million dollars airing a commercial based solely on your sage advice: "Hey, business dudes, I think this spot rocks."

Used correctly, research is great. What better way is there to get inside the customer's head? To be what Marshall McLuhan called the "frog men of the mind" and find out what people like and don't like, to understand how they live. There is no better way. Most of the good research isn't done in little buildings outside of town, either, but right downtown in the bars, asking drinkers about their favorite booze, asking shoppers how they choose a product, eavesdropping on real people as they talk about a category or a brand.

The thing is, the best people in the business use research to generate ideas, not to judge them. They use it at the beginning of the whole advertising process to find out what to say. When it's used to determine how to say it, great ideas suffer horribly.

Should your work suffer at the hands of a focus group, and it will, there isn't much you can do except appeal to the better angels of your client's nature.

What follows are some arguments against the reading of sheep entrails. Or the subjective science of copy testing.

Testing storyboards doesn't work.

Testing, by its very nature, looks for what is wrong with a commercial, not what is right. Look hard enough for something wrong and you'll sure enough find it. (I could stare at a picture of Miss November and in a half hour I'd start to notice, is that some broccoli in her teeth? Look, right there between the lateral incisor and left canine, see?)

Testing assumes that people react intellectually to commercials, that people watching TV in their living rooms dissect and analyze these interruptions of their sitcoms. (*"Honey, come in here. I think these TV people are forwarding an argument that doesn't track logically. Bring a pen and paper."*) In reality, both you and I know their reactions are visceral and instantaneous.

Testing is inaccurate because storyboards don't have the magic of finished commercials. Would a focus group approve this copy had it just been read to them? "Chestnuts roasting on an open fire. Jack Frost nipping at your nose." Probably not. I can just see a focus group member putting down his doughnut to protest: *"I hate those chestnut things. And also, who wants to sing about wind chill? Can't the song be about something happy?"* But in spite of the lyrics, generations of people love this song.

Testing is inaccurate because customers simply do not *know* what they'll like until they see it out in the world. It's like what William Goldman said about movies and Hollywood: "Nobody knows what works." If we did, every movie would be a blockbuster.

Testing rewards commercials that are vague and fuzzy because vague and fuzzy doesn't challenge the viewer.

Testing rewards commercials that are derivative because commercials that have a familiar feel score better than commercials that are unique, strange, odd, or new. The very qualities that can lift a finished commercial above the television clutter.

If tone is important to a client, testing is inaccurate because 12 colored pictures pasted to a board will never communicate tone like actual film footage, voice-over, and music.

Testing, no matter how well disguised, asks consumers to be advertising experts. And invariably they feel obligated to prove it.

Finally, testing assumes we really know what makes a commercial work and that it can be quantifiably analyzed. You can't. Not in my opinion. It's impossible to measure a live snake.

Bill Bernbach said, "We are so busy measuring public opinion, we forget we can mold it. We are so busy listening to statistics that we forget we can create them." This simple truth about advertising is lost the minute a focus group sits down to do its business. In those small rooms, the power of advertising to affect behavior is not only subverted, it's reversed. The dynamic of a commercial coming out of the television *to* consumers is replaced with consumers telling the commercial what to say.

I say, big deal if a group says your storyboard doesn't reflect their opinions. With a good director and a couple of airings on the right programs, their opinions may reflect your commercial's.

These arguments, for what they are worth, might come in handy someday, especially if you have a client who likes the commercial you propose, but has to defend poor test scores to a management committee.*

Extensive research has proven that extensive research is often wrong.

From a book called *Radio Advertising* by Bob Schulberg, I bring this research study to your attention:

> J. Walter Thompson did recall studies on commercials that ran during a heavily-viewed mini-series, "The Winds of War." The survey showed that 19 percent of the respondents recalled Volkswagen commercials; 32 percent, Kodak; 32 percent, Prudential; 28 percent American Express; and 16 percent Mobil Oil. The catch is that none of these companies advertised on "The Winds of War."[6]

In the mid-1980s, research told management of the Coca-Cola company that younger people preferred a sweeter, more Pepsi-like taste. Overlooking fierce customer loyalty to this century-old battleship of a brand, they reformulated Coca-Cola into New Coke, and in the process packed about $1 billion down a rat hole.

"We forget we can mold it."

Research people told writer Hal Riney that entering the wine cooler category was a big mistake. Seagram's and California Cooler had it locked up. Then Riney began running his Bartles & Jaymes commercials, and a year later his client had the number one wine cooler in America.

"We forget we can mold it."

Research people told writer Cliff Freeman when he was working on Wendy's hamburgers, "Under absolutely no circumstances run 'Where's the Beef?' " After it ran, sales shot up 25 percent for the year and Wendy's moved from fifth to third place in fast-food sales. The 20,000 newspaper articles lauding the commercial didn't hurt, either.

"We forget we can mold it."

And what some call the greatest campaign of the 20th century, Volkswagen—none of it was subjected to pretesting. The man who helped produce that Volkswagen campaign had a saying: "We are so busy measuring public opinion, we forget we can mold it."

---

*For more information about the pitfalls of testing concepts, I refer you to Jon Steel's excellent book on planning, *Truth, Lies, and Advertising: The Art of Account Planning* (John Wiley & Sons, 1998). In particular I direct you to Chapter 6: "Ten Housewives in Des Moines—The Perils of Researching Rough Creative Ideas."

Because focus groups can prove anything, do they prove anything?

British ad star Tim Delaney, in a famous article on the value of intuition, wrote:

> Have you noticed what happens when five agencies are competing for an account? They all come up with completely different strategies and ideas—and yet, miraculously, each of them is able to prove, through objective research, that their solution is the right one. If nothing else does, this alone should devalue the currency of focus groups. . . . Researchers think that if you spend a lot of time analyzing a problem beforehand, it will bring you closer to the advertising solution. But the truth is, you only really begin to crack advertising problems as you get deeper and deeper into the writing. You just have to sit down and start writing on some kind of pretext—and that initiates the flow of ideas that eventually brings a solution. In [my] agency, we start writing as early as possible, before the researchers have done their analysis. And we usually find that the researchers are always trailing behind us, telling us things we've already thought of.[7]

The writing itself is the solution to the problem. It's in the writing itself that the answers appear, when you're in there getting your hands dirty mucking about in the mud of the client's marketing reality. The answers are right there in that place where there's direct contact between the patient and the doctor. And if the doctor has a question about how to proceed, who would you want him to ask for advice? A focus group of grocers, lawyers, and cab drivers? Personally, I'd want it to be another doctor.

I have a friend who walks around the agency trying to find out if a concept he's done is any good. He keeps going around until the "It's cool" votes outnumber the "It sucks." Sometimes he doesn't get the answer he wants and keeps working.

You know what? In my opinion, it's the only pretesting that works. The agency hallway.

Science cannot breathe life into something. Dr. Frankenstein tried this already.

David Ogilvy once said that research is often used the way a drunk uses a lamppost: for support rather than illumination. It's research used to protect preconceived ideas, not to explore new ones.

Another way that research can be used poorly is what I call *Permission Research*. Permission Research happens when agencies show advertising concepts to customers and ask if they like them or not. *("Man, it would be really great if you guys all say you like this, 'cause then we can put it on TV. C'mon, whattaya say?")*

What's unfortunate about Permission Research is that it's often used by clients and agencies to validate terrible advertising. Yes, it all looks and sounds like science, but as prudent as such market inquiries appear on the surface, the argument is specious. Because the very process of Permission Research and all its attendant consensus and compromise will grind the work into either vanilla or nonsense.

As an example of what the process of Permission Research can do, I cite an interesting and very funny study done in 1997 by a pair of Russian cultural anthropologists—Vitaly Komar and Alexander Melamid.[8] With tongue firmly planted in cheek, these two researchers set out to ask the public, "What makes for a perfect painting? What does a painting need to have in order for you to want to hang it in your home?"

They did massive amounts of research, hosting hundreds of focus groups all over the world. Their findings, meticulously prepared and double-checked with customers, were as follows: 88 percent of

Figure 11.3   Here's what happens when you ask customers to art-direct a painting. And yes, that's George Washington standing to the left of a modern-day family.

customers told them, "We like paintings that feature outdoor scenes." The color blue was preferred by 44 percent of respondents. "Having a famous person" in the painting got the thumbs-up from a full 50 percent. Fall was the preferred season. And animals! You gotta have some animals.

All this research was compiled, and an actual painting was commissioned. The final "art" that came out of the lab (to nobody's surprise) was very bad, as you can see here (Figure 11.3).

The point? Research is best used to help craft a strategy, not an execution. As journalist William F. Buckley once observed, "You cannot paint the *Mona Lisa* by assigning one dab each to a thousand painters."

PROTECTING YOUR WORK.

Well, so much for research. If your concept manages to limp out of the focus groups alive, congratulations.

But even if your idea fares well in tests, if it's new and unusual the client is still likely to squirm. As the scientist W.I. Beveridge noted, "The human mind likes a strange idea as little as the body likes a strange protein and resists it with a similar energy."

Even if they like your idea, they'll begin suggesting "minor changes." The Chinese call this "the Death of a Thousand Cuts." Minor changes kill great ads, very slowly and with incredible pain. By the time they've inflicted their thousandth minor change, both you and your ad will be begging for a swift bullet to the head.

Sometimes you're going to need to deliver that bullet yourself. If client changes have hurt your original idea, pull the trigger. You think it's hard to look at your "fixed" ad on a layout pad? Wait till you see it as a spread in *Time* magazine.

Over the years, I've heard clients bring up the same minor changes time and again. Here are a few of them.

Your client asks that you feature more than one product or benefit.

Clients often ask for an ad to tout their full line of fine products. Who can blame them? The page they're buying seems roomy enough to throw in five or six more things besides your snappy little idea, doesn't it? But full-line ads are effective only as magazine thickener, nothing else.

The reason is simple. Customers never go shopping for full lines of products. I don't. Do you? *("Honey, start the car. We're going to the mall to buy everything.")* Customers have specific needs. It stands to reason that ads addressing specific needs are more effective. There's that old saying, "The hunter who chases two rabbits catches neither."

Smart companies know this. Coca-Cola owns nearly 80 brands of soft drinks, but they've never run an ad for all of them with some catchall claim like, "Bubbly, sugar-based liquids in a variety of vastly different tastes for all your thirst needs."

So if your client says he has three important things to say, tell the account executive the client needs three ads.

If that doesn't work, perhaps you'll just have to convince your client that there's a certain part of the audience that he's just not going to reach. Filling his ad with extraneous claims or peripheral products may attract some of this fringe audience, but the dilution will be at the cost of the main audience he needs most.

It's this simple: You can't pound in a nail that's lying on its side.

Somebody says, "Negative headlines are wrong."

Well, you can start by pointing out that what he just said was negative but communicated his position quite respectably. But there are some other rebuttals you can try.

Take a look at the photograph reprinted here (Figure 11.4). It's a very positive image, isn't it? There's happiness and cheerful camaraderie all around, and everybody's enjoying the client's fine product. It's also so boring I want to saw off my right foot just so I can feel something, feel anything.

It's boring because there is no tension in the picture. No question left unanswered. No story. No drama. And consequently, no interest.

Perhaps you could begin by explaining to your client that one of the basic tenets of drama (and we are indeed in the business of dramatizing the benefits of our clients' products) is conflict. The bad guy (competition) moseys into town, kicks open the saloon door, and Cowboy Bob (your client) looks up from his card game.

Conflict = drama = interest. Without it, you have no story to tell. No friction between the tire and the road. No beginning, middle, or end. And consequently, no interest.

"Humorists have always made trouble pay," said E.B. White.

Figure 11.4   Q: "Why can't you do something positive?" A: This is why.

The brutal truth is that people don't slow down to look at the highway, they slow down to look at the highway accident. Maybe we're ashamed to admit that, but trouble and conflict are always riveting.

The thing to remember about trouble and conflict in a commercial is this: As long as your client's product is ultimately portrayed in a positive light or is seen to solve a customer problem, the net takeaway is positive.

As Tom Monahan pointed out, "The true communication isn't what you say. It's what the receiver takes away."[9]

Here are some other arguments you might try on an intransigent client.

Remind your client that one of the biggest success stories in marketing textbooks is Federal Express, a tiny outfit in Memphis that became an international commodity. This company owes its success almost entirely to a series of television commercials featuring terrible conflict—things going wrong, packages arriving late, nitwits getting fired.

Tell your client about a small classified ad that ran in 1900. (This is another story stolen from Neil French.) The ad read: "Men wanted for Hazardous Journey. Small wages, bitter cold, long months of complete darkness, constant danger, safe return doubt-ful. Honor and recognition in case of success—Ernest Shackleton."

When the famous explorer placed this ad looking for fellow adventurers to trek with him in search of the South Pole, he received many responses. Should it instead have read "Happy snow bunnies needed for Popsicle Party"? Probably not. It worked because readers were piqued by the honesty of the ad and the chal-lenge of the imminent journey.

If that doesn't convince your client, try this one from copywriter Jim Durfee: "Would you call the following statement positive or negative: 'Don't step back or you'll fall off the cliff'."

Negatives have power. Try writing the Ten Commandments posi-tively. If you did, I bet it wouldn't all fit on two stone tablets. Negatives are a linguistic construction we're all familiar with, one we've been hearing since we were caught dangling the cat over the baby. They're neither good nor bad; they are merely an executional detail.

So try to keep your client from focusing on the details. It isn't the details customers remember anyway. If you look at most day-after testing results, you'll find that customers may not remember a sin-gle word of a commercial. Just the main idea and what's good about the product—which is all that matters.

Somebody says, "Our competitors could run that same ad!"

They'll usually go on to say, "If you cover up our logo, this could be the other guys' ad."

"We said it first" is the simple answer. "Their logo isn't down there. Yours is."

Sometimes clients need to be reminded that their product isn't substantially different from the competition's. All that may distin-guish the two is the advertising you propose. Nothing else.

Your client needs to see that while there's no explicit claim in the ad different from what his competitor might be able to say, the ad and its execution have many implicit messages the client can call his own. Whether it's the strategy, the concept, the tone, or the look of the campaign—together, they are giving the client a personality like no other.

Don't force your hand, though. If you can get the client to find in their product a unique selling proposition, all the better. Agree to start over if any significant difference can be found.

If not, you need to get your client to see that execution can be content and that personality can be proprietary. They're called *pre-emptive claims*—claims any competitor could've made had they moved fast enough. Your client may see that it's simply a matter of which company's going to get first dibs on the ground staked out by your concept.

It comes down to "We were here first."

It's been pointed out many times that it could've just as easily been "Winston Country." But Marlboro got there first.

They ask you to print the phone number in big, bold type.

Ask if they'd also like to have their number shouted in radio spots. Will people be more likely to call the number if we scream it at them? No? Then why do it in print?

If readers want your phone number after seeing the ad, they'll get it. From the ad, from the phone book, or from 411—somehow they'll get it.

Picture this: A woman (man) at a bar slides a folded matchbook across the mahogany and under your napkin. You open it and see a phone number. Are you more likely to call if the number is written in inch-thick numerals with a fat red crayon? Of course not.

Yes, the phone number should be in there, probably in the last sentence or maybe by the logo. But advise the client that trans-mogrifying the type so you can needlessly shriek a phone number is not only desperate and without class, it adds yet another element to a crowded space and can only hurt the effectiveness of an ad.

Somebody asks, "Why are you wasting 25 seconds of my TV spot *entertaining* people?"

Other ways clients ask this is, "Can we mention the product sooner?" Or "Can't we just get to the point?"

This is a client who mistakenly believes that people watch television to see his commercial. *("Honey, get in here! The commercial's almost on!")*

There is no entitlement to the customer's attention. It is earned.

And make no mistake, we're not starting from zero with customers. Thanks to Whipple, Snuggles, and "Digger" the dermatophyte nail fungus, we're starting at less than zero. There is a high wall around every customer. And every day another brick is added.

You need to get your client to see that those 25 seconds of "wasted" time in the commercial are his ticket through the gate. You're not welcome until customers like you. And they won't like you until they listen to you. And they won't listen to you if you open your pitch with bulleted copy points of your product's superiority.

To visit the door-to-door salesman analogy again, you can't just dispense with knocking on the door. Clients who say, "Let's lose all that entertainment stuff" are really saying, "Forget the introducing ourselves at the door. Forget that doorbell crap, too. In fact, let's just jimmy the lock with a brochure and barge into their kitchen with a fistful of facts. We'll *make* 'em listen."

You can't. You're not welcome until they like you. Ring the doorbell and straighten your tie.

Your client takes your concept literally.

This is a hard one.

Let's use one of Cliff Freeman's hilarious Little Caesars pizza spots as an example (Figure 11.5)—the ones featuring the famous

Figure 11.5   Out in TV-Land, nobody ever wondered,
"Gosh, if Little Caesars cheese stretches that much, doesn't that
mean it's kind of rubbery? Let's go to Domino's instead."

"stretchy cheese." In these spots, goofy-looking customers pull slices of pizza out of the box and attempt to carry them away to their supper table. The cheese, connecting the slice with the pizza still in the box, stretches like a rubber band, snaps them back, usually causing some sort of cartoon injury along the way.

"Well, I don't know," says the client. "Our cheese doesn't really stretch that far. And if it never breaks, doesn't that mean it's kind of rubbery?"

The client is taking the storyboard literally. It would be pleasant if simply pointing that out would make the client say, "Oh, my mistake. By all means, produce the spots." This is known as a hallucination.

What the client needs is someone to shift his paradigm so that he can see the commercials as a TV viewer does and not as the product manager of a large corporation.

But first, back him up.

Is it agreed that the job of advertising is to dramatize the benefit of the product? (In this case, the extra helpings of cheese.) Not *show* the benefit, *dramatize* the benefit. If showing the benefit is the goal, we need only picture someone holding a slice of pizza and saying, "Look at all this extra cheese. Now that's value." We could also throw our money down the middle hole of an outhouse and achieve the same effect, since no one will watch or remember Smiley Pizza Man.

So it's agreed that dramatizing the benefit is our goal?

"Yes, but the cheese never breaks," says the client. "Maybe the stretching part is funny, but rubbery cheese is no good. I'm telling you, I've been in food services for 15 years and I've watched focus groups and heard customers say those very words."

Here's where the client needs to take a leap of faith. Take his hand. Lean out over the precipice and tell him this: "In TV-Land, the rules are different."

And jump.

The rules of acceptable logic are different in TV-Land. Not only do viewers know the rules are different, they *expect* them to be. If the rules aren't different, they might as well be watching the news. TV-Land is not reality. It is entertainment. Television is watched by tired people needing escape from reality.

In reality, cops don't catch the bad guy. In TV-Land, they do. In reality, coyotes kill roadrunners. In TV-Land, coyotes end up under the big Acme-brand anvil.

And while rubbery cheese isn't appetizing in reality, in TV-Land

the comic device of stretchy cheese that's both rubbery and delicious is perfectly acceptable logic. The device, one the viewer tacitly
knows is created for entertainment, transcends all reality-based
concerns about edibility, leapfrogs all taste issues of rubbery/non-
rubbery cheese, and lands with a big, welcome splash in the mind of
the customer with its intended message—this pizza has lots of
yummy cheese.

The rules are different in TV, but they're still rules. You must
obey them as long as you wish to retain the attention of your audience. Stretchy cheese, rubber logic, and other dramatic devices are
the accepted currency in TV-Land. They are the only way to communicate what is often a bland corporate message.

In fact, that rubbery cartoon cheese is a bland corporate message
(*"Our pizza has more cheese"*), but one that's seen through the fun-
house prisms of TV-Land. At a certain level, all corporate messages
that show up in TV-Land are bland because they weren't invited. In
order to come to the table, the ante is entertainment.

But the chasm between the cool fluorescent lights of America's
corporate meeting rooms and the play-school colors of TV entertainment is deep and wide. It takes a client who's either imaginative
or brave to make the leap. Clearly, Little Caesars was both.

In a wonderful book for clients called *That's Our New Ad
Campaign?,* Dick Wasserman takes on this sticky issue:

> When [clients] evaluate advertising executions, they do not under-
> stand that consumers react to ads in a generalized, unanalytical, emo-
> tional way. . . . Consumers are much more imaginative than many
> advertisers are willing to give them credit for. Readers and viewers
> do not have to be led by the hand to understand what a client's adver-
> tising is getting at. All they need is a couple of key verbal and visual
> guideposts, and they are quite capable of filling in the blanks.[10]

Your client will be uncomfortable in TV-Land. Once you get back
to the safety of the conference room, you need to convince him that
the literal approach is actually riskier than obeying the wacky rules
of TV. A literal approach, where you simply tell the client's story is,
as Wasserman says, a speech; what viewers want is a play.

Your client may be agreeing with you at this point, but he's not
going to like it. He's going to be like that one guy in every disaster
movie, up to his knees in mud but still checking his hair in the mirror. He is out of his element.

Remind him his discomfort is natural. This isn't Wall Street. But it isn't Sesame Street, either. It's the intersection—that place where the odd bedfellows of business and advertising meet. The corner of Art and Commerce.

Bill Bernbach was perhaps talking to this same kind of client when he said: "Is creativity some obscure, esoteric art form? Not on your life. It's the most practical thing a business [person] can employ."[11]

Somebody asks, "Why do you have to cast such goofy-looking characters for my TV spot?"

We're talking about those concepts where some kind of nerd or schmuck or victim is key to the execution, not those spots where a normal-looking everyday Joe will suffice.

When a client has a problem with the casting, it's usually because he's taking the commercial literally. Often at the root of it is a fear that your commercial is making fun of his customers.

Some clients seem to think their customers can't relate to anyone who doesn't look like them. (I'm tempted to ask, "Then why are you wearing a suit you first saw in a store window worn by a brainless, bald-headed mannequin?" A workable analogy, but probably not a good idea.)

You need to convince them that the same rules of TV-Land apply to the actors in commercials.

To be even allowed into TV-Land, and welcomed into America's living rooms, your characters must have some scratch, something about them that's funny or unusual. Viewers are either bored by or secretly angry at nice-looking models with good haircuts. (Or "AMWs," as they're called in Los Angeles—actress, model, whatever.)

Tell your client that viewers weren't offended by that slightly overweight geek who was knocked around the room by the pizza with stretchy cheese.

Viewers weren't offended by the jacklegs, yes-men, and bootlicks that made up Federal Express's confederacy of dunces. The late Patrick Kelly, who wrote the FedEx spots, said, "People identify with the schlemiel. We've all been that way at one time or another. . . . The identification comes on a subconscious level. At the *conscious* level, we see the idiot as someone else."[12]

What will offend viewers is having their sitcom or football game interrupted by a cheerful Stepford Wife lip-reading a cue card full of benefits. They want to be en-ter-*tained*.

Your client needs to be reminded that when it comes to mass communication, all customers are smart. Even a mouth-breather in a trailer park watching commercials on a stolen TV set with tinfoil on the antenna knows the rules of TV-Land. He was raised on them.

And the truth be known, there are a lot of funny-looking people out there in Real Life Land.

Your client says (as the law requires them to), "Can you make the logo bigger?"

Clients are about their logos like guys are about their . . . you know.

They love talking about them. They love to look at them. They want you to look at them. They think the bigger they are, the more effective they are. And they try to sneak looks at other guys' logos when they can.

But as any woman will tell you, nobody cares.

Just the same, when you swagger into a client's boardroom with a full-page newspaper ad punctuated by a logo you could cover with a dime, fur's gonna fly.

I remember we had one client who called the agency, very angry. He had just seen an outdoor board our agency had done for his company, and he couldn't see the logo very well.

"Uh-oh," said the account executive who fielded the call. "Where did you see this billboard?"

From a plane.

The client was angry because he couldn't see his logo from a *plane* as it circled LaGuardia airport.

But let's back up a little. If your client has a problem with the size of the logo, ask him first, "Do you agree the ad is good? Is it strategically correct and creatively memorable?" It is?

If it's agreed the ad successfully stops readers and engages them with an offer that intrigues, what do you suppose the readers will look for next? It's doubtful they'll look at the logo of some other ad. It's doubtful they'll take their attention off the leash and let it wander into the park like a stray dog. There's a *dynamic* involved here. The readers have just seen something they want. Where can they get it? The logo. Unless you're using a watermark, readers will almost certainly find it, no matter what its size.

"But why can't you just make it a little bigger? What does it hurt?"

It's a matter of taste. The Latin saying is *De gustibus non est disputandum.* "Taste cannot be disputed." But, forget Cicero; let's dispute.

In every ad there are explicit and implicit messages, both equally important. The explicit message is what the headline and visual are saying. But implicitly, the layout of the ad is sending many messages about the quality of the product, about the class, the demeanor, the personality of your client. They are all subtle. And while explicit messages can sometimes be adjusted with a wrench, implicit messages need an expert's touch.

Your client needs to know that the art director's decision to make the logo the size it is was arrived at after careful consideration of these implicit messages. Too much logo and the ad becomes a used-car salesman. Increase the size of the logo a little more and the lapels on his suit become wider; increase it again and the plaid of his coat becomes louder.

The biggest logo I've ever seen towered 20 stories over Times Square: a giant Prudential logo, easily 30 yards square. No sales message, no headline, just yards and yards of blue logo. When people look up and sees this giant logo, what are they to do with the information? Would it be more relevant or more persuasive if it were 50 yards square? Ooooh, what if we made it a *hundred* yards square?

Where is it written that large logos increase sales? When introducing yourself, do you say your name in a booming voice? "Hi, my name is

Do the large bottles of Coke with bigger logos sell faster than the cans? Are your business cards the size of welcome mats? If cattlemen heated immense brands and seared the entire sides of cows, would fewer be rustled?

Ads without any logos at all are often the most powerful. I know, clients aren't likely to buy this argument, but it's valid nevertheless. A logo says, "I'm an ad!" and an ad says, "Turn the page!" But an intriguing message without any logo to defuse it can be a riveting interruption to a magazine. It doesn't say, "This message brought to you by . . ." It says, "This message." Some of the most effective ads I've ever seen worked without the benefit of a logo. Three of them are in this book.

The reason they worked is that customers don't buy company logos. They buy benefits. If an ad successfully communicates benefit, logo size is relevant only in terms of quality of design, something best left to the art director's well-trained eye—his intuition.

Find a way to give the client a gentle reminder that this intangible thing, this intuition, is our business. Ask him if he would presume to tell his doctor what the diagnosis should be and what prescription to write. Or if he would instruct his lawyer in the nuances of contract law. I know I wouldn't.

I won't even tell the trashman not to lift the garbage can with his back. I figure he knows what he's doing.

Your client gets a few letters from "offended" customers and pulls the campaign.

Many clients worry that their ad may offend somebody, somewhere. And they begin yanking commercials off the air after they receive one or two phone calls about the commercial. Or they begin telling their ad agencies to write everything in such a way that not one soul in a country of 250 million will find a scintilla of impropriety.

This is advertising by fascism, pure and simple. The marketing plan to the many, overruled by the pious sensibilities of the few. It is a form of political correctness, which is itself a politically correct word for fascism. It may be Fascism Lite, but it's still book burning, only we're burning them one adjective, one headline, and one script at a time.

Don't give in. Tell the truth and run.

In the next ad you craft, say what you think is the right thing. Remember, your job is to sell the client's wares to as many people as you can. To appeal to the masses, not the minority. Tell the truth and run. And let the chronically offended pen their lugubrious letters. Let them whine.

The trick will be to get your client to see what a quark-size minority these Kleenex-dabbing, career whiners are. The way I put it: "The letter flooded in." Hey, it's a *letter*, not Omaha Beach.

I say: B-F-D. The letter flooded in. Fine. Even if it's a hundred letters, big deal. Smart clients know they'll get angry letters just for hanging out their shingle. You build a factory, you get a letter. Sell a product, get a letter. I'll wager you could publish the cure for AIDS in tomorrow's paper and by Friday you'll get a missive scribbled in crayon on the back of a Burger King place mat from someone sniveling, "Why didn't you cure cancer *first*?"

Advise your client to run the ad. The world, amazingly, will not stop. 99.99 percent of the people who see the ad will somehow manage to get on with their lives. The other .01 percent will turn down the volume of whatever wrestling show they're watching and reach for the nearest number 10 envelope. Fine. Let them mewl.

To soften the ad in advance or pull the ad once it's run is to surrender your company's marketing to a consumer group you could fit in a phone booth—an angry clutch of stamp-licking busybodies with nothing better to do than peruse *Redbook* magazine for imagined slights to their piety. Ask your client, "Do you want your company being run out of a church basement? Do you want to give every pursed-lipped, pen-wielding, moral policeman with a roll of stamps free rein to sit on your board of directors and dictate marketing plans?"

Tell your client these people are the minority. That's the fraction with the "1" above the line and the really *big* number on the bottom. And this is America. Where the Constitution says in so many big, fancy words, "What the majority says, *goes*."

Outlast the objections.

I hope that having one or two of these counterarguments tucked away in your quiver helps you save an ad one day. But the reality of this business is that sometimes nothing you can do or say is going to pull an ad out of the fire. If a client doesn't like it, it's going to die.

The reasons clients have for not liking an ad often defy analysis. I once saw a client kill an ad because it pictured a blue flyswatter. Why the client killed it, he wouldn't say. "Just consider it dead." When pressed for an explanation months later, he implied that he'd had a "bad experience" with a blue flyswatter as a child. The room grew quiet and we changed the subject.

So get ready for it.

All is not lost, though. You have one last weapon in your arsenal: persistence. I once read that the definition of success is simply getting up one more time than you fall.

To that end, I urge you to simply outlast the client. I don't mean digging in your heels, but rolling past their resistance like a stream around a rock. I once did 13 campaigns on one assignment for a very difficult client. Thirteen different campaigns over the period of a year, and each one was killed for increasingly irrational reasons. But each campaign we came back with was good.

They kept killing them, but they killed the campaign only 13 times. The thing is, we presented 14.

Remember who the enemy is.

Lest these last few pages give the impression I think the client is the enemy, they're not. Remember, the enemy is the client's competition—the other guys across town with the scummy, overpriced products. But like any marriage, there are going to be arguments with your client. Unlike marriage, in advertising you can actually win some.

━━━━━

PICKING UP THE PIECES.

There's always another ad.

Instead of fighting, here's another idea. After you come up with an idea, do what Mark Fenske told me. "Pat it on the rear and say 'Good luck, little buddy' and send it on its way." Mark believes you shouldn't make a career of protecting work. Alex Bogusky has said the same thing. He says the agency is an idea factory. "You don't like this one? Fine. We'll make more." Maybe they're right. Perhaps the best thing to do in the end is this: Come up with an idea and then walk away. There's going to be another opportunity to do a great ad tomorrow.

Don't lose vigilance when work is approved.

I find that when I have sold an ad I didn't think I'd ever sell, I become so happy I lose my critical faculties and blithely allow the ad to go off into production unescorted. I forget to keep sweating the details.

Moral: Don't fumble in the end zone.

Don't get depressed when work is killed.

The ads you come back with are usually better. And when you're feeling down in the dumps, remember that nothing gets you back on your feet faster than a great campaign.

Sometimes the playing field changes when a campaign is killed. For one thing, you know more now about what the client wants. Also, you'll probably be left with a shorter deadline. A curse, but a blessing, too. A time crunch may force a client to buy your next campaign. If the media's been bought, they may have to buy your ideas. So make it great.

A short deadline also has remarkable motivating properties. Someone once told me that the best amphetamine is a ticking clock.

If they don't buy number two or three or four, hang in there. The highs in the business are very high and the lows very low. Learn not to take either one too seriously.

James Michener once observed, "Character consists of what you do on the third and fourth tries."

After you've totaled a car, you can still salvage stuff out of the trunk.

Okay, so the client killed everything. (I actually had an account executive come back from a meeting and say, "They approved the size of the ads!" Yaaaay.) But you know what? You can still get something out of the deal.

If you're part of the presentation, you can at least improve your relationship with the client. I don't think there's any client who actually enjoys killing work. Ask any creative director; it's easier to say yes and avoid the confrontation. They know you've worked hard on it. But remember, they're not completely without insight into what sells their product.

If you can take the loss like a professional and still sit there and be your same funny self and ask, okay, so what the hell do you want?, you can build rapport. They're going to like you for it. And they're going to trust you more the second time around.

Even if your work is killed, produce it.

This is another piece of advice from Mark Fenske. If you're working at an agency where most of your stuff is fed to the Foamcore Furnace, you need to begin worrying now what you're going to show at your next interview. *("Well, see, the client really sucked and they made me do this one. . . . And this one, too. . . . Yeah, but I had this other idea, no really, you shoulda seen it, . . . Hey, why are we walking to the elevators?")* If you can somehow get to tight layouts, even on the dead ads, at least you'll have something to show a prospective CD what you're capable of.

If you're not producing agency work, do freelance.

This is dicey advice. Some agencies don't like it. They figured they invited you to the dance, you should dance with them.

But you do have to watch out for yourself. You need to keep adding to your portfolio. So if you find yourself in an agency that's producing only meeting fodder, foamcore, and rewrites, maybe it's fair to flirt with a small client who needs a few ads. Just don't pin it up in the company break room.

Not only will doing the occasional freelance campaign keep your book fresh, it can keep your hopes alive, keep you excited about the possibilities of this business.

Keep a file of great dead ideas.

I've referred back to mine many times and have reanimated lots of old ideas, sometimes for the same client that originally killed them. I know many creative people who do all their writing in big, fat blank books that they put on the shelf when the books are full. Nothing gets thrown away. Except by clients.

Fig 1. Ca Ca.

DON'T HATE ME because I'm beautiful.

I'm not a doctor, but I play one on TV. Did

somebody say deal? A double pleasure is

waiting for you, tra la la la. I liked it so

much I bought the company. Colt 45, works

every time. He loves my mind <u>and</u> he

drinks Johnny Walker. If any of this reminds

you of your portfolio, please get on your

Pontiac and ride. THE CREATIVE REGISTER.

Advertising Talent Scouts. (212) 533 3676.

Figure 12.1   A good portfolio should attract job offers, not flies.

12

A Good Book or
a Crowbar

Some thoughts on getting into the business

GONE ARE THE DAYS WHEN JUNIORS were hired off the street because of a few promising scribbles on notebook paper and the fire in their eyes. The ad schools are pouring kids out onto the street, many of them with highly polished portfolios.

Do you need to go to an ad school?

If you can afford it, if you can put in a couple of years, by all means, go for it. When I got into the business, there were only a few such schools in the country. Now they're popping up all over. There's a list of eight first-rate schools I include here, but the list may change by the time this book reaches your hands and will likely keep changing.

As of this writing (key phrase—*as of this writing*), the top-rated professional schools on my list are the Art Center College of Design in Pasadena, the Academy of Art University in San Francisco, Brainco in Minneapolis, The Creative Circus and the Portfolio Center in Atlanta, Miami Ad School, New York City's

School of Visual Arts, and Virginia Commonwealth University's Ad Center in Richmond.

In the United Kingdom, I hear good stuff about West Herts College, Buckinghamshire Chilterns University College, and Central St. Martin's College of Art and Design.

Up in Canada, my friends Nancy Vonk and Janet Kestin say they've seen good students come out of Ontario College of Art and Design as well as Humber College. And here in my neck of the woods is one of the few universities in America producing students with good books, the University of Texas-Austin.

If you simply haven't got the money and can't attend a school, don't give up. You will have a much steeper hill to climb, undoubtedly, because you'll be competing with students who've set aside a year or two of their lives to fully concentrate on putting together a terrific portfolio. In the end, however, it all comes down to the work you can put together—your book.

To get a job in the creative side of this business, you will need a portfolio, or a *book*, as its called—some 25 to 30 pages of speculative ("spec") ads you've put together to show how you think. If you can put together eight or nine great campaigns, the top graduate of the best school has nothing on you. On the other hand, if you're still pounding the pavement after a year with your homemade book, maybe it'll be time to think about enrolling in one of the creative schools. (This is particularly true if you want to be an art director. Unlike copywriting, even junior art directors must have certain graphic, production, and computer skills to get in the door.)

Once you decide to go for a book, give it everything. Your portfolio will be the single most important piece you work on in your career. It is your foot in the door, your resume, your agent, spokesperson, and a giant fork in the road to your eventual career. And like a good chess opening, the better it is, the more advantages you will discover through the rest of the game.

Don't worry right now what kind of portfolio to buy or what it should look like. You'll figure that out later. For now, here's some advice on what to put *in* it.

PUTTING TOGETHER A BOOK.

If you're a writer, team up with a promising art director.

And if you're an art director, find a writer you get along with. You need each other's skills, and together you will add up to more than the sum of your parts. More than anything, look for someone with energy, with drive. Someone who's hungry. It's a long, uphill battle putting a great book together, so you'll need all the firepower you can muster.

An art director can help the ads look great, and given the rise of the advertising schools out there, the way your work *looks* is getting more important—even if you aspire to be a copywriter. Books that are full of really good ideas but are poorly art-directed will simply not get the same attention from agencies. (And when you think about it, it's not any different from high school. The good-looking kids got all the attention. Oh . . . excuse me. I digress.) Bottom line: The competition is fierce. Look your best.

If you're a writer working alone, you can still pull it off.

To see what you're up against without an art director (and to learn what you should at least shoot for), ask an agency recruiter or a helpful person at one of the professional ad schools to show you samples of the better student portfolios.

What you'll see will probably be daunting, but you have to remember that many creative directors will also be looking for the quality of your ideas. So, with headlines set on somebody's computer, some imaginative use of scrap art or existing photos, and a few hours at a copying shop, it is possible put together a respectable spec ad.

Here's the big piece of advice, and I don't care if you're alone or at a top ad school. If you remember nothing else, remember this: *Spend the time making the concept great, not the execution.*

Here's an example of a concept that's so good, even a bad drawing doesn't get in the way. I am right-handed. With my left hand, I have rendered a famous Nike ad from a British agency (Figure 12.2). The concept still looks great. Even if your portfolio is a tattered shoe box full of concepts like this, I don't care if they're written in crayon on wet napkins, you will get a job. I guarantee it.

Come up with great ideas, not just great ads.

My friend Mike Lear (a copywriter and teacher at one of the ad schools) gives students this advice: "A book full of cool ads doesn't guarantee you a great job. A book full of brilliant thinking does."

The point is, when you sit down to work don't just "do an ad."

Do something big and marvelous and wonderful. Position a shoe

*Figure 12.2   To make my point, I have redrawn this famous Nike ad
with my left hand, although I'm right-handed. A highly polished
layout of a so-so concept won't hold a candle to a great idea,
even one produced like this.*

company as environmentalists (as they did for Timberland).
Reinvent the whole idea of driving (as they did for BMW's MINI).
Improve the product (like they did by bringing iPod and running
together in Nike+). Brilliant thinking has less to do with what's in
the ad than what's behind it—the thinking you do strategically, the
brass-tacks business ideas you come up with that can move a brand
forward.

It was brilliant business thinking that moved Vegas's tourism
away from a me-too Disney strategy to the naughty idea that
reversed their declining visitor counts—"What happens in Vegas,
stays in Vegas." R&R Partners' simple and refreshingly honest idea
was the engine for years of incredible advertising, one sample of
which is this fabulous ad (Figure 12.3). A lint roller covered with
naughty detritus like spangles, sequins, and false eyelashes brings to
life the strong business idea underneath all of the Vegas work. The
brilliant thinking came first. The brilliant ads, later.

Famous copywriter Ed McCabe once described the size of the
ideas we're talking about here: "I'm not interested in day-after
recall of ads. I'm interested in 10-year recall."

*Figure 12.3   The best advertising is true to the core of the product.
Few campaigns did this better than the advertising for Las Vegas.
"What happens in Vegas, stays in Vegas."*

For your first portfolio, concentrate on print.

If you're new to the business don't try to tackle television or radio. Print's hard enough, and most creative directors I've talked with agree that thinking conceptually in print is probably the best place to start. Concentrate on print, which for the purposes of this discussion can include outdoor advertising, posters, point-of-purchase, collateral, and interactive. If you have a monstrous idea for television, go for it; do a simple storyboard. Just remember that TV boards (and radio scripts) in a portfolio present themselves *slowly*. I tend to think it's better to have a book that presents great print ideas fast, one page after another—whap, whap, whap.

But print isn't the only thing that presents fast. What other advertising venues can you explore? Start with print and once you feel your confidence grow, branch out. Do something amazing.

Remember, in tough economic times clients are looking for ways to reach customers beyond the usual (and expensive) methods of print and TV. Let your book show that you know this.

If there's ever a time to study the awards annuals, this is it.

Study them. Read, learn, memorize. Don't just concentrate on the most recent issues, either. Dig up old annuals. Go online. Go to the ad blogs. Design fads come and go, but the classic advertising structures endure. See what makes the ads work. Take them apart. Put them back together. Some of the ads are humorous and work. Some are straight and work. Why? What's the difference?

One way to start is simply to redo some existing ads.

Page through *Time* magazine and look for a bad ad. You probably won't have to go past page three. Find the idea buried in the body copy, where it almost always is. Pull it back out and turn it into an ad.

Round out your portfolio with a variety of goods and services.

If you're just starting out and doing spec ads, don't try to add to the latest, award-winning Nike campaign. It's tempting to do so, but you set yourself up for a harsh comparison to work that's extremely good.

Just pick some products you like. Start a file on them. Fill it with great ads from the awards annuals and bad ads from the magazines. Start jotting down every little thing that feels like an idea. Don't edit. Just start. You like music? Start building a campaign on, say, how this new portable disc player doesn't skip every time you step off the curb. Now find two other products you like. Find what makes them different and do two campaigns there.

Then choose some boring products—products without any differences that distinguish them (besides the ads you're about to do). Insurance. Banking. You figure it out. But find a way to make them interesting.

You might try writing ads for a product you've never used and likely never will. If you're a guy, write subscription ads for *Brides* magazine. The fresh mind you bring to the category may help your concepts ring new.

And, finally, take a shot at a campaign for a packaged good. Like lipstick, soup, or bouillon cubes. But don't touch Hot Wheels toy cars or Tabasco sauce. Everybody in the space-time continuum is doing ads on these. Also, I implore you, please, no pee-pee jokes, potty humor, and for the love of God, no porn shops, not even condoms. All of these things have been done to death. You won't just be beating a dead horse. You'll be beating the dust from the crumbling rocks of the fossilized bones of an extinct species of horse crushed between two glaciers in the Precambrian Age.

To get you started on the kind of products that might make for a good student book, I provide the following list. It's by no means a definitive list, just stuff I've seen in some of the better student books.

Nicorette	A bookstore
The local newspaper	Tiffany & Co.
Lasik Eye Centers	Sealy mattresses
Prudential Insurance	Scope
Blackberry	24 Hour Fitness
A wine	Secret deodorant
Tupperware	Silent Air purifier
Trash bags	Western Union
Domino Sugar	La-Z-Boy recliners
Fidelity Investments	Sirius radio
DirecTV	Sherwin Williams

AARP	Snapple
Brawny towels	Laundry detergent
Polaris	Nasdaq

When you're done, your book should show the ability to think creatively and strategically on goods and services, both hard and soft.

One last thing. Avoid public service campaigns. They're too easy. (*"Hey, look at these fish I caught. Sorry the holes in their heads are so big, but they were at the bottom of a barrel when I shot them."*)

Now is not the time to play it safe.

As you put your book together, err on the side of recklessness. It's the one time in your career you get to pick the client and write the strategy. If you're not pushing it to the edge now, when are you going to start? A junior book should be the most fun thing a recruiter gets to look at all day, just for the reasons above. It's not real, so live a little. It's better to have stuff that's fresh and strategically naïve than a nice, sensible portfolio of ads so dull you have to laminate them just to cut down on the smell.

Nor is this the time to be clueless and naive.

Don't fill your book with outrageous ads that have no chance of ever running.

Swearwords in the headlines, pee-pee jokes, stuff like that is all fine and dandy when you're working with your partner, telling jokes, and messing around. But when you actually include stuff like this in your book, what it says about you isn't flattering. (*"Hello, I'm a clueless young creative. My work is 'edgy' and 'provocative' and I think putting a sanitary-pad belt on the real Statue of Liberty would be a cool outdoor idea for Tampax."*)

Do stuff that actually has a chance of running.

Fill your portfolio with campaigns, not one-shots.

Almost anybody can write a decent headline if they work at it long enough. Only skilled ad people can think in campaigns. Don't send your book out until it has five or six great campaigns in it. And remember, the best campaigns aren't three one-shots strung together by a common typeface, but one big idea executed in a variety of ways. The Absolut Vodka or *Rolling Stone* print campaigns shown in Chapter 2 are good examples.

If you have a couple of great one-shots, go ahead, throw 'em in. But they should be icing. Not the cake.

Don't fill your portfolio with cute campaigns for microscopic clients.

A book full of ads for the local bakery, your brother's auto shop, and the dry cleaner will not be very impressive. You need to do ads for checking accounts, newspaper subscriptions, a brand of clothing, a cologne. Real stuff.

These are the tough day-to-day projects you'll actually be working on most of the time in this business. Ads on products like these are a better measure of your abilities than dashing off a zippy headline for portable toilets or an acupuncture parlor.

Jamie, my agency recruiter friend, told me: "My favorite books are ones that come from shops with crappy clients. If a person can make something good from some of the godawful products I see . . . *that*, my friend, is someone with brains and drive."

My friend Bob Barrie concurs: "Do great ads for boring products."

In addition to having a variety of clients, make sure you show a variety of styles in your book.

Not all headline ads, not all visuals, but a good mix of everything you're capable of. This advice applies particularly to aspiring art directors. Show ads that demonstrate your ability to handle type. And ads that are all visual, ads that are all headline, ads with a lot of stuff in them that require a good sense of design. Flex a lot of muscles. The same advice applies to writers. Show a range of voice. I've seen books written entirely in one wiseass voice, and the only brand that comes through is the writer's.

Let me repeat: *Flex a lot of muscles.*

In the last couple of years, 90 percent of the student portfolios that I've seen are made up almost entirely of visual solutions. A visual solution is fine; I've been harping about them in this book, yes. But they're not the only solution out there. I see so many of these ads now that it's getting to feel a little formulaic. (This trend, I'm guessing, is driven by the predominance of visual solutions currently filling the awards annuals.)

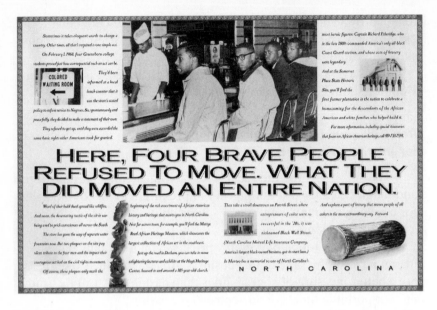

Figure 12.4   There is attention to detail, graceful design, and craftsmanship evident in this marvelous ad for North Carolina. As an art director, you should have work like this in your portfolio.

A book full of visual solutions will not show your prospective employer how good a designer you are. How could it? The typical visual-solution ad is a photograph with a teeny copy line down next to the logo.

So, show off. Do a long-copy ad. Do one that's all type. Dazzle us with your art direction. Show us you know how to handle headlines and body copy. Show us you know how to bend those 26 letters to your will and make them hop through any hoop you hold, no matter how high. Show us you know how to assemble a page that is blazing with the craft of design.

This ad for North Carolina's tourism commission from Loeffler Ketchum Mountjoy (Figure 12.4) is an example of excellent craft. (The reprint here doesn't do it justice. You can see a better version in *Communication Arts* #38, page 46.)

Remember, as an art director your job isn't over when you come up with the concept; it begins all over again. And it's at this phase that you have a chance to move a great concept into the orbit of perfection with a booster push of amazing design and execution. You probably won't get into this orbit with a book full of picture ads with teeny lines down by the logo.

Take your best campaign idea, and blow the sucker out into a big integrated one.

This is where the big brands play. It's the stage on which big ideas can best show their stuff. It's what clients are asking for. And it's what creative directors are looking for in student books. It's all that stuff we talked about in Chapter 8, the Big Honkin' Ideas.

So, as you approach completion of your first workable portfolio, pick that one campaign idea with the most flexible, media-infinite idea and put it through its paces.

Keep in mind that I'm not suggesting you devote 10 pages of your portfolio to the same idea sized to fit newspaper, then outdoor, then brochures, and so on. Show us how muscular and flexible your core idea is with different executions across a variety of media. Could your print campaign extend to the side of a coffee cup? Could it be a guerrilla marketing and web site combination? Could you write something on a Post-it Note that, applied to a lamppost, becomes a cool concept? How would it work as a handout at a trade show? As a place mat?

Remember, this isn't a nice-to-have. It's a must-have.

If you're looking to land a copywriter's position, show some writing, for Pete's sake.

Visual solutions are all the rage. Fine, do some. But as a junior copywriter in an agency, your first 500 assignments are all likely to be writing headlines for an airline's 500 destinations or a telco's 500 calling plans. Show me you can write. Show me some muscular, intelligent headlines. (For a reminder of what muscular, intelligent headlines look like, revisit the *Economist* on pages 93–94.)

If you're looking to land a copywriter's position, have a few samples of body copy in your book.

One of the big recruiters in New York City, Tiffany Warin, reminded me that having at least one great, well-written, long-copy ad is a good idea.

Ms. Warin said, "When I was the recruiter for Deutsch, we'd hire these young kids and they'd sometimes get the hardest projects right off the bat. Like radio. Well, radio is one of the toughest assignments you can get. So these young kids would be handed five or six radio assignments on their second day and just choke. So I always look for a long-copy ad to see if they can sustain a thought in a witty, intelligent manner."

Remember that Land Rover ad in Chapter 3 (Figure 3.7)? That's a great example of a long-copy ad. Will your prospective employers read every word? Probably not. But have it in there.

Think about the order in which you want your work to appear in the book.

My advice: Start strong; end strong. Put your very best piece first. Right on page one. Put your next-strongest campaign at the end. And in between, vary the styles and the emotions. Funny-serious-sexy-funny-serious, just keep the flow moving along.

Just before you put the final book together, get out a big knife and cut everything that isn't great.

Novelist Elmore Leonard had this great line that went, "I try to leave out the parts people skip." That's good advice about writing as well as for assembling your final book. But it's hard advice to follow. All of those creations are your babies, I know. But some babies are ugly. Thin the herd. If you have doubts about something, cut it. It's weird, but people often judge you based on the weakest work in your book, not the strongest. Cut the weakest stuff. Even if that means cutting a campaign of five down to two, cut.

There's another reason to pare the book a bit. If a pared-down book you've sent an agency lands you an interview, you'll have something new to show once you're face-to-face. Perhaps the best candidates to leave out are any one-shots you have or perhaps a campaign from the middle of the book.

If you're going to make minibooks, make sure that reading them doesn't require tweezers.

A minibook is a portable portfolio. Typically, the ads are sized down to an 8½- by 11-inch format to make it cheap and something you can pop in the mail. Minibooks are a good idea.

And when you make one, make a whole bunch—hundreds, if you can. Direct-mail companies profit on a response rate of just 1 and 2 percent. So make a whole bunch of minibooks and send them out to every agency you're interested in.

But don't make the work too small. I receive lots of these minibooks, and more than half of them I cannot read. I cannot read the body copy. And worse, I cannot read the headlines.

Don't reduce your book to bits of highly art-directed particles of sand.

Put your book on the Internet.

It's easy to do, easy to update, and amazingly cheap. It doesn't eliminate the role of a minibook or your main portfolio, but it's there in a pinch if you need it and it shows a fair bit of e-savvy. Personally, I happen to prefer looking at print as print and generally ask juniors to simply send me their minibooks. But I know of many creative directors who actually prefer to see work online.

Another possibility is posting your work on one of the online portfolio showcases. There are some free services; some cost money. How well they work, I don't know, but at the minute I don't see a downside to it.

Put an online presence in your arsenal. When you're out there networking with e-mails, include your site as a link. It also helps if you can put a "comments" link below your work. You'll get some good feedback.

The same rules apply to your web site as to your main book. Don't get hung up in the presentation. The work is everything. Showcase the work.

Don't gussy up your portfolio.

Don't spend money on the portfolio case itself or put felt on back of the ads. For one thing, felt backing makes an ad look too important. Come on, it's not the Magna Carta. It's a coupon ad for Jell-O. Felt also takes up too much room, and I can make my portfolio beat your portfolio with more great work in the same amount of space. I refer you again to my left-handed drawing of the famous Nike ad. Forget the packaging. The work is everything.

Here's more advice from my friend Jamie, the recruiter at a huge agency:

> Keep in mind that the person on the other end of your portfolio mailing has an average-sized desk with about 100 other portfolios on top of it at any given moment. So if you decide to send your giant metal box with heavy laminated ads, that recruiter's probably gonna say some words that would make your momma blush and then they'll move onto the next portfolio because yours is a pain to deal with.

Don't do "clever" mailers.

It's tempting to demonstrate your creativity this way. But don't. I've seen the weirdest things sent to the agency. A foot from a department store dummy in a box topped with the expected line: "I'd love to get my foot in the door of your agency." I saw about 20 of those. One guy tiptoed into the mail room and sat inside a Federal Express box. And in the creepy category, we note an Igloo cooler that arrived with a label stating "creative brain inside." And then there was that envelope stuffed with "bloody" bandages with some message about how "I'd kill to work at your agency."

Don't do a mailer. I've never seen anything as clever as a good portfolio.

Don't do a cute resume.

Your portfolio is where you should showcase your creativity. Your resume should say who you are. Keep it to one page and get right to the point. This is my name. I'm a writer or I'm an art director. This is the job I want. Here's my experience, my address, and my phone number. Thank you and good night.

Dropping your minibook or portfolio off at the agency isn't enough.

This is a people business.

While there may be a small sense of accomplishment in securing a name and sending your book off to one of your target agencies, don't check that agency off your list, lean back at the pool, and wait for the phone call. You need to get *in* there. You need to follow up with phone calls, letters, e-mails. You need an interview. It's rare that a dropped-off book results in a phone call.

This is a people business. While the ante to the game is a great book, the winning hand is a great interview where you impress the person who actually has the job opening.

If you're just beginning, don't count on a headhunter to find you a job.

Typically, headhunters work with midlevel to senior positions that have higher salary potential. (They make their money on a percentage of the salary.) Most agencies aren't interested in paying recruiters' fees to fill entry-level jobs when they're getting all the applicants they can handle walking in off the street.

Just the same, you may decide you want to use a creative recruiter to supplement your search. Fine. They're great people to get to know in this business, and, who knows, if they can't place you now, they could be of great help down the road. Keep in touch with them. It's called *networking*.

"Networking."

I swore I'd never use the word as a verb, but nothing else seems to fit here. If you don't have relatives working in the business, networking's precisely the thing you'll have to do. You'll have to send out feelers far and wide.

Tell every living person you know you're trying to land a job at an ad agency. You may find that the friend of a friend has a name. And a name is all you need to start building your contacts.

So you ask around and get a name. Maybe he or she doesn't even work in the creative department. It doesn't matter—you call. Even if they're not hiring, you ask for an "information interview" or advice on your book.

When you meet this person, be your usual charming self. Don't be too flip or go through the mail on his desk. Just listen. Then politely ask if he knows of job openings anywhere. Get the name of another contact. Ask if you can use his name to get in the door somewhere else. Keep this up, and over time you'll slowly build up a list of names, numbers, and contacts. One day the phone will ring.

I was lucky. In my case, it went like this: My college roommate's wife's brother was the president of a local agency. So I called my old buddy. He talked to his wife. She talked to her brother. And he said to have me call some guy in the creative department—some guy named Tom McElligott.

Establish a phone or mail relationship with a working writer or art director.

There are plenty of friendly and helpful people in the business who will be willing to coach you along. The trick is finding one.

Take a risk. Write a letter to somebody whose work you admire. Or call 'em. (Call before 9 A.M. or after 6 P.M. It's less crazy then.) Tell them you really like the stuff they do. No brownnosing. Just fact-of-the-matter. Tell 'em you're trying to get into the business and ask if they could take a look at your work and give you advice on how to improve it.

Once you get a dialogue going, there are two important things to do. One, take the advice you get. And two, don't stalk the person. Keep a respectful distance. Don't call more than once or twice. If somebody doesn't return your call after three tries, take the hint—stop calling, at least for six months or so. And get back to them only when you've significantly improved your book.

Get a cell phone.

And when you go on the road for interviews, bring something to read.

——————

THE INTERVIEW.

Before each interview, study the agency.

It's probably smart to begin your search by looking closely at the agencies that are doing work compatible with your style.

Read the latest awards books and familiarize yourself with their best work. Memorize the names of their top clients. Learn the names of the people who created their best work and check to make sure they still work there.

You'll find client lists, billings, and other stuff in a big fat book called *The Standard Directory of Advertising Agencies*, known in the business as the Red Book. There's a similar sourcebook, *Adweek's Agency Directory*, available through the magazine. If neither book is available at your local library, borrow one from a friendly agency, photocopy the places you want to hit, and study them.

Of course, none of this is for the purposes of brownnosing. *("Gee, Mr. Crawford, I thought your work for Spray 'N' Wipe was so meaningful.")* What it says is that you're a student of the business and you're serious enough about getting into it that you've done your homework.

Avoid the rush at the front door. Try the side door, or even a window.

Many agencies now employ creative recruiters. These people are generally not writers or art directors, just folks with a decent sense of what makes for a good portfolio. As good as some of them are, try to get your book into the agency somewhere over their head. If you can do so, you stand a better chance because you're removing a layer of approval. Yes, it's good to get to know the names of the recruiters in your target agencies. Keep their names in your address book, but don't limit your calls only to them.

If you can't get in to see the general, talk to a lieutenant.

You don't have to get an interview with the creative director to get your foot in the door at an agency. If you have a great book, see if you can get 15 minutes of time with a senior creative person. They know when the agency is hiring, even if they're not the ones doing it. If they like you, it's relatively easy for them to slide your port-folio under the CD's nose at the right moment.

It may happen for you this way. If it does, someday maybe you can return the favor to a kid who comes into your office with a bad tie and a great book. Take the time to help. We're all in this together.

In the interview, don't just sit there.

I don't care how good your book is, you can't just throw it on a CD's desk, park yourself on his sofa, and wait to discuss company health plans and vacation time. You must make it clear you have a pulse. Advertising is a business that requires a lot of people skills, and it will help if the CD sees you have them—that you're personable, that you can handle a business meeting with verve and confidence, and that generally you aren't a stick-in-the-mud.

One famous creative director I know is more interested in your hobbies than anything else. "They tell me a lot about you." And Andy Berlin once confided to a recruiter that hiring sometimes comes down to chemistry. "A lot of people could probably do this job," he said, "but what it's really about is . . . who would we want to have a beer with?"

Have an opinion.

This is another version of "Trust your instincts."

If the interviewer asks you what kind of advertising you like or what campaigns you wish you had done (and many do), don't be afraid to have an opinion. Say what current or classic campaigns you like and describe why. It's a subjective business, and unless you pick Mr. Whipple as your dream campaign, you'll probably do fine.

What's bad is having no opinion at all. "Oh, I like . . . well, I like whatever's good is what I like."

Don't explain your book.

When you are finally in the creative director's office and watching her page through your book, resist the temptation to explain anything (unless, of course, you've actually been asked a question). I know it's tempting to explain. You'll want to set up what a certain assignment was or how you had this "way better" idea that was killed.

Don't.

The fact of the matter is this: You won't get a chance to explain your ad to a person reading it in *Time* magazine at the airport. *("Excuse me, I see you're reading that ad for the new Toyota Camry. If you'll allow me to explain, basically those blur lines right there, they really don't need to be behind the car but we felt it was the only way to indicate the vehicle was in motion . . . which makes the whole concept work quickly, which it does, right?")*

If you ever feel the slightest urge to explain something in your book, cut it. That urge means the piece is not working. As someone once said, "If your work speaks for itself, don't interrupt."

If you are asked about some work, be ready with an articulate explanation of how you came up with it.

"So, I like this campaign," says the creative director. "How'd you come up with it?"

"We just thought it up, man. Just sorta . . . poof! And I went like, whoa, dude, this rocks."

You are being considered for employment at a firm that sells the intangible. Agencies sell ideas. So your ability to precisely articulate how you created an idea and to persuasively pitch it to a neutral (and sometimes hostile) audience is key.

Have your answers ready.

Trust your instincts.

Go to 10 different interviews and you're going to get 10 different opinions on your work. It will be confusing. *("The guy with the goatee liked this campaign, but the guy with the ponytail said it sucked.")*

If the majority say the same thing, take the hint. But you don't have to agree with everybody. If you do, you'll water down your book. Trust your instincts. Keep what you believe in. Change what you don't. Keep reworking your book until the weak parts are out and the good parts are great.

One way to get a good read on what needs improving is to ask each person you meet in an interview what he thinks is the weakest campaign in your book. If more than a couple point to the same campaign, take it around the back of the barn. You know what to do.

Relax. Ask some questions.

Keep in mind as you interview that you can learn as much about them during this meeting as they can about you. Remember that even though you're young and on the street, you have options. You don't *have* to take this job, even if it's offered. You have choices.

With that in mind, relax a little bit. Your interviewer is not there to pin you to the felt like a butterfly. If they invited you to come in, they already like your book. They're trying to see if they like you. So be yourself. Have an opinion.

Offer to do the grunt work.

My very first assignment in the business was to write some 50 "live" radio scripts for a hotel corporation. Live radio is simply a script read by the local DJ in between the farming updates and wrestling reports. I suspect if that awful live radio job hadn't come through the agency door, I might not have, either. But I was more than happy to do it.

I recommend you take the same attitude. Express your willingness to take on any assignment they throw at you. Many young people come in wanting to work on an agency's national TV accounts. My advice is, offer your shoulder to any wheel, your nose to any grindstone they have. I overheard a junior creative wisely coach a student by saying, "Trust me, you don't *want* to be on a TV shoot. You can't imagine how clueless you are right now."

While it's possible you could land some TV relatively early on in your career, it's more likely you'll have to first pay your dues. Get ready to do some live radio, or what we cynics call "the brochures of the airwaves."

Sell your ability to think strategically.

Many students concentrate too much on presenting their creative ability when it's already evident in their portfolio. That's understandable, given all the effort you've put into the ads. But trust the creativity to speak for itself. Instead, it might pay to talk about the strategic thinking behind the ads you're presenting. Creative directors probably don't hear much of this kind of talk during interviews, and your strategic abilities and overall business acumen are just as important in estimating your worth.

Let them know if you are willing to freelance.

Agencies often have more work than their staffs can handle, and even if they don't need another full-timer, they may need temporary help. Ask if this is the case at your target agencies. Let them know you're willing to freelance. It gives the CD a chance to work with you, to see if you should keep "dating" before you get married.

If you can't get into the creative department, get into the agency.

I can name quite a few good creative people who started their agency careers in the mail room, or as coordinators, assistants, even account executives. Ed McCabe, for example—mail-room boy. Jamie Barrett—junior account guy.

The thing is, once you're in, you can learn more. You'll be able to watch it happen firsthand. You'll also start making friends with people who can hire you or help move you into the creative department. Unlike companies such as IBM, ad agencies are loosely structured places that often fill job openings with any knucklehead who proves he can do the work. They don't care what he majored in.

So get in there, do the job, keep your ears open, your book fresh, and when a creative position opens up, whom do you think they'll hire? A stranger off the street or the smart young kid in the mail room who has paid his dues and is still chomping at the bit?

How to talk about money.

I had a long discussion about money matters with Dany Lennon, one of the best creative recruiters in the ad business. (The ad that opens this chapter, for "The Creative Register," that's her.) She gave me this advice, and I pass it on to you.

"Do your homework," Dany told me. "Before you go into an interview you should know what the starting salary levels for that city, and that area, are. Talk to headhunters, talk to the agency recruiters, make phone calls, but find out. Then, when you and the creative director begin to talk about money, you won't be left in the position of saying, 'Okay, so what do you think I'm worth?' An agency might be tempted to low-ball you.*

"Instead you say, 'Well, this is what I understand to be the starting salary at comparable agencies in this area.' Drop the name of an agency if you like. But take the responsibility of knowing about money. Don't leave it up to the agency. If you do it forthrightly, your CD is going to see an intelligent person who's done their homework and money won't be a federal case. Just one of fairness. It's not so much the money you get that matters anyway, but the way in which you conduct yourself during the negotiation. A mature, intelligent, and fair negotiation says a lot about your character, also very important in an interview.

"Once you've negotiated your salary," Dany went on, "you may want to tell your CD you would appreciate a review in six months. Not a raise, but a review. This says to him, 'I'm going to work my tail off for this place and I'm confident in six months you'll see you've made a great hire.' And six months is all it usually takes for a CD to get a good read on you: on how hard you work, your attitude, your overall value to his company."

More than anything, Dany warned me, don't cop an attitude and start pitting one agency's offer against another. According to Ms. Lennon, there is, unfortunately, a burgeoning "brat pack" movement within the industry. Standard starting salaries, which were once etched in stone, are a thing of the past, and negotiations are more common. Not a bad thing in itself, but it has created a situation where talented newcomers are swaggering into agencies with good portfolios and bad attitudes.

I heard this story from the president of one of the country's top ad schools. He happens to be visiting a New York agency, chatting in the office of the creative director. Phone rings, and it's a young graduate of another ad school. (The agency had previously agreed

---

*The Internet may also be a good source for assessing average salaries. Currently the sites talentzoo.com and salary.com seem to be fairly accurate. Whether they're still operating by the time this book reaches your hands is another matter.

to fly this kid up to New York for a better look at him and his book—translation: a real interview and a likely job offer.)

But on the phone, the kid cops a 'tude and tells the agency CD he isn't coming unless he makes such-and-such kind of money (a salary way outside of what juniors usually make). Before slam-welding the phone receiver to its cradle, the creative director shrieks into it a string of invectives so toxic that common decency prevents their retelling here.

A man named Frederick Collins once said, "There are two types of people in the world. Those who come into a room and say, 'Well, here I am!' and those who come in and say, 'Ah, there you are.'"

Be that second type of person.

Don't choose an agency based on the salary they offer.

If you're lucky enough to get a couple of offers, you may find that the better salary is offered by the worse agency. It has always been thus. And Lord knows, it will be tempting to take that extra 10 grand when it's held out to you. Don't.

One of Bill Bernbach's best lines was "It isn't a principle until it costs you money." In this case, the principle in question is the value you place on doing great work. I urge you to go with the agency that's producing good advertising. You may work for less, but it's more likely you'll produce better ads. And in the long run, nothing is better for a great salary than a great book.

More than once I've seen a talented kid go for the bigger check at a bad agency and a year later take a cut in pay just to get the hell out of there. The bad part was that even after a year in the belly of the beast, he hadn't added so much as a brochure to his original student portfolio.

If you get a fair offer from a good agency, take it. Take in four roommates if you have to, live in your parents' basement, but get on board—that's the trick. I read somewhere not to set your sights on money anyway. Just do what you do well and the money will come. McElligott once told me, "You'll be underpaid the first half of your career and overpaid the second."

Take a job wherever you can and work hard.

All you need to do to get on a roll is produce a couple of great campaigns and have them run. And it's possible to do great work at almost any agency in America. (Note judicious use of the word *pos-*

sible.) Once you do a great campaign, once it gets in the books, creative directors everywhere will see your name. And you can make the next move up.

Don't be crestfallen if you can't get into one of the "hot" shops. The agency offering you the job will be your stepping-stone. (However, it's probably not a good idea to tell them this as you're shaking hands: "*Thank you, sir. I guess this will just have to do until something opens up at Wieden + Kennedy. In fact, I think I'll just leave my coat on if you don't mind.*")

Here's the other thing: You don't *wanna* have your first job be at an elite shop. First of all, you'd probably be so intimidated your butt cheeks will fuse together. Second, you won't appreciate how good you have it at an elite shop if it's your first job in the industry. Mike Hughes of The Martin Agency notes: "People who start in [great places like] Goodby and leave are forever disappointed in their other agencies. And when they were at Goodby, they didn't think it was that good."[1]

Remember, wherever you land a job, there'll be plenty to learn from the people you'll meet. Think of that first job as continuing your education.

Just get on board and work like hell. Early in your career's the time to do it, too, when you don't have children calling you on the phone asking how to get the top off the gasoline can in the garage.

It may seem that you can't outthink those senior creatives right now, but you can definitely outwork them. Make hard work your secret weapon.

"Interns? Clean-up in Aisle 3, please."

The answer on whether to intern or not depends on the agency. Look for a paid internship, and expect to work hard. It's not likely you'll be creating Super Bowl spots; doing image searches for an art director or making copies for a pitch is more like it. But that's life in an agency, and an internship can be a great place to learn what it's really like. Offer to do anything for anyone. If you see a senior team working late, lean into their office and offer to help. They may take you up on it. That's the break you need.

A word of advice: Don't stay in an internship too long; a couple of months is enough. And whatever else happens, make sure you're not taken advantage of, either financially or personally. Sadly, it's been known to happen.

SOME FINAL THOUGHTS.

Once you land a job, stick with it awhile.

There are going to be rough spots no matter where you work. There are no perfect agencies. I like to think I have worked at a couple of the best, and there were plenty of times I thought just about everything that could be wrong was wrong.

Hang in there for a while. Things can change. An account that's miserable one year can suddenly become the one everybody wants to work on. There's also value in learning to stick with something long enough to see it through. Plus, it doesn't look good to bail on a place inside of a year. Show some patience.

If you've heard that the best way to increase your salary is to change jobs, it's true. But I advise against job-hopping solely for that reason. If you're at a good agency making a fair wage, stay there. Every six months or so, take a long, hard look at your portfolio. If it's getting better, stay. Move on only when you've learned as much as you possibly can. You don't want a resume that's a long list of brief stints at agency after agency.

Don't let advertising mess up your life.

On the same page that I say work hard, I also warn against working to the exclusion of all else. We all seem to take this silly advertising stuff so seriously. And at some shops, the work ethic isn't even ethical. People are implicitly expected to work till midnight pretty much full-time.

When this happens, we end up working way too hard and ignoring our spouses, our partners, our friends, and our lives. Remember, ultimately, it's just advertising. Compared to the important things in life, even a commercial that runs on the Super Bowl is still just an overblown coupon ad for Jell-O. Love, happiness, stability, sanity— those are the important things. Don't forget it.

Don't underestimate yourself.

Don't think, "I shouldn't bother sending my book to that agency. They're too good."

All people are subject to low self-esteem, and I think creative people are particularly prone to it. I can think of several people in our creative department who didn't think they were good enough but sent their book on a lark, and we took them up on it.

Don't overestimate yourself.

For some reason, a lot of people in this business develop huge egos. Yet none of us is saving lives. We are glorified sign painters and nothing more.

Stay humble.

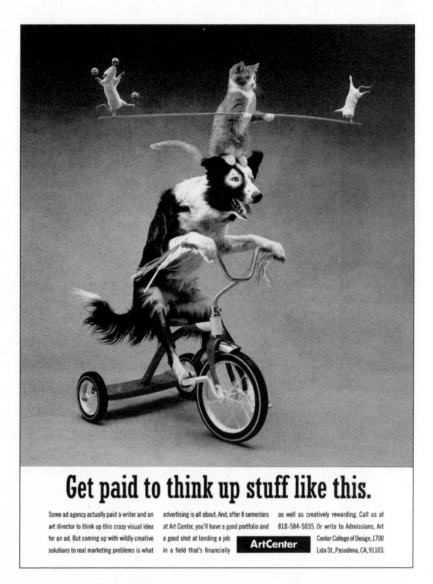

Get paid to think up stuff like this.

Some ad agency actually paid a writer and an art director to think up this crazy visual idea for an ad. But coming up with wildly creative solutions to real marketing problems is what advertising is all about. And, after 8 semesters at Art Center, you'll have a good portfolio and a good shot at landing a job in a field that's financially as well as creatively rewarding. Call us at 818-584-5035. Or write to Admissions, Art Center College of Design, 1700 Lida St., Pasadena, CA, 91103.

ArtCenter

Figure 13.1   Although Joe Paprocki and I did this ad, we didn't think up the visual for it. We just borrowed it from some other ad. Then we went to lunch. What a great business.

13

Making Shoes versus Making Shoe Commercials

Is this a great business or what?

THIS IS A GREAT BUSINESS.

What makes it great are all the knuckleheads. All the people just slightly left of center. This business seems to attract them. People who don't find fulfillment anywhere else in the business world somehow end up on advertising's doorstep, their personal problems clanking behind them like cans in back of a just-married car. They come for very personal reasons, with their own agendas. They bring to the business creativity, energy, and chaos, and from the business they get discipline, perspective, and maturity.

All in all, they make for an interesting day at the office, these oddballs, artists, misfits, cartoonists, poets, beatniks, creepy quiet guys, and knuckleheads. Every one of them seems to have a great sense of humor.

David Ogilvy once wrote, "People do not buy from clowns." He was suggesting there is no place for humor in effective advertising. Forgetting for a moment whether Mr. Ogilvy was right, wrong, or *extremely* wrong, the thing is this: People do buy from clowns. Every day, millions of Americans use something sold by a clown, because the ad industry employs clowns by the tiny-circus-car-load.

Don't get me wrong, most of the people in the stories that follow are smart businesspeople. You'd want them on your team. But they're world-class knuckleheads as well. Agencies are full of 'em.

It's just one clown after another all the way down the hallway. Knuckleheads in the mail room, knuckleheads answering the phones, knuckleheads in the CEO's office . . . they're everywhere.

Why this should be so eludes me. I know only that most of every working day I spend laughing—at cynical hallway remarks, tasteless elevator bon mots, and bulletin board musings remarkable for their political incorrectness.

Submitted for your approval: this collage of images, incidents, and idiocy culled from agency hallways and stairwells around the nation. All true. And all stupid.

———

A finicky agency president has his own executive bathroom. No one else is allowed to use it, much less step in there. One day when the president is out to lunch, creatives are seen going into the bathroom carrying two muddy cowboy boots and a cigar.

Cut to boss coming back from lunch. He goes into his private restroom and immediately comes back out, really pissed off. "Who in God's name is the dumb *cowboy* sittin' in my stall smokin' a stogie?" His assistant has no clue.

The boss waits outside for the cowboy to emerge. Ten minutes pass, and the boss peeks back in. The same creepy tableau presents itself—muddy boots below the stall door, blue smoke curling above it.

Cigars can smolder for about half an hour. Bosses, even longer.

———

A creative director at a big agency decides to build a "communal area where creatives can relax." The problem is, he builds it right outside his office. Any creatives with enough time to hang out there are usually spotted by the CD and handed one of those awful last-minute assignments nobody wants. *("Hey, can you write this live promotional tag?")*

Creatives dub the area "The Meadow," inspired by the movie *Bambi*—a dangerous wide-open area where hunters can put you in the crosshairs. The name catches on. Everybody starts referring to the area as The Meadow. So does the creative director, though he never understands the reference and wonders why his happy new area is *constantly* deserted.

———

Left behind in an empty conference room, a piece of paper with this idea for Penn tennis balls, using a spokesman (well, a spokesperson): "I got rid of my old balls and now I use Penn."
—*Renee Richards*

———

A senior account guy decides to hose the "new meat." Sends an e-mail to all the junior account people in their modular offices, informing them that the building management has hired "burlap rakers" to come in and spruce up the walls of the cubicles.

"Please remove all materials tacked, stapled, or taped to your walls until you receive further notice from the burlap rakers."

The young account executives obey, but never receive further notice. A week later, the receptionist's left eyebrow goes way up when a young account guy asks him, "Hey, do the burlap rakers come in at night or on the weekends?"

———

Retrieved from the wastebasket in a writer's office, this headline for a new dog shampoo: "Gee Your Ass Smells Terrific!"

———

A big New York agency lands the Revlon account. The client says that only females understand the market and they want only women to work on the account. But a staffing crunch forces the traffic manager to assign a male writer—a guy named Mike. Mike is assigned a new name—Cindy. The client never meets Cindy, but receives e-mail from Cindy and reviews and approves great work from Cindy. "Cindy understands women."

———

Quotes from actual creative work sessions:
    "Which is funnier? ADHD or narcolepsy?"
    "Obviously, it needs more vomiting references."
    "I'm serious, man. I just don't think Julie Andrews would ever *do* that."

———

A writer, notorious for rummaging through people's desks to steal food, purloins some specially made brownies containing four bars of Ex-Lax. Writer is seen a half an hour later in the hallways, looking pale, and is not seen again till the following Monday.

———

Another account guy and a creative are having a heated discussion about the creative person's vision for the agency.

"So," asks the account guy, finally getting testy. "What kind of work *do* you want to see the agency doing?"

Creative says: "I wanna do the kind of work that's in *CA*."

Account guy goes: "Then move back to California!"

———

Junior account person writes this note next to every single paragraph of a rough ad layout with greeked-in text: "Please translate."

———

Favorite brave comeback to a client who said to make the logo bigger: "Put your face closer to the ad."

———

Okay, this next story, a prank, happened to me.

I'm on a morning flight to a client meeting in St. Louis. It's just me and my old boss, the president of a large advertising agency.

It's not a full flight, so I stake a claim to an empty row, set up shop, and get a little work done. My boss settles down a row behind me. After a while, I doze off. When I wake up 20 minutes later, my tray table is down, and on it, wide open to the centerfold, is a *Penthouse* magazine.

Behind me I can hear my boss, snickering.

God only knows how many *stewardesses* have walked by, seen me slumped there, my mouth gaping open. Twitching, probably.

———

The "I quit" and the "You're fired" stories are usually pretty good in this business; more florid and dramatic than what you'll find in, say, the banking business. From my "Pathetic" file, here's my favorite "You're fired" story.

Okay, so they have to fire this art director—lay him off is more accurate, because the agency had lost some business. They need to lay him off that very week, but the problem is, the guy's suddenly in the hospital—some infection or something, but no big deal.

Still, the gears of capitalism must grind on, even if they're in reverse, and so the guy's boss shows up at the hospital asking to see him. The boss is told he's not allowed in the infectious wing of the ward, so the poor schmuck is summoned from his hospital bed out to the lounge area, where he is fired and handed his severance check.

The boss returns to the agency with a sad story that ends with the image of this poor guy limping back down the hospital hallway, one hand wheeling his IV apparatus, one hand holding his walking papers, and no hand left to hold his hospital gown shut. His freshly fired ass is last seen peeking out of his thin hospital gown as he walks back down the infectious hallway.

The "You're hired" stories aren't bad, either.

An aspiring ad student wants to get a job at one of the elite ad agencies in the country. But interviews there are hard to get.

He cuts a picture of the agency's creative director from a trade magazine, mounts it on a fake driver's license, and laminates it perfectly. He tucks the fake ID into an old, tattered wallet and then puts small copies of his best student work into the photo holders.

Here's the cool part.

He visits the agency, asks to use the bathroom, and then abandons the wallet on the sink counter.

The wallet's "returned" to the desk of the CD, and the kid's hired.*

You have to admit it, this is a great business. Can you imagine breaking into the *banking* business with a stunt like that? *("Jenkins, people are* still *talkin' about how you scribbled your investment portfolio on the mirror in the executive washroom. Another round for my man Jenkins here!")*

"ADVERTISING: THE MOST FUN YOU CAN HAVE WITH YOUR CLOTHES ON."
—Jerry Della Femina

This is a great business.

Look at what you're doing. You're an image merchant. You're

---

*Yes, in Chapter 12 I wrote, "Don't do clever mailers." But in Chapter 1, Ed McCabe said, "I have no use for rules. They only rule out the brilliant exception."

weaving words and pictures together and imbuing inanimate objects with meaning and value.

Mark Fenske said advertising is the world's most powerful art form. Is he right? Well, Picasso was great, but I've never looked at one of his paintings and then walked off and *did something* Pablo wanted me to do. I know that sounds silly, but advertising is like no other form of creative communication, because it has the power to affect what people do. It works.

In the 1920s, Claude Hopkins sat down in his office at Lord & Thomas and wrote "Drink an orange." A nation began drinking fruit juice.

Steve Hayden sat down in his office at Chiat/Day and wrote "Why 1984 won't be like 1984" for Apple computers. A nation began thinking maybe computers belong in living rooms, not just in corporations.

Dan Wieden sat down, wrote "Just Do It," and changed the world.

In 1978, there weren't many joggers on the side of the road. (Even the *word* didn't exist. *Jogging*. What the hell was that?) Now you can't throw a stick out the window without hitting five of them.

"Nike killed the three-martini lunch," says Fenske. Nike told us to get off our collective butt and just do it, and suddenly it wasn't okay anymore to lie around on the couch wallpapering our arteries with lard. We started taking the stairs. At the wheel of this national change of heart: an advertiser, a great agency, and the world's most powerful art form—advertising.

Whether you agree with Fenske that "Nike and Coke brought down the Berlin Wall," the power of advertising to globalize icons and homogenize the buying habits of whole continents is undeniable.

In *Adcult USA,* James Twitchell wrote:

[Advertising] has collapsed . . . cultures into a monolithic, worldwide order immediately recognized by the House of Windsor and the tribe of Zulu. . . . If ever there is to be a global village, it will be because the town crier works in advertising.[1]

This is a great business.

Look at what you're getting paid for: putting your feet up and thinking. This is what people with real jobs do when they get time *off*—put their feet up and daydream, drift, and think of goofy stuff. You, you're getting a paycheck for it.

I remember we had this new secretary in the creative department.

He kept walking into the offices of art directors and writers, interrupting their work, just to chat. Somebody finally said to him, "Listen, we'd love to talk another time, but we have to get this done. So if you could . . ."

He backed out of the room, apologizing, "Geez, I'm sorry. You had your feet up. You were talking, laughing. It didn't look like you were working."

———

This is, indeed, a great business.

This fact was recently brought home to me during a train ride from downtown Chicago to O'Hare airport.

I'd just left a very bad meeting where a client had killed a whole bunch of my work. I fumed for the first couple of miles. *("That was a really good campaign! They can't kill it!")*

As I sat there feeling sorry for myself, the gray factories passed by the train windows. Miles of factories. On the loading docks, I could see hundreds of hardworking people. Laborers forklifting crates of Bic pens onto trucks, hauling boxes of canned peaches onto freight cars. They'd been there since six o'clock in the morning, maybe five o'clock. These were hardworking people. With real jobs.

And then there was me, feeling sorry for myself as I whipped by in an air-conditioned train on the way to my happy little seat on the plane with its free peanuts. Peanuts roasted and packed by some worker in another gray factory as he looked up at the clock on the high brick wall, waiting for the minute hand to hit that magic 10:30 mark so he could get out of the noise for 15 minutes, drink a Coke, smoke a Winston, and then it's back to packing my stinkin' peanuts.

I must remember this.

There are research firms out there that will tell me the sky isn't blue. Clients who will kill an ad because it has a blue flyswatter in it. And agencies that will make bloody fortunes on ideas like Mr. Whipple. Yet tomorrow I'll be back in the hallways telling jokes with the funniest people in corporate America, putting my dirty sneakers on marble tabletops, and getting paid to think. Nothing more. Just to think. And to talk about movies.

You should remember this, too.

You'll be paid a lot of money in this business. You'll never have to do any heavy lifting. Never have dirt under your fingernails or an aching back when you come home from work. You're *lucky* to be talented. *Lucky* to get into the business.

Stay humble.

Please feel free to give me your thoughts on this text and how I might improve subsequent editions. Probably the easiest way to send me your thoughts is to log on to the *Hey, Whipple, Squeeze This* page on amazon.com. Just look up the title of this book and you'll see they have a place there for reader comments.

SUGGESTED READING

Which doctor would you have perform your next surgery? The doctor who has a dusty biology textbook from med school moldering high on the shelf behind his desk? Or the doctor whose desk is piled high with copies of the last four years' worth of the *New England Journal of Medicine?*

I'm serious. Which doctor do you want standing over you with a scalpel? Well, if you propose to sell yourself as an expert to your clients, you'll actually have to *be* an expert. You'll have to read. And learn. And learn a lot. There is no shortcut to being the best. No easy way around it. You have to know your stuff and know it cold.

The short list of books and online resources I've included here is only the beginning. They happen to be my favorites in the creative area. But there are many other disciplines you should be studying—marketing, branding, interactive—all of which will be relevant to your craft.

There is no shortcut. This is how we learn it. Bit by bit. Remember: "Chance favors the prepared mind."

Read every old One Show and *Communication Arts* you can get your hands on. Read every British *Design & Art Direction* annual you can find.

Become a student of advertising history. On the subject of history, I'll list these titles: *When Advertising Tried Harder,* by Larry Dubrow; *Remember Those Great Volkswagen Ads?* by David Abbott; *From Those Wonderful Folks Who Brought You Pearl Harbor,* by Jerry Della Femina; *Inside Collett Dickenson Pearce*, by Ritchie and Salmon; *A Book About The Classic Avis Advertising Campaign of the 60s,* by Ericksson and Holmgren; *Helmut Krone. The Book*, by Clive Challis; and also *Advertising Today*, by Warren Berger.

Then there's Warren Berger's other book, *Hoopla: A book about Crispin Porter + Bogusky.* Expensive, but a good look inside that agency.

Advertising: Concept and Copy, by George Felton, is a wonderful textbook on the craft. Excellent, detailed advice on how to think, how to write. Good stuff.

Cutting Edge Advertising, by Jim Aitchison, is one of the better books out there on how to write a decent print ad.

Ernie Schenck is the author of *The Houdini Solution: Put Creativity and Innovation to Work by Thinking Inside the Box.* The smaller your budgets, the more you need this book.

Creative Advertising: Ideas and Techniques from the World's Best Campaigns, by Mario Pricken. This hard-to-find and kind of expensive book is very good. Great ideas on *getting* great ideas. Lots of cool ads in it, too.

e, by Matt Beaumont, is a novel of life inside an agency told entirely in e-mails. It is hilarious.

Truth, Lies, and Advertising: The Art of Account Planning, by Jon Steel, is the single best book on how smart brand planning adds value to the whole creative process. Steel is also the author of *Perfect Pitch: The Art of Selling Ideas and Winning New Business.* He's a joy to read and so smart.

Eating the Big Fish: How Challenger Brands Can Compete Against Brand Leaders, by Adam Morgan. Such a brilliant read. The title pretty much explains what this book is about: how to outsmart the competition when you can't outspend them.

Strunk & White's *The Elements of Style* is required reading for anyone who holds a pencil anywhere near paper.

For the sheer joy of writing, I recommend Natalie Goldberg's *Writing Down the Bones* and Anne Lamott's *Bird by Bird.*

If you're just trying to break into the business, I recommend Vonk and Kestin's *Pick Me: Breaking into Advertising and Staying*

There. A little older, but still helpful, is Maxine Paetro's *How to Put Your Book Together and Get a Job in Advertising.*

And, if you can get them to, have your *client* read Dick Wasserman's wonderful *That's Our New Ad Campaign?* It's out of print, but if you find one, get it. It's great.

Also, next time you're in Czestochowa or Gdansk, pick up a copy of the excellent *Jak Robic Switene Reklamy.* And for you readers in Constantinople, I highly recommend the incredible *Satan Reklam Yaratmak.* (Okay, I'm kiddin'. They're just translations of this book.)

BIBLIOGRAPHY

Adams, James, L. *Conceptual Blockbusting.* Reading, MA: Addison-Wesley Publishing Co. Inc., 1974.

Aitchison, Jim. *Cutting Edge Advertising: How to Create the World's Best Print for Brands in the 21st Century.* New York: Prentice Hall, 1999.

Berger, Warren. *Hoopla: A Book about Crispin Porter & Bogusky.* Brooklyn, NY: Powerhouse Books, 2006.

Bernbach, Bill. *Bill Bernbach said . . .* New York: DDB Needham, 1995.

Burton, Phillip Ward, and Scott C. Purvis. *Which Ad Pulled Best: 50 Case Histories on How to Write and Design Ads That Work.* Lincolnwood, IL: NTC Business Books, 1996.

Clark, Eric. *The Want Makers.* New York: Viking, 1988.

Cook, Marshall. *Freeing Your Creativity: A Writer's Guide.* Cincinnati, OH: Writer's Digest Books, 1992.

Corporate Report magazine, Minneapolis, MN, 1982.

D&AD Mastercraft Series. *The Art Director Book.* Switzerland: Rotovision, 1997.

D&AD Mastercraft Series.*The Copy Book*. Switzerland: Rotovision, 1995.

Dru, Jean-Marie. *Disruption: Overturning Conventions and Shaking Up the Marketplace.* New York: John Wiley & Sons, 1998.

Foster, Jack. *How to Get Ideas*. San Francisco: Berret-Koehler Publishers, 1996.

Fowler, David. *The Creative Companion*. New York: Ogilvy, 2003.

Goodrum, Charles, and Helen Dalrymple. *Advertising In America: The First 200 Years.* New York: Harry N. Abrams, Inc., 1990.

Gossage, Howard Luck. *The Book of Gossage*. Chicago: The Copy Workshop, 1995.

Higgins, Denis. *The Art of Writing Advertising*. Lincolnwood, IL: NTC Business Books, 1965.

Hoff, Ron. *I Can See You Naked*. Kansas City, MO: Andrews & McMeel, 1992.

Ind, Nicholas. *Great Advertising Campaigns*. Lincolnwood, IL: NTC Business Books, 1993.

Jaffe, Joseph. *Life After the 30-Second Spot: Energize Your Brand with a Bold Mix of Alternatives to Traditional Advertising.* Hoboken, NJ: John Wiley & Sons, 2004.

Lamott, Anne. *Bird by Bird*. New York: Doubleday, 1994.

Landa, Robin. *Advertising by Design*. Hoboken, NJ: John Wiley & Sons, 2004.

Lee, Bruce. *Acting on TV: Direct Response Television and How It Works.* From the Ogilvy web site, visited June 28, 2007, http://www.ogilvy.com/viewpoint/index.php?vptype=TOC&iMagaId=4.

Lyons, John. *Guts: Advertising from the Inside Out*. New York: Amacom, 1987.

Matthews, John E. *The Copywriter*. Glen Ellyn, IL: self-published, 1964.

Mayer, Martin. *Whatever Happened to Madison Avenue?* Boston, MA: Little Brown & Company, 1991.

McAlhone, Beryl, and David Stuart. *A Smile in the Mind: Witty Thinking in Graphic Design.* London: Phaidon Press Ltd., 1996.

Minksy, Laurence. *How to Succeed in Advertising When All You Have Is Talent.* Chicago: The Copy Workshop, 2007.

Monahan, Tom. From *Communication Arts* magazine, Palo Alto, CA.

———. *The Do-It-Yourself Lobotomy*. New York: John Wiley & Sons, 2002.

Ogilvy, David. *Confessions of an Advertising Man*. New York: Atheneum, 1963.

One Club, The. *Pencil Pointers* newsletter. New York, 1995.

Paetro, Maxine. *How to Put Your Book Together and Get a Job in Advertising.* Chicago, IL: The Copy Workshop, 1990.

Pricken, Mario. *Creative Advertising: Ideas and Techniques from the World's Best Campaigns.* London: Thames & Hudson, 2002.

Ries, Al, and Jack Trout. *Marketing Warfare.* New York: McGraw-Hill, 1986.

Ries, Al, and Jack Trout. *Positioning: The Battle for Your Mind.* New York: McGraw-Hill, 1981.

Roman, Kenneth, and Jane Maas. *The New How to Advertise.* New York: St. Martin's Press, 1992.

Schenck, Ernie. *The Houdini Solution: Put Creativity and Innovation to Work by Thinking Inside the Box.* New York: McGraw-Hill, 2006.

Schulberg, Bob. *Radio Advertising: The Authoritative Handbook.* Lincolnwood, IL: NTC Business Books, 1994.

Steel, Jon. *Truth, Lies, and Advertising: The Art of Account Planning.* New York: John Wiley & Sons, 1998.

Twitchell, James. B. *Adcult USA: The Triumph of Advertising in American Culture.* New York: Columbia University, 1996.

———. *Twenty Ads That Shook the World.* New York: Crown Publishers, 2000.

Vonk, Nancy, and Janet Kestin. *Pick Me: Breaking into Advertising and Staying There.* New York: John Wiley & Sons, 2005.

Wakeman, Frederick. *The Hucksters.* Scranton, PA: Rinehart & Company, 1946.

Wallace, Dave. *Break Out!* Grand Rapids, MI: Ainsco Incorporated, 1994.

Wall Street Journal, Creative Leaders Series. New York: Dow Jones & Company, 1993.

Warren, Jim, and Sheena Paul, *Smart Advertising.* (Unpublished paper.)

Wasserman, Dick. *That's Our New Ad Campaign?* New York: The New Lexington Press, 1988.

Weiner, Ellis. *Decade of the Year.* New York: Dutton, 1982.

Wypijewski, JoAnn, ed. *Paint by Numbers: Komar and Melamid's Scientific Guide to Art.* New York: Farrar, Straus & Giroux, 1997.

Young, James Webb. *Technique for Producing Ideas.* Chicago, IL: Advertising Publications, Inc., 1944.

ONLINE RESOURCES

One of the best ways to learn about the world of advertising is to bookmark the better web sites that are out there. Some are blogs, some are rants, and some are just cool places to look at new commercials.

I did a survey with my ad friends, asking them what their fave online resources are. They were all nice enough to return e-mails positively glowing with underlined links in blue type ready to whisk me into the ether. I went down the rabbit hole and must've studied two or three hundred of them by the time I realized that trying to publish a list of the best sites (on paper, in a book, at least) would suck. The online world constantly changes, and any working Web address I list here today may get a "Can't find server" tomorrow. You'll also find that a single address is enough to get you started, because most of the sites (the blogs, anyway) include a list of favorite links; one attaches to another like coat hangers at the bottom of your closet. Grab one, you get the rest.

I happen to like my buddy's site: Ernie Schenck Calls This Advertising? Also, some folks in Canada put out a great site called ihaveanidea.org. If your agency subscribes to adcritic.com, check that one out. Start with those.

NOTES

CHAPTER I

1. Martin Mayer, *Whatever Happened to Madison Avenue?* (Boston: Little, Brown & Company, 1991), 46.
2. Kenneth Roman and Jane Maas, *The New How to Advertise* (New York: St. Martin's Press, 1992), 38.
3. John Lyons, *Guts: Advertising from the Inside Out* (New York: Amacom, 1987), 115.
4. Frederick Wakeman, *The Hucksters* (Scranton, PA: Rinehart & Company, 1946), 22.
5. Ibid., 45.
6. *Wall Street Journal*, Creative Leaders Series (New York: Dow Jones & Company), 12.
7. Phillip Ward Burton and Scott C. Purvis, *Which Ad Pulled Best: 50 Case Histories on How to Write and Design Ads That Work* (Lincolnwood, IL: NTC Business Books, 1996), 24.
8. Bill Bernbach, *Bill Bernbach Said . . .* (Not paginated).
9. William Souder, "Hot Shop," *Corporate Report* (September 1982).

10. Al Ries and Jack Trout, *Positioning: The Battle for Your Mind* (New York: McGraw-Hill, 1981), 24.
11. Ted Morgan, *A Close-Up Look at a Successful Agency* p. 300.
12. Bernbach, *Bill Bernbach Said . . .*.
13. John Ward, "Four Facets of Advertising Performance Measurement," in *The Longer and Broader Effects of Advertising*, ed. Chris Baker (London: Institute of Practitioners in Advertising, 1990), 44.
14. Sandra Karl, "Creative Man Helmut Krone Talks about the Making of an Ad," *Advertising Age* (October 14, 1968).
15. Bill Bernbach, *Bill Bernbach Said . . .* (Not paginated).

CHAPTER 2

1. James Charlton, ed., *The Writer's Quotation Book: A Literary Companion* (New York: Viking-Penguin, 1980), 55.
2. *Wall Street Journal*, Creative Leaders Series, 5.
3. Eric Clark, *The Want Makers* (New York: Viking, 1988), 24.
4. James Webb Young, *Technique for Producing Ideas* (Chicago: Advertising Publications, Inc., 1944).
5. D&AD Mastercraft Series, *The Copy Book* (Switzerland: Rotovision, 1995), 68.
6. *Wall Street Journal*, Creative Leaders Series, 41.
7. Jean-Marie Dru, *Disruption: Overturning Conventions and Shaking Up the Marketplace* (New York: John Wiley & Sons, 1998), 151.

CHAPTER 3

1. Tom Monahan, *The Do-It-Yourself Lobotomy* (New York: John Wiley & Sons, 2002), 84.
2. Clark, *The Want Makers,* 54.
3. Warren Berger, *Hoopla: A Book about Crispin Porter & Bogusky* (Brooklyn, NY: Powerhouse Books, 2006), 160.
4. Al Ries and Jack Trout, *Marketing Warfare* (New York: McGraw-Hill, 1986), 70.
5. Dru, *Disruption*, 157.
6. Anne Lamott, *Bird by Bird* (New York: Doubleday, 1994), 23.
7. Mario Pricken, *Creative Advertising: Ideas and Techniques from the World's Best Campaigns* (London: Thames & Hudson, 2002), 22.
8. Marshall Cook, *Freeing Your Creativity: A Writer's Guide* (Cincinnati, OH: Writer's Digest Books, 1992), 7.

9. David Fowler, *The Creative Companion* (New York: Ogilvy, 2003), 7.

10. Jim Aitchison, *Cutting Edge Advertising: How to Create the World's Best Print for Brands in the 21st Century* (Singapore: Prentice-Hall, 1999), 135.

11. D&AD Mastercraft Series, *The Art Director Book* (Switzerland: Rotovision, 1997), 44.

12. Bernbach, *Bill Bernbach Said . . ..*

13. *New York Times Magazine* (December 10, 2006), 68.

14. James L. Adams, *Conceptual Blockbusting* (Reading, MA: Addison-Wesley Publishing Co., 1974), 66.

15. Beryl McAlhone and David Stuart, *A Smile in the Mind: Witty Thinking in Graphic Design* (London: Phaedon Press Ltd., 1996), 19.

16. Howard Luck Gossage, *The Book of Gossage* (Chicago: The Copy Workshop, 1995), 114, 115.

CHAPTER 4

1. Monahan, *The Do It Yourself Lobotomy*, 90.

2. Phillip Ward Burton and Scott C. Purvis, *Which Ad Pulled Best: 50 Case Histories on How to Write and Design Ads That Work* (Lincolnwood, IL: NTC Business Books, 1996), 26.

3. Karl, "Creative Man Helmut KroneTalks about the Making of an Ad."

4. Lyons, *Guts*, 167.

5. Fowler, *The Creative Companion*, 19.

6. Nancy Vonk and Janet Kestin, *Pick Me: Breaking into Advertising and Staying There* (New York: John Wiley & Sons, 2005), 83.

7. George Kneller, *The Art and Science of Creativity* (New York: Holt, Rinehart & Winston, 1965), 55.

8. *Wall Street Journal*, Creative Leaders Series, 20.

CHAPTER 5

1. Fowler, *The Creative Companion*, 31.

CHAPTER 6

1. Jim Warren and Sheena Paul, *Smart Advertising* (Unpublished paper).

2. Bruce Lee, *Acting on TV: Direct Response Television and How It Works* (From the Ogilvy web site, visited June 28, 2007, http://www.ogilvy.com/viewpoint/index.php?vptype=TOC&iMagaId=4).

3. Ibid.
4. Vonk and Kestin, *Pick Me*, 112.

CHAPTER 7

1. Tom Monahan, *Communication Arts* (July 1994), 198.

CHAPTER 8

1. "New media" (Wikipedia web site, visited July 7, 2007, http://en
   .wikipedia.org/wiki/New_media).
2. Laurence Minksy, *How to Succeed in Advertising When All You Have
   Is Talent* (Chicago: The Copy Workshop, 2007), 313.
3. Quotation from Tony Granger, *Creativity* (June, 2007), 10.
4. Berger, *Hoopla*, 406.
5. Robin Landa, *Advertising by Design* (Hoboken, NJ: John Wiley &
   Sons, 2004), 236.
6. Joseph Jaffee, *Life After the 30-Second Spot: Energize Your Brand
   with a Bold Mix of Alternatives to Traditional Advertising* (Hoboken,
   NJ: John Wiley & Sons, 2004), 219.
7. Rob Schwartz, *Shoot* (June 7, 2002), 24.

CHAPTER 9

1. Karl, "Creative Man Helmut Krone Talks about the Making of an
   Ad."
2. Daniel Pope, *The Making of Modern Advertising.* (New York: Basic
   Books, 1983), 4.

CHAPTER 10

1. *Wall Street Journal*, Creative Leaders Series, 44.
2. "The average length of a CMO's tenure across corporate America
   has been dropping in recent years—down from 23.6 months in 2003 to
   23.2 months in 2006, according to a Spencer Stuart study," *Adweek*
   (June 4, 2007).
3. Ellis Weiner, *Decade of the Year* (New York: Dutton, 1982).

CHAPTER 11

1. Ron Hoff, *I Can See You Naked* (Kansas City, MO: Andrews & McMeel, 1992), 30.
2. Dick Wasserman, *That's Our New Ad Campaign?* (New York: New Lexington Press, 1988), 3.
3. Alastair Crompton, *The Craft of Copywriting: How to Write Great Copy That Sells* (Englewood Cliffs, NJ: Prentice-Hall, 1979), 166.
4. Fowler, *The Creative Companion,* 3.
5. Tom Monahan, *Communication Arts* (May/June 1994), 29.
6. Bob Schulberg, *Radio Advertising: The Authoritative Handbook* (Lincolnwood, IL: NTC Business Books, 1994), 234.
7. Tim Delaney, "Basic Instincts," *One to One: Newsletter of One Club for Art & Copy* (November/December 1994), 1.
8. Alexander Melamid and Vitaly Komar, *Paint by Numbers: Komar and Melamid's Scientific Guide to Art*, ed. JoAnn Wypijewski (New York: Farrar, Straus & Giroux, 1997).
9. Tom Monahan, *Communication Arts* (September/October 1994), 67.
10. Wasserman, *That's Our New Ad Campaign?*, 37, 38.
11. Bernbach, *Bill Bernbach Said . . . .*
12. A. Jerome Jeweler, *Creative Strategies in Advertising* (Belmont, CA: Wadsworth-ITP Publishing, 1995), 171.

CHAPTER 12

1. Laurence Minksy, *How to Succeed in Advertising When All You Have Is Talent*, 183.

CHAPTER 13

1. James B. Twitchell, *Adcult USA: The Triumph of Advertising in American Culture* (New York: Columbia University, 1996), 43.

ACKNOWLEDGMENTS

Cover design by Craig Denham and David Crawford of GSD&M, Austin, Texas.

I would like to thank the following people for help in writing this book: My wife, Curlin Reed Sullivan, Dan Ahearn, Richard Apel, Kim Baffi, Bob Barrie, Jamie Barrett, Betsy Barnum, David Bell, Andre Bergeron, Andy Berlin, Kevin Berigan, Bob Blewett, Alex Bogusky, Laurie Brown, Rob Buchner, Pat Burnham, Cathy Carlisi, Tim Cole, Scott Cooley, David Crawford, Markham Cronin, Russell Curtis, Gina Dante, Clay Davies, Craig Denham, James Embry, Mark Fenske, Kevin Flatt, Ashley Fortune, Anne Fredrickson, Betty Gamadge, Yosune George, Tom Gibson, Wayne Gibson, Glenn Gill, Kevin Griffith, Tiffany Groglio at Wiley, Al Hampel, Phil Hanft, Cabell Harris, Sam Harrison, David Jelly Helm, Carol Henderson, Joel Hermann, Bill Hillsman, Adrian Hilton, Sally Hogshead, Blue Hopkins, Clay Hudson, Paul Huggett, Mike Hughes, Gary Johns, Pruie Jingle James Jones Johnson, KatMo, Kathy Jydstrup, Claire Kerby, Lori Kraft, Jim Lacey, Greg Lane, Mike & Kelley & Henry & Owen Lear, Dany Lennon, Andy Lerner, Mike Lescarbeau, Tom Lichtenheld, John Mahoney, Tom McElligott, Tom McEnery, Doug

Melroe, Karen Melvin, Lucy Meredith, Ruth Mills, Larry Minsky, Andrea and Natalie Minze, Mister Mister, Tom Monahan, Marina Monsante, Ty Montague, Ken Musto, Richard Narramore (my kind editor at Wiley), Ted Nelson, Tom Nelson, Diane O'Hara, Judy Popky, Gene Powers, Kevin Proudfoot, Cathy Orman, Johnathan Ozer, Hal Pickle, Margot Reed, Col. William Preston Reed, Joey Reiman, Mike Renfro, Hank Richardson, Tania Rochelle, Isvel Rodriguez, Tom Rosen, Nancy Rubenstein, Daniel Russ, Cecily Sapp, Elizabeth Stickley Scott, Ron Seichrist, Fred, Marty, and Jennifer Senn, Mal Sharpe, Joan Shealy, Montrew Smith, Pete Smith, Roy Spence, Thad Spencer, Myra Longstreet Sullivan, good ol' Joe Sweet, Kirsten Taklo, Diane Cook Tench, Mary Tetlow, Tom Thomas, Rob Thompson, Jerry Torchia, Judy Trabulsi, Eric Valentine, Rob Vann, Carol Vick, Christa von Staaveren, Tiffany Warin, Mary Warlick, Jim Warren, Mike Weed, Craig Weise, Jean Weisman, Howard Willenzik, Judy Wittenburg, Bill Wright, and Steve & Charlie Wolff.

INDEX

A

Adjective, brand equals,
26–29, 33
Ad schools, 271–272
Anvils, Acme® brand,
259
Apple computer, 23, 98, 100,
119, 134, 189

B

Barrie, Bob, 14, 202,
233–234
Bernbach, Bill, 140
on being provocative,
57–58
on execution, 9, 200
on formula, 14
on founding an agency, 5
on primary purpose, 67
on principles, 292
on the product, 30, 68
on research, 249
on truth, 6, 23
Body copy:
in ads, 98–106
avoiding long introductions
in, 101
basic structure of, 101
conversational style,
99–100
details in, 103
long-copy, 216–217,
281–282
Brands, 20–21, 134, 176
equals adjective, 26–29, 33

Budgets, for television
    commercials, 118, 123
Bullies, 223–224

C

Casting, in radio, 167–169
Charmin, 1, 2, 3, 8, 26
Chiat/Day, 118
Clichés, 153, 241
Clown suit, washing blood
    out of, 233
Clutter, simplicity as the cure
    for, 72–73
Communication Arts
    magazine, 12, 89, 109,
    114, 119, 151, 280,
    300
Commercials:
  radio, 149–172
  TV, 127–129
Copy-testing. *See* Reading of
    sheep entrails
Creative leverage, 189
Creative process, 21–24,
    37–79, 82, 200
Crispin, Porter + Bogusky, 40,
    56–57, 142, 182, 183, 185,
    188
Cubicle plankton, 213

D

D&AD, 34, 114
Day in the life, 176–177
Design, 95
Details (in body copy), 103
    sweating the, 105
Direct-response television,
    131–147
"Doing a 360°", 212

E

Economist, The, 61–62, 93–94,
    95, 96, 180, 184
Emotion, 43, 46, 143, 145, 151,
    202, 203, 243–244, 260
Equity, 20
Exaggeration chip, 59–60

F

Fascism Lite, 264
Fenske, Mark, 266
  on advertising, 302
  on big ideas, 196
  on defending work, 231
  on DRTV, 144
  on logic, 203
  on open-mindedness, 30
  on producing dead ads, 267
Foam Core Furnace, 209
Focus groups, 34, 217–222,
    247–253
Fowler, David, 45, 107, 125,
    245
Froggy Lady, 220–221

G

Gossage, Howard, 67, 78, 189
GSD&M, 40, 47, 187–188
Guerrilla advertising, 181,
    189–190

H

Hacks, 224–227
  on crack from Hackensack,
    107
Hallway Beasts, 224–234
Hayden, Steve, 22
Headline, 84–95

clichés, 92, 94
completing the visual,
    88, 92
doing methodically,
    84–89
negative, 254–255
puns in, avoid like
    plague, 84
Hogshead, Sally, 89, 107
Home for Tired Old
    Visuals, 55
Hour Gobbler, 232–234
Hughes, Mike, 114, 136, 293

I
Idea:
    coming up with, 37–79
    generation, 21–24,
        112
    getting from the
        marketplace, 107–109
    Linus Pauling on, 82
    over the wall, 81
Index, that would be, um, this
    page
Infomercials, 133, 142–147
Interning, 293
Interviewing, 286–295

K
Kestin, Janet, 107, 146–147,
    194
Koncept Krusher 2000®,
    217–222
Krone, Helmut, 7, 14
    on design, 96–97
    on how to do an
        ad, 37
    on "new," 199–200

L
Lamott, Anne, 43, 223
Lear, Mike, 187, 273
Literally, taking an idea,
    258–262
Logic, 134–136, 141, 142, 145,
    203, 244, 259–260
Logo, 57
    ads without logos, 264
    can you make it bigger?,
        262–265

M
Martin Agency, 98, 114, 122,
    136, 293
Martini, Yesman &
    Longlunch, 214
McCabe, Ed, 15, 102, 150,
    226, 274, 290
McElligott, Tom, 12, 74, 242,
    285, 292
Meat Puppets, 209–214
Meetings, run from, 232–234
Metaphor:
    ad examples, 62–64
    description, 61
    stop sign as, 69
MINI, 57, 174, 185–186,
    274
Monahan, Tom, 39, 89, 169,
    247, 255
Money, 227–228, 294

N
Naughty, on the value of
    being, 183–188
New media, 175–196, 281
Nike, 61–62, 68, 200–201, 274,
    302

Norwegian Cruise Line,
189–190

O
One Show, 12, 24, 34, 72,
78–79, 89, 96, 109, 110,
114, 120, 175
Outdoor advertising, 74–78

P
Pablum Park, 214–217
People People®, 214–215
Planning, account, 31
Portfolio, 271–285
Positioning, description,
9, 29
Presentation, 239–247
Production, radio, 169–172
Protecting work, 253–266
Public Relations (PR),
191–192

R
Radio, 149–172
dialogue in, 157–160, 168
humor in, 151–155
jingles in (*see* poisonous
toads)
writing for, 150–163
Rectal itch, 451
Reductionism, 73–74
Research, 29, 217–222, 238,
247–253
arguments against
pretesting concepts,
248–250
creating "art," 251–253
huge mistakes in, 250

S
Simplicity, 68–74
in billboards, 74–76
Cezanne on, 70
Henry David Thoreau
on, 68
Maurice Saatchi on, 68
Michelangelo on, 69
in television, 118, 123
Sisyphus, 208–209
Slash Weasels, 230–232
Sound effects, in radio,
163–167
Story, 121, 125, 136, 144
Strategy, 21, 31–34, 37–38,
42–43, 181, 243
Stuck, what to do when
you're, 106–111

T
Tag lines. *See* Schmag lines
Television commercials,
116–129
15-second, 127
visual solutions in,
120–121
Testing. *See* Research
Tommyrot, flimflam and,
141
Twitchell, James B., 143, 302

U
Unique selling proposition, 5

V
Viral, ad, 192–195
Visual:
clichés, 35, 55

solutions in print, 46–47,
52–57
solutions in television, 120,
125
Voice:
in radio, 151–155
in writing, 100–102, 139
Voice-over, 167–171
Volkswagen, 6, 7, 8, 39, 50,
65–66, 101, 182, 250
Vonk, Nancy, 107, 146–147,
194

W
Wack Jobs, 230–232
Wasserman, Dick, 211, 243,
260
Whiners, 229–230
Whipple, 1–5, 8, 26, 112, 226,
257, 303
White, E.B., 102
Wieden & Kennedy, 123,
200
Writing, 43–44, 82–106, 118,
251